DISABLED FUTURES

In the series *Dis/color*,

edited by Cynthia Wu, Julie Avril Minich,
and Nirmala Erevelles

DISABLED FUTURES

A Framework for Radical Inclusion

Milo W. Obourn

TEMPLE UNIVERSITY PRESS

Philadelphia • *Rome* • *Tokyo*

TEMPLE UNIVERSITY PRESS
Philadelphia, Pennsylvania 19122
tupress.temple.edu

An earlier version of Chapter 3 was originally published as Milo Obourn, "Racialized Disgender and Disruptive Futurity in Lorde's and Engelberg's Cancer Narratives," *Genders* 1.2 (Fall 2016), http://www.colorado.edu/genders/issue-12-fall-2016-0.

An earlier version of Chapter 4 was originally published as Megan Obourn, "Octavia Butler's Disabled Futures," *Contemporary Literature* 54.1 (2013): 109–138. Copyright © 2013 by the Board of Regents of the University of Wisconsin System. Reprinted courtesy of the University of Wisconsin Press.

Library of Congress Cataloging-in-Publication Data

Names: Obourn, Milo Woolf, 1976– author.
Title: Disabled futures : a framework for radical inclusion / Milo Woolf
  Obourn.
Description: Philadelphia : Temple University Press, 2020. | Includes
  bibliographical references and index. | Summary: "This project reads
  disability alongside race, gender, and sexuality in order to
  problematize the roots of the field of disability studies in the
  experience and writings of white, straight, cis-gendered men. Obourn
  coins the term 'racialized disgender,' a resistant way of reading
  dominant representations of disability."— Provided by publisher.
Identifiers: LCCN 2019010531 (print) | LCCN 2019981146 (ebook) |
  ISBN 9781439917305 (cloth : alk. paper) | ISBN 9781439917312 (paperback
  : alk. paper) | ISBN 9781439917329 (ebook)
Subjects: LCSH: People with disabilities. | Intersectionality (Sociology) |
  Discrimination.
Classification: LCC HV1568 .O26 2020 (print) | LCC HV1568 (ebook) |
  DDC 305.9/08—dc23
LC record available at https://lccn.loc.gov/2019010531
LC ebook record available at https://lccn.loc.gov/2019981146

9 8 7 6 5 4 3 2 1

For Woolf Erin Obourn and Winter Garland Obourn

Wherever you are, my love will find you.*

*With a nod to the book *Wherever You Are, My Love Will Find You*, by Nancy Tillman.

Contents

Preface and Acknowledgments

During the years that I was completing this book, a number of experiences—including the death of my child in infancy, coming out as trans, and taking a one-year position in diversity administration work—started to bring together the thinking I had been doing on an academic front over the better part of a decade. When I came to this project, I was excited about the broadened possibilities for conceptualizing the future of identity-based politics and studies made possible by the growing field of critical disability studies. As I come to the end of the project, I recognize that my understandings of and ways of relating to my body, the cultural capital of my whiteness, and my awareness of what it means to wield that capital alongside the set of socially cultivated ignorances that accompany it are in a state of constant change and negotiation. The idea of the "future" as a linear next or even progressive move forward has given way to a shifting relationship with the concept of futurity. What does it mean to move "forward" as a parent of a dead child? What does it mean to carry with me white privilege as I claim a transmasculine gender identity in a society in which I cannot escape the meanings of white masculinity even as I continue not to identify as or be treated as a white man? What does futurity feel like for my relation to hormone therapy for both fertility and gender dysphoria? What does it mean to do professional work in the service of a future tense of more equity and inclusion within an inequitable, racist, and ableist system that provides me the cultural capital and material privilege to be paid for such work in the first place?

The questions this project has raised for me only make me more certain of the importance of continuing to try to think through the complexities of social identities from and with a critical relation to my own vantage point—a vantage point that is thoroughly situated within and informed by my experiences as a white queer and trans person, raised female, and as someone not constructed by my culture as a person with disabilities, though I have received both mental and physical diagnoses of various sorts. These statuses, including the diagnoses, have, when combined with my white-collar academic job and first world citizenship status, allowed me exceptionally easy and broad access to medical coverage and medical care, as problematic as that care has at times been. I am also influenced by an academic genealogy of white queers writing about the radical political potentials of marginalization, transgression, and deviant embodiment. Such writing has frequently ignored, buried, and/or co-opted the experiences and experiential and intellectual knowledge of people of color and undocumented persons, particularly those who are also queer or disabled. This project begins from the knowledge that it is influenced by such traditions, attempts to expand and critique them, but does not assume that a radical alterity to them is either achievable (given both my social and educational background) or an effective form of internal critique. What is necessary and, I believe, both achievable and effective is to continue to expand our ways of thinking about the multiple intersections between the cultural power of disability as an idea; ideologies of inclusion, normativity, and wellness; and our multiple lived experiences within a range of social identities, including but not limited to disability, that are created and maintained by structures of power and privilege.

Academic writing too often understands itself as primarily part of a conversation with other academics. While it is certainly true for any peer-reviewed project that most of its direct interlocutors are other professional academics, I believe it does a disservice to the multiple arenas in which we learn and process our knowledges and perspectives to act as though those are our only or most important influences. In an effort to expand this awareness, I want to recognize that it has been primarily in working through loss, connection, shifts in health and illness in interpersonal relationships—my own and others'—as well as participating in more activist work around LGBTQ inclusion, accessibility for persons with disabilities, and working with various racial justice groups, that much of my deepest thinking around intersectionality and social identity has occurred. It has been in these spaces that I have discovered the value of mining intersections and disjunctures in the ways we experience power. This value is not solely academic, though it is also that. What is most valuable, in my opinion, is how such mining can ultimately provide more expansive and necessarily complex strategies for building more inclusive spaces and resisting the replication of oppressive power in areas in which we have some agency to do so.

Thus, I start by thanking people I have loved with, worked with, and organized with, some of whom are not even aware of this book but all of whom have contributed to its arguments. I thank The Movement at The College at Brockport, in particular its founding and early members—Eemane Boadu, Calvin Butler, Kerlyne Colin, Diamond Cotton, Will Dillard-Jackson, Anastajah Hayes, Keara Knight, Imani Lawrence, Sidnee MacDonald, Jordin Paige, and Isaiah Patmon—for letting me learn from co-conspiring. I am grateful to Brockport's President's Council on Diversity and Inclusion (PCDI) Committee on Accessibility, particularly its brilliant and tireless chair, Jessica Sniatecki. I thank Brockport's Office of Community Development for being an ongoing model of not only collaborative learning that does not compromise rigor but also broad inclusiveness and accessibility, in particular Karen Podsiadly (a fabulous mentor), Kim Piatt, and the outstanding graduate assistants. I am grateful to Brockport's Student Accessibility Services team, especially Director Sherri Micheli. I thank the many folks who have staffed Brockport's Office of Diversity, Equity and Inclusion for their work and support. I especially appreciate Heather Packer, whose generosity and labor have made more change happen than I think most people realize. I thank the Brockport Pride Alliance; Brockport's Office of Residential Life; Brockport's Academic Success Center Team; Brockport's Faculty and Staff affiliation groups and their leaders; and the PCDI Professional Development Committee, especially my current co-chair, Melody Boyd. My deepest gratitude goes, as well, to the off-campus groups that have helped deepen my thinking about identity, power, and inclusion, including SURJ ROC (Showing Up for Social Justice, Rochester) and the Opening Doors Diversity Project—Ricardo Adams, Kathy Castania, Betty Garcia-Mathewson, and Eduardo González, who are all inspiring and supportive role models. I also thank my yoga families, particularly my teachers Aimée Senise Conners and Tisah Leigh Milner Brederson; studio owners Pete Nabozny and Lindsay Wech Nabozny, Jesse Amesmith and Julie Olney, and Joy Ebel; the wonderful interpreters for ASL Interpreted Yoga (Tru Yoga, Rochester), especially Dee Herera and ash harper for their organizational work and partnership; and everyone who comes to Queer & Trans Yoga (Yoga Vibe, Rochester) and ASL Interpreted Yoga. They have all made more space for me to practice knowing myself more honestly so that I can practice knowing others more honestly. And I am grateful to two incredibly generous mentees, Lucky Summer Light and Jermaine Meadows—working with them has both challenged and shaped my thinking in highly substantive ways.

I must also acknowledge the insight I have gained from my students, particularly those in my graduate course, "Queer Theory, Disability Theory, and Contemporary American Literature," and my undergraduate courses, "Introduction to Intersectional Disability Studies" and "Disability Studies in American Literature." I thank them all for learning with me. Much gratitude goes, as well, to my colleagues in both English and Women and Gender Studies. I thank Rachael Mulvihill for the helpful edits and input on Chapter 3. I am grateful to Barb LeSavoy for constant support, wonderful feedback, and life mentorship. I also thank my English Department mentors, Jennifer Haytock and Janie Hinds, who continue to support and guide me well past the hoops of the tenure process. I thank Cherise Oakley for knowing everything and for offering such generous support. My gratitude goes to Alissa Karl for the insightful feedback on Chapter 1. And my deepest thanks go to Kristen Proehl—whose insight and support have truly been invaluable—for reading and commenting on many portions of the manuscript, some at multiple stages.

I also owe my deepest thanks to several local colleagues outside of my home departments and institution. I am grateful to Emilie Wasserman for getting me access to the grand rounds lecture, discussed in this book's Coda. I thank Jennifer Ratcliff for ongoing intellectual discussion, support, humor, and perspective. I am grateful to June Hwang for feedback on Chapter 1 and for providing engaging and thought-provoking conversation about not only the possibilities and limitations of critical social theories of identity but also how they play out within academic life. I thank Kristen Hocker and Faith Prather for being so dang smart, for being amazing personal and professional supports, and for modeling the enactment of the changes we long for without ever compromising the awesomeness that they embody. And I am grateful to Jennifer Ashton for being my teammate in all things disability studies related and for giving me the most generous feedback on Chapter 3 that I may have ever received in my life.

To my long-distance and long-term collaborators, I extend my great esteem. I thank Anthony Casciano, Inge De Taeye, Tania Friedel, Tom Jacobs, and Ben Turner for continuing to be a hub of friendship and intellectual engagement in New York. I am grateful to Annie Lee Jones for writing with me and for helping me process ways to talk about the trauma of identity, and the subject position of whiteness in particular, without pulling away (or with the strength to go back if I do). I owe thanks always to Jean Wyatt, who gave me tremendously insightful feedback on Chapters 1 and 3 and who continues to include me in some of the most productive scholarly communities I have known. I am grateful to Brooke Conti for many years of processing relations between time, identity, and care and for modeling a practice of professionalism that does not compartmentalize or deny the personal. Though it has been too long since we talked about these things, Joe Ortíz's academic and personal thoughts on identity and literature have made their way into my thinking in numerous and expansive ways. I thank Sara Morrison and Rachel Weeks for helping me better understand the often inextricable relation among embodiment, empowerment, grief, and struggle. To Jacoby Ballard I offer my sincerest gratitude for modeling awareness, care, consistency, and love in all pursuits. I thank my former graduate school colleagues Aliyyah Abdur-Rahman and Leigh Claire La Berge for their feedback and support over the years, in relation to both specific portions of this project and its claims more generally—I wish for more time with them both. I am grateful to andré carrington for providing the rich social media feeds and for pointing me to the Macharia essay cited in this book's Coda. To Allison Hobgood, Roy Pérez, and Rachel Steck, I extend my appreciation and gratitude for hosting me as a speaker and visitor to their classes at Willamette, which gave me the opportunity to explore the ideas in this book with collegial and student communities outside my own. I also express my gratitude for and acknowledge the influence of my graduate school mentors— Phillip Brian Harper, Elizabeth McHenry, José Esteban Muñoz, Cyrus Patel, Ross Posnock, and George Schulman. Though I did not begin the writing of this book until after I left New York University, many of the ways I approach theories of social identity were formed under their instruction and mentorship. José's work on disidentification and his generosity of spirit and drive to align theory with possibility and pleasure have been particularly influential to my thinking, and I am so deeply saddened that he is not here to receive this acknowledgment.

I thank the participants and organizers of the 2018 National Women's Studies Association session "Knowledge, Identity, and Place: Resisting Binaries and Re-envisioning a Gender Expansive University"; the 2017 SUNY Conversations in the Disciplines Conference "Disability Studies: An Interdisciplinary Conversation"; the 2016 American Comparative Literature Association (ACLA) Seminar "Race and Narrative Form"; the 2016 Modern Language Association (MLA) session "Disability and Interdependence"; the 2013 ACLA Seminar "Getting Lost: Contemporary Fantasies of Isolation, Withdrawal, and Disconnection"; the 2012 "After Queer, After Humanism" conference at Rice University; and the 2012 Northeast MLA session "Revenge of the Queers." Each of these sessions facilitated constructive and supportive input on this project. In particular, I am grateful to Rosemarie Garland-Thomson for her keynote and conversation at our SUNY "Disability Studies" Conference and to Andrea Gadberry and Sheldon George for their extended feedback, conversation, and support at and following ACLA.

Earlier versions of Chapters 3 and 4 appeared in *Genders* and *Contemporary Literature*, respectively. I thank the series editors at *Genders*, Judith Roof and Alanna Beroiza, for supporting my work. I am grateful to the University of Colorado at Boulder and the University of Wisconsin Press for permission to reprint and the anonymous reviewers at both journals for their insightful feedback. I also thank the anonymous reviewers at Palgrave, who—although the press was not the best match for this project—gave me substantial and important input that helped me develop this project into its final form. My deepest gratitude goes to the staff at Temple University Press—Aaron Javsicas, Gary Kramer, Nikki Miller, Ginny Perrin, Ashley Petrucci, and Joan Polsky Vidal—who have been amazingly supportive and such a pleasure to work with. I owe a very special and substantial thank-you to Sara Jo Cohen, a truly outstanding editor, interlocutor, and supporter of this project. I am grateful to the *Dis/color* series editors, Cynthia Wu, Julie Avril Minich, and Nirmala Erevelles—and especially the editorial board and anonymous readers at Temple University Press, who saw the potential in the manuscript and gave the precise feedback it needed to reach it.

I thank Cedric Johnson for permission to use his artwork on the cover of this book and Jessica Daniel at Creative Growth Art Center for helping to make its use possible. I am grateful to HarperCollins for permission to reprint Miriam Engelberg's comic "Personal." I thank Craig Froehle for making his "Equity vs. Equality" illustration public domain so that it could be included here and in many other locations as a site for continued discussion of the meaning of true equity.

Always and above all, I am grateful to my family. Candy, Ted, Peter, Chelsea, and Erin Obourn; Elliott Mealia; Janice Carello; Eric Scoles; and Brad McKay make it possible to live, think, and write as me, and I could not possibly want for a more brilliant, strange, loving, amazing family. I am heartbroken that Brad is not here to receive this gratitude. I thank Tuesday Obourn, my partner in everything; my favorite and most brilliant interlocutor, academic and otherwise; and the greatest supporter of this project from its beginnings, for always holding my wrists and my heart. Finally, I am grateful to Woolf and Winter, my beauties and greatest joys, who have both taught me so much about love and grief and frailty and the messiness of beauty and pain, about limitations, and about infinite expansions. I shape these words for them. May they always know, wherever they are, my love will find them.

DISABLED FUTURES

Introduction

On the Future of Disabled Identities

I consider myself both an academic theorist immersed in disability studies, gender and sexuality studies, and critical race studies and a practitioner of institutional equity and inclusion work. I have frequently experienced this balance of theory and practice as a paradox in which I am employed to perform labor aimed at raising awareness of and decreasing systemic and interpersonal oppression by an academic institution and within a set of national and professional structures that are built on and complicit with neoliberal capitalist domination. Thus, I often find myself engaging social justice work within higher education that utilizes many of the concepts and related practices that I critique in my academic writing. There is a friction here that affects not only me. From the perspective of professional practitioners concerned with equity and inclusion, critical social and other academic theory can be perceived as too abstract, inaccessible, or impractical. From the perspective of critical social theorists, the practice of diversity work may be understood to be assimilating radical ideas into neoliberal and depoliticizing institutional structures. Such frictions remind me that one of the barriers to building more equitable and inclusive spaces is the fiction that theory and practice are separable and opposing things. This fiction circulates not only at the theoretical level in academic writing, where we are often most comfortable pointing out the limitations and flaws in concepts like identity, diversity, and inclusion, but also in the ways we divide work within our institutions— "student affairs" versus "academic affairs," for example. How are academic affairs not student affairs, and how is the support and well-being of our students not an academic matter? This book takes as a foundational assumption that critical social theories such as critical disability studies, critical race studies, and feminist/gender studies grow out of social justice movements and continue to inform the practices we utilize to create greater equity and justice within the flawed systems in which we find ourselves.

Disabled Futures enters into conversation with work in disability studies, gender and sexuality studies, and critical race studies in hopes of building a framework for thinking about how to more effectively address inequity as a set of interlocking systems that both disable and constitute human subjects. In this book, I use readings of literature and film to explore the constitutive and oppressive intersections between ableism, racism, and sexism/cissexism/heteronormativity.[1] These ideologies and systems of power work in particular and historically informed collaborations to constitute subjects in the contemporary United States. I consider race, gender, and disability to be distinct and identifiable subject positions and self-identifications. At the same time, I argue that the ways we conceptualize these aspects of our identities and the power structures and liberation politics that may attend to them continue to be treated in false isolation from one another.

Recently, while preparing several internal equity/diversity/inclusion-related trainings at my home institution, I found myself engaging in a set of debates about how and whether to include information for participants on the difference between equity and equality. Primarily, these debates centered on the now widely used and fairly widely critiqued comparative illustrations designed by Craig Froehle of three human figures of different heights trying to look over a fence to see a baseball game. In the illustration on the left, frequently labeled "equality," each figure stands on a single box of uniform size—unnecessary for the first figure, who is the tallest; just high enough for the second figure, who is slightly shorter; and not high enough for the third, who is the shortest. In the illustration on the right, most often labeled "equity," "justice," or "fairness," the first figure stands on no box, the second stands on one box, and the third stands on two boxes, allowing all to see over the fence.

While reviewing an online diversity training, which focused largely on power and privilege, our faculty/staff committee decided to leave this illustration out. We were all aware of the critiques of the illustration, including its unmarked whiteness and how it reinforces a deficit model by implying that the source of inequity is located in individual bodies (i.e., the height of the figures) rather than in the histories of systemic oppression, exclusion, and stigma that have created deep barriers to access and resources. A few weeks later, when a different group of faculty/staff reviewers was making some final revisions for a more focused internal training on ableism and accessibility, the

Craig Froehle's "Equity vs. Equality."

question of whether to include this illustration arose again. Again, the critique was made that while the illustration is useful for pointing out that different bodies need different accommodations, it does not address the histories of systemic oppression of people with disabilities or the hegemonic environmental barriers themselves, represented in the illustration by the static fence. To address the issue this time I replaced the original illustration with a revised version designed by Paul Kuttner, which includes staggered ground and an inclined fence, and in which figures look more like plastic cut-outs that are all the same height and are colored red, yellow, and blue. Kuttner's version suggests that histories of power have put some people on lower ground and given some people more barriers than others, and it attempts to take away bodily social identity markers like race, gender, and disability status. This time, however, there was more pushback. In the context of raising awareness about ableism, our group wanted to stress that difference *is*, in fact, located in bodies and that to make the figures all the same height actually carries ableist assumptions about how we represent equity and inclusivity. To make the figures all the same size suggests that we are not, in fact, talking about real embodied differences—differences that frequently matter very much to people with disabilities.

It was not until I attempted to use Froehle's illustration in the context of social justice awareness work that I started to think that the problem may be less the illustration itself and more the ways we conceptualize various forms of oppression and avenues for their redress. Numerous illustrations have emerged to address the limitations of Froehle's original.[2] Some have changed it so that the figures read as people of color. Several illustrations include people who appear to be of varying racial backgrounds. Some include more femme-appearing folks. One replaces two blocks with a ramp and shows the third person at the top in a wheelchair. Many include a third illustration labeled "liberation" or "justice" that has a chain-link fence or no fence. Such revisions are ways of attending to what is a conceptually helpful but not particularly inclusive representation with illustrations that increase the types of bodies, experiences, and ways of thinking about power represented. No matter how much we add to this illustration, however, there remains an impasse in inclusive representation that stems from a lack of a shared way of thinking about oppression that is *both* historical/systemic/environmental *and* deeply rooted in bodies and bodily experience. Understanding how multiple forms of oppression, including racism, (cis)sexism, and ableism, intersect to create inequity necessitates a conception of oppression and liberation that understands bodyminds,[3] histories, and environments to exist in dynamic relation to each other to produce privilege, oppression, agency, power, subjectivity, and subjection.[4]

Working at the Intersections of Race, Gender, and Disability

This book attempts to theorize social identity and power as always already *both* embodied and historically and environmentally created. To do so, it looks to close textual analyses as sites for illuminating how we are all constituted as subjects within an intersectional racist, sexist, and ableist society. My hope is that such understandings can contribute to strategies for intervening in ableism, racism, and sexism that can be understood to impact and benefit people who identify as disabled and able-bodied, people of all and no gender identity/ies, and people of all racial identities in the United States. This, I consider, to be a radical framework in that it looks to some of the historical and environmental roots of our identities and to the oppressions, limitations, and privileges that arise in relationship to them. I also consider it a radical form of inclusivity in that it is concerned with the ways our liberations really are bound up in one another, and therefore provides a foundation for engaged allyship work across and within identity groups. In particular, the readings in this book (1) examine and unpack specific ways that race and gender construct and are constructed by historical notions of ability and disability, sickness and health, and successful recovery versus damaged lives and (2) consider how affective and representational relationships to futurity impact how we currently do and potentially can imagine embodiment within raced, gendered, and dis/abled subjectivities. In applying a disability studies lens to readings of race and gender, and critical race and gender and sexuality studies lenses to representations of disability, what begins to emerge is not only a more complex and deeper understanding of the intersections between ableism, racism, and (cis)sexism but also, and equally as important to imagining alternate and more radically inclusive futures, an expanded space for holding and acknowledging the simultaneous limitations and power of our embodied identities, and the ways they are intertwined with the identities, experiences, freedoms, and oppressions of others.

The readings in this text attempt to decipher the distinct but interdependent workings of ableism, racism, and (cis)sexism in a number of different representations and in so doing to refract or change the directionality of our common ways of perceiving gendered, raced, and dis/abled identities. In the service of referring to such an interpretive lens without repeatedly explaining it at length, I have coined the term "racialized disgender." This term is meant to capture how (1) all gender identities are always already raced, (2) all racialized gender identities are constituted in relation to the able/disabled binary, and (3) racialized gender acts on the body via a process of disablement, not only through limiting access to physical and political spaces for those with marginalized racial and gender identities but, moreover, by constituting raced and gendered bodies through external violence, impairment, and social control over our physical, emotional, and mental engagement with the world and others.[5] Racialized disgender as I use it here is not a metaphor for race and gender. Racism and (cis)sexism have their own distinct set of violences and logics. And people with disabilities have been used as metaphors for harm, marginalization, or dysfunction for far too long. Racialized disgendering is a description of a set of linguistic, ideological, and physical practices that constitutes racialized gender identity in direct relation to ideas about healthy and able bodies as well as in relation to physical, emotional, and psychological limitations on and violences done to individuals.[6]

My thinking here is deeply indebted to the concept of intersectionality. Intersectionality as a political and theoretical idea comes out of Black feminist politics and theory and was historically necessitated by the "single axis" thinking of white-dominated feminisms and male-dominated Black liberation movements (Crenshaw 138). The term itself was coined by Kimberlé Crenshaw to better address "the particular manner in which Black women are subordinated" (140). The importance of attending to the specific experiences and knowledges of women of color is also often traced to arguments by the Combahee River Collective, as well as theorists such as Gloria Anzaldúa, Angela Davis, Audre Lorde, Cherríe Moraga, and Barbara Smith, who stressed the importance of not only race and gender but also sexuality, size, ethnicity, language, and ability status as mutually constitutive identities and systems of power. Patricia Hill Collins coined the term "matrix of domination" to describe how power works through various forms of interdependent oppressions (*Black Feminist Thought* 18) and reminds us in her 2016 Key Concepts series monograph, *Intersectionality,* co-written with Sirma Bilge, that "intersectional frameworks understand power relations through a lens of mutual construction [in which] power relations . . . gain meaning in relation to one another" (27). That the term "intersectionality" has been at the center of much critical debate in the past few years suggests to me not that it has been overdone or irredeemably co-opted by a conservative neoliberal academy (as some have argued).[7] Rather, it points to the need for ongoing work to develop critical practices that both attend to intersectionality's foundational claim that the perspectives of those multiply marginalized by structures of identity-based oppressions can provide needed insight into the workings of those systems and also deepen our understanding of the ways we are all constituted by and all simultaneously limited by these systems.[8]

Disabled Futures draws on the double work of intersectional theory—attending to specific marginalizations and clarifying broader workings of power—to explore the interdependence and co-construction of race, gender, and disability in James Cameron's film *Avatar,* J. J. Abram's television series *Lost,* Arturo Islas's novel *The Rain God,* Cherríe Moraga's play *Heroes and Saints,* Audre Lorde's essay collection *The Cancer Journals,* Miriam Engelberg's comic memoir *Cancer Made Me a Shallower Person,* and Octavia Butler's *Xenogenesis* trilogy (published most recently in one volume titled *Lilith's Brood*). I pursue these readings not only in the hope of revealing more about how the matrix of domination that uses ableism, racism, and (cis)sexism as tools to replicate itself functions but also in the hope of highlighting that we are all impacted by the intersections of these forms of domination and that each of our bodyminds is constituted within them. The close analyses in this book proceed not by assuming preexisting categories of race, gender, or ability/disability but rather by thinking about how these categories are inconceivable without the others. Each reading takes as a premise that becoming raced is also a gendering process, that becoming gendered is also a racializing process, and that becoming racially gendered is for every social subject simultaneously enabling (in terms of gaining access to subjecthood) and disabling (in terms of both how it can limit social, political, and economic access *and* how it can cause harm to the bodyminds of those subjects). I posit these analyses as a set of models for talking about how such forms of power, and the subjects and identity groups that they construct, are always already informing one another and how they affect every bodymind that comes into being as a social and political subject within them.

In approaching intersectionality between ableism, racism, and (cis)sexism, this book aims to bring together the disability and race-focused critiques of scholars such as Christopher Bell, Nirmala Erevelles, Julie Avril Minich, and Therí Pickens with the disability and gender-/sexuality-focused critiques of scholars such as Eli Clare, Alison Kafer, and Rosemarie Garland-Thomson. As Clare, Kafer, and Garland-Thomson argue, normative gender is both a highly ableist and racialized category itself in the United States. Similarly, Bell, Erevelles, Minich, and Pickens make arguments that suggest not only that bodies that inhabit intersections of disability and racial nonwhiteness are targets of violence and social erasure but also that racial nonwhiteness has historically been a category defined heavily in relation to disability in ways that reproduce and reinforce practices of violence against people of color. Like Minich's desire to "emphasiz[e] similarities, not differences, between people with disabilities and other minoritized groups" (22) and Pickens's intent to "push back against the idea that normalcy or belonging is a state to which [one] should aspire" (*New Body Politics* 12), my argument looks for moments in which representations of racialized and gendered bodies highlight the histories of disablement that have created their material and social realities and identities, without aspiring to heal or overcome these histories.

Disability and Futurity

While intersections between race, dis/ability, and gender are far from exhaustive of the many identities and power relations that constitute us as subjects, race, disability status, and gender are three aspects of our social and political selves that have historically been theorized not only in isolation from one another, a fact to which the intersectional critiques of Crenshaw and others attest, but often in purposeful antipathy to one another. Ableist ideology has been used as a tool to distance feminist, LGBTQ, and racial justice movements from identification with people with disabilities. As Vivian May and Beth Ferri argue, "An impairment or deficit model has been used by those in power to characterize marginalized groups . . . as incapable of full citizenship," which has in turn led to the use of ableist concepts and metaphors within many social justice movements that do not understand themselves to be aligned with the disabled (120).[9] This logic appeared in the reading of the "equity vs. equality" illustrations that opened this Introduction, in which locating difference in individual bodies is read as inherently a "deficit" model. If we are to truly use intersectionality as the radical—as in reaching to the roots—tool that many believe it to be, we need to keep sharpening its edges and looking for the most subtle and nuanced ways we can use it to decipher and thus hopefully intervene in workings of power.[10] We also need a way of attending to a complex understanding of social identities and oppression as constructed by our environment and simultaneously lived at the material level of the body. Such an understanding can help us to think about how we can live in the present with a full awareness of the histories of woundedness, disempowerment, limitation, and harm done by our coming into subjecthood within a matrix of oppression that marks and forms our bodyminds to serve dominant forms of power, without letting that awareness pull us away from conscious and conscientious action, activism, and allyship in the present. Such a model enables us to think about futures that we may desire that are not free from histories of or even present experiences of woundedness, limitation, frustration, or barriers.

Disability studies provides models for holding conceptual space for both the negative and positive experiences of our lived identities and relations to power. Holding those experiences and affective relations in the present provides a foundation for future imaginaries that can prompt action in resistance to power that limits and confines us while simultaneously understanding that liberation is not freedom from all limitations, wounds, or pain. While the critique of identity-based politics that it is too attached to histories of pain and marginalization continues to circulate in critical social theory, disability theory provides alternate ways of thinking about ambivalent but necessary and even potentially productive relations to pain and current/historical woundedness.[11] Susan Wendell argues that there is potential epistemological value to pain and that we must "learn to talk about . . . that which cannot be noticed without pain and that which cannot be celebrated without ambivalence" (179). Tobin Siebers articulates this ambivalence on a political/theoretical level, arguing that while "opponents of identity politics are not wrong . . . when they associate minority identity with suffering," they are mistaken in that "they do not accept that pain and suffering may sometimes be resources for the epistemological insights of minority identity" (20). This study, following Wendell and Siebers, foregrounds the value of historical and contemporary wounds of identity in relation to the potential epistemic privilege they provide.[12] Pain and other physical and emotional negative feelings like fatigue, guilt, trauma, and anger may be bodily signals of social inequities that those who embody minority social identities have more access to. Physical and psychological pain can be both experiences we may want to mediate and sources of knowledge and connection.[13]

Suffering, particularly when shared with others in similarly oppressed positions, can create theoretical knowledges about the functioning of power, privilege, and inequality. Heather Love gestures toward this in her work on queer negativity, where she suggests that the turn toward pride and hope in queer politics has harmed our ability to incorporate the "dark side" of queer representation and histories of queerness as histories of erasure, violence, and exclusion. Tellingly, she gestures toward a need to better understand how to "liv[e] with injury—not fix[] it" (4). Bodies marked as queer and bodies marked as having disabilities have incurred different kinds of histories of violence, marginalization, and physical and psychological wounding. Nevertheless, Love's use of injury to talk about aspects of queer history that may get lost in the push toward more optimistic futures suggests that disability theory, which has thought deeply and complexly about injury, impairment, and disability as an inextricable part of one's social identity, could be a rich source to approach a politics that looks toward a more accessible, equitable, and less violent future without having to sever affective attachments to disability, impairment, and wounds.

The concept of "disabled futures" attends to the need to hold space for the value and the pain of identity even as we resist systems and ideologies of ableism, racism, and (cis)sexism that function through the creation of unwanted pain and domination. As Alison Kafer points out, disability is so often used to mean tragedy that the very presence of disability can signal "a future that bears too many traces of the ills of the present to be desirable" (2). Eunjung Kim suggests that ideologies of cure "fold" time into a relation to past cause and future healing that prevents one from living fully in the present with a disability. Such dominant forms of ableist thinking not only put people with disabilities in a position outside of valued human life and contribute to eugenicist thinking that aims to rid the world of people with disabilities; they also disallow the traces of ills that have constituted all of us as subjects a place in our realities and in the ways we move toward less oppressive and more aware futures. Anna Mollow's concept of the "disability drive" is also useful for thinking through U.S. culture's ambivalent relationship to disability, woundedness, and marginalization. Disability drive, according to Mollow, is our individual and cultural attraction to and repulsion from the loss of self that a queer and/or disabled future would threaten/promise. Mining this ambivalent affective and subconscious relation to such a future can help us explore possible alternatives to what Mollow terms "rehabilitative" futures that conserve current power structures and promote fear of loss, pain, and disability, all of which are inevitably part of our human experience and deeply embedded in our gender, racial, and dis/ability identities. The concept of disabled futures I employ in this text resists rehabilitative and curative models and intervenes in critiques of identity-based politics that suggest we must rid ourselves of or detach ourselves from wounded identities in order to imagine a more liberated future.

Racialized Disgender as Inclusive Framework

I argue that all bodies constituted as subjects in the United States come into being as racially gendered subjects directly and inextricably in relation to assumptions about able-bodiedness, mental health, normative expectations for movement and social relationality, and imposed/internalized limitations to body and mind. I argue in the chapters that follow that while some texts may be more useful for unpacking the ways that racialized gender constitutes bodies in relation to disability—and these are often texts written by and with the epistemic privilege of disabled or ill women and queers of color—the framework that I am constructing can be used to talk about the effects of these power structures on any body. Social power functions not only through the ways bodies experience material privilege and marginalization along lines of social identity but also through the psychological and emotional harm to all bodies and the threat of further harm if one does not accept the limits of their racially gendered position. While the types of harm and the extent to which bodies are stigmatized and experience (the threat of) direct physical violence varies hugely across racial, gender, and dis/ability categories, all U.S. subjects are constituted as raced, gendered, and dis/abled subjects via histories of violence.

The idea that gender and race are constituted through impairment and disability is not a new one. There is a fairly long genealogy of work theorizing the creation of race and gender through disability and impairment, though it is not always named as such. Iris Marion Young has argued that ideologies of womanhood "physically handicap" women and girls. Susan Bordo has demonstrated how agoraphobia, hysteria, and anorexia have been created by cultural expectations for white middle-class women. Diane Herndl notes that the emergence of the white "invalid woman" in the mid-nineteenth century was directly related to ideals of bourgeois femininity that reinforced the embodiment of female ideals through debilitating clothing and practices that deprived girls of protein-rich foods, exercise, and hygiene (*Invalid Women* 27–28). Tamara Beauboeuf-Lafontant suggests that the cultural myth of the strong Black woman results in illness for many Black women. Jim Downs has studied the emergence of current categories of disability in relation to labor in the treatment of freed Blacks during Reconstruction. Dennis Tyler Jr. argues that during the Jim Crow era, "the law's proclivity to disable functioned as another way to discipline and control Black bodies that it deemed deviant and unruly" (186). And Jay Dolmage has studied the entwined constructions of disability and racial nonwhiteness via eugenics-informed immigration practices in the early twentieth-century United States. Such readings clarify ways that raced forms of gender indoctrination

and gendered forms of racial indoctrination harm, limit, and constitute bodies as identifiable subjects.

It is not only in studies of marginalized racial and gender identities that
intersections with disability and illness arise. Thandeka argues that white
racial identity in the United States is formed developmentally though "an
injury to [the white child's] core sense of self" and that this injury is "too
traumatic to retain in consciousness" (17, 87). Steve Martinot argues that
white racial identity and community is constituted by a kind of shared "social
paranoia" (57). Michael Kimmel studies how men are created through "codes"
of boyhood that leave them "disconnected from a wide range of emotions,"
making them "more prone to depression [and] suicidal behavior," and more
likely to be diagnosed with emotional disturbances and ADHD than children
of other genders (53–54). And James Harrison, James Chin, and Thomas Ficarrotto have suggested that cultural expectations for masculinity are not
only unhealthy but can also be literally "lethal" for men (282).

I do not cite these texts because I find myself in full agreement with their
methodologies or assumptions, or because they are all equally useful to the
readings I engage with in this text. Rather, I reference them to highlight that
relations between race and disability and gender and disability have been a
part of race and gender studies even as they have not always been named as
such and have only more recently been studied through an explicitly critical
disability studies lens. In fact, several of the arguments cited above replicate
ableist ideology by figuring injury and disability as solely negative aspects of
social identities that might be recovered from. This is all the more reason that
when we talk about race and gender, we must attend to how they form and
inform each other in relation to disability—both in the form of violent impo-
sitions of impairment and in the form of the stigmatization of bodies. The
disability aspect of gender and racial formations is often hidden via ableist
ideologies that pressure bodies not marked as disabled to not recognize or
identify with the stigma of disability. It is also often hidden via racist ideologies that mark white bodies as safe from and bodies of color as vulnerable to
social violence and impairment, thus normalizing certain forms of disablement. Finally, it is hidden via dominant gender ideologies that associate some
mental, emotional, and physical disabilities with normative gender embodiment—for example, emotional pain or instability might be read as a sign of
normative womanhood, rather than as a disability. Despite their sometimes
ableist assumption that disability or impairment is inherently negative, the
texts cited above do address ways that race and gender are processes of disablement. I read against the grain of the ableist assumption that we want to
be free of disability, while at the same time acknowledging the inseparability
of injury, disablement, race, and gender to which such work points. Becoming

more aware of the ways racialized disgender functions not only nuances our understanding of racism and (cis)sexism but also can help us to perceive the effects of ableism on our bodies and identities, thereby making us all more effective and engaged advocates for a less ableist society.

To explore this mutual constitution of race and gender via disability, I turn to Hortense Spillers's "Mama's Baby, Papa's Maybe: An American Grammar Book" and bell hooks's *The Will to Change: Men, Masculinity, and Love*. I choose these texts in part as an acknowledgment of the impact of intersectional Black feminisms to the concept of racialized disgender, in part because of their long-standing impact on critical race and gender studies, and in part because each has been taken up as a key text for exploration by contemporary scholars in disability studies working on the relationship between gender, race, and disability, albeit to slightly different ends. Spillers's and hooks's essays together provide an outline for ways of thinking about how power uses physical/mental/emotional impairment and ideologies of ableism to constitute racial and gender identities in the United States. They also point to the fact that the ways we conceptualize normative bodies are inextricable from historical racial and gender formations. And they provide some orientation for navigating the ethical dilemma of claiming identities created in violence without replicating or celebrating the violence itself.

In Spillers's "Mama's Baby, Papa's Maybe," she notes that a primary form of dispossession resulting from chattel slavery was "the loss of gender." This fact necessitates an "altered reading of gender" for Black men and women in the United States (77). Spillers's argument is that the history of human captivity and enslavement on which the United States' culture and economy was founded created a gendering outside of dominant patriarchal understandings of maleness and femaleness for Black Americans. The "social-political order of the New World," argues Spillers, denied normative gender possibilities to Black Americans via "*actual* mutilation, dismemberment, and exile" (67). That is, the category of racial Blackness was constructed through the ungendering of bodies that occurred through imposed and unwanted physical impairment and the related stigmatizing and dehumanizing of the disabled and desexed body.

Erevelles argues that Spillers's "essay is as much about disability as it is about race" in that it reveals that "it is precisely at the historical moment when one class of human being was transformed into cargo to be transported to the New World that black bodies become disabled and disabled bodies become black" (40). Erevelles insightfully traces the unnamed but continually present concept of disability in Spillers's essay, concluding that the "markings on the flesh" that begin under slavery "produce impairment" on

Black bodies such that it becomes almost impossible to "claim the sovereign subject, now mutually constituted via race, disability, and gender as a dehumanized commodity" (44). Erevelles uses this reading to stress an attentiveness to the ways that racial Blackness has been constructed via violent impairment-creating practices that turn the Black disabled body into a commodity, and therefore to problematize poststructuralist and disability studies rhetorics that celebrate the deconstruction of the subject as inherently emancipating or transgressive.

I too want to resist patterns of depathologizing disability that turn immediately and only to a celebration of disability as difference or resistance. However, I approach this not so much by situating the cocreation of race, gender, and disability in transnational capitalism and the exchange of bodies as commodity as by thinking about the ways this cocreation has situated our current politics and possibilities for conceptualizing a future. In Erevelles's reading, gender is "stripped" from enslaved Black bodies, and it is this "erasure of gender" that enabled the impairment of the Black female body. While Spillers does suggest that gender disappears in the Middle Passage and becomes reinscribed as a site of commodification rather than the subject-enabling identity that maleness and femaleness are in our society, she also suggests at the end of her essay that there is room for a reclaiming by Black men and women of the identities this historical dissolution has created. While the history of violence done to Black bodies via the Middle Passage and the institution of chattel slavery is impossible to reclaim in and of itself as a site for celebration, transgression, or emancipation, the *effects* of such a history do, in fact, offer up a possibility for reclamation. At the very least, Spillers suggests, there is the possibility of "claiming" the inheritances of this history, not to reify or celebrate trauma and violence, but to "make a place for" the Black female body as one that is gendered outside the "traditional symbolics of female gender" such that a claiming of this "monstrosity"—that is, a female body that is not subject to patriarchal norms—"might rewrite . . . a radically different text for female empowerment" (80). What Spillers points out as an "un-gendering" of flesh does not result in a complete lack of gender, but rather offers us a historical reading of how racial disgendering functions. Gender, race, and disability are all historically and inseparably structured, such that all genders, all racial identities, and all dis/ability statuses are created in relation to one another. There is no true and preexisting gender that is stripped from Black female bodies, even as the way that those bodies experienced dehumanization and commodification happened through denying them legibility within dominant symbolics of maleness and femaleness. Rather, those bodies come to experience their gendering via the historical imposition of extreme violence.

While Spillers is most invested in exploring how this history impacts current (mis)understandings of the power and marginalization of Black women, she attends, as well, to how this history has created Black manhood, white womanhood, and even white manhood. Spillers argues that chattel slavery and its work in the creation of racialized gender create Black men as the "*only* American community of males" who have the potential to know "the female within itself" (80). She suggests that white women's racialized gender was formed in relation to "the same fabric of dread and humiliation" as Black women's, though to very different ends (77). And in her statement that "'sexuality' as a term of implied relationship and desire, is dubiously appropriate . . . to *any* of the familial arrangements under a system of enslavement, from the master's family to the captive enclave," I would suggest that Spillers at least gestures toward the fact that the racialized gender of slave masters was also constructed in relation to violent practices of disablement and human commodification (76).

In my expansion of Spillers's critique to all bodies under slavery, I want to continue to highlight the specific violences done to Black female bodies but also to suggest that her framework for understanding how the Middle Passage and chattel slavery constructed race, gender, and dis/ability as interdependent and nationally and historically specific categories can be applied to the construction of all identities formed out of these historical violences. Here I understand myself as working in alignment with Crenshaw's conception of intersectionality—that it is created specifically to address the multiple marginalization of Black women, and that in examining that marginalization it offers a framework for understanding power and its effects more broadly.[14]

One might take issue with this expansion on the grounds that intersectionality has been theorized as the intersections of oppressions and marginalizations and that Spillers is specifically talking about racial and gender identities constructed as the Other to the full subjectivity of white maleness. This is where bell hooks's *The Will to Change: Men, Masculinity, and Love,* a foundational text for current work in men and masculinity studies that perceive manhood as impairing men's bodies, can offer us additional insight. Here hooks forwards the reading that men have been just as traumatized and disabled by patriarchy as women and that if feminism cannot understand and incorporate this fact, it cannot work to end the cycle of violence that is men's domination of women. Itself imbedded in ableist language, hooks's reading is not informed by a disability studies approach. This becomes clear in her use of the term "emotional cripples" to describe what happens to men under patriarchy, as well as her conclusion that in order to attend to the "self-mutilation" that patriarchy requires, we must "reunit[e] the severed parts" (27, 66). Thus, hooks uses language suggesting that disability is something wholly negative and takes a medical model approach that understands it as in need of rehabilitation or repair.

Sami Schalk has pointed to how hooks's metaphor must either be read as ableist—implying that disability is "a negative, anti-relational state of injury and brokenness," or as antifeminist—that men have a disability and thus their world and environment need to be more accommodating of their violent expressions of love, thereby "shift[ing] the focus away from patriarchy as a damaging system of oppression" ("Metaphorically" n.p.). I want to offer another possible reading here, which goes against the grain of hooks's ableist framework but not necessarily against her overall point. What if we read hooks less metaphorically and we accept her diagnosis but not her ableist prescription for treatment? In other words, what if we read her argument not as a metaphor for what patriarchy does to men but as a literal description of mental/emotional impairment that is the result of the workings of (cis)sexism on all bodies? Schalk suggests that a disability studies approach would not place the responsibility to change on the disabled person, but rather on their environment. Schalk here is referring to the social model of disability in which disability can be attended to entirely by changing the environment. As other disability studies scholars have noted, however, a person with a disability may experience pain, fatigue, and mortality, which are not necessarily alleviated by changing the environment. A diagnosis of mental illness can be a way to situate and respond to psychic pain. A person with a disability might want regular and affordable access to medical care, even if they do not want or align themselves with a medical model that puts the problem of disability in their body.[15] Using a disability studies perspective that takes a more complex approach to embodiment, one might read hooks as suggesting, along similar lines to Spillers and Erevelles, that gender identity is formed in relation to violence, in this case a psychic violence targeting men, that results in disability. Rather than taking hooks's approach to curing the disability by fixing the men, what if we accepted racialized disgender as inherently part of the formation of our social identities, including manhood, and both tried to decrease that violence and to think about men having access to knowledge about power through the ways they have experienced disability. A disability studies perspective used in this way might help us to perceive patriarchy as a damaging system of oppression that recreates itself though disablement, and to understand the effects of that disablement to be the formation of gender identities that are both wounded and valuable sites for knowledge production and political change. This might allow people who identify as able-bodied men to perceive their own liberation in the work of disability studies as well as in feminist thinking.

My reading of hooks here suggests, like my reading of Spillers, that social identities as we know them originate in the impairment and disabling of bodies along identity lines, including but not limited to race and gender. While the ideologies around which bodies are marked as disabled differs along racial and gendered lines, the concept of racialized disgender helps us to talk about ways that disability is both socially constructed and lived in the body and that racial, gender, and disability identities are aspects of the self that one might take great pride in, while simultaneously being lived as a material embodiment that may involve impairment, pain, and unwanted bodymind limitations. Understanding racialized disgender as an inescapable part of the embodied experiences of all U.S. subjects offers a possibility for claiming, rather than trying to fix or distance oneself from, these impaired and disabled racialized genders. Such a claiming might constitute an act of inclusion that could take us into a disabled future in which we do not need to fix the harm done by these histories so much as to learn to live with it in a way that does not replicate its history of physical, emotional, and psychological violence.

Selection of Texts and Chapter Overview

This book discusses "race," "gender," and "dis/ability" as categories produced by systemic apparatuses of power, rather than looking at a specific historical articulation of a racial, gender, or disability identity or formation. It addresses whiteness, Jewishness, Chicanidad/Mexican Americanness, and Blackness; cisgender manhood and womanhood; characters with and without socially marked disability; and straight and queer sexualities. It does not address Native American, Asian American, Muslim American, or other racial and ethnic identities in the United States, nor does it address any texts with transgender, intersex, or nonbinary characters. This is not a function of these identity categories; each could certainly be read through the lens of racialized disgender. Rather, it is a result of choosing texts that usefully illuminate and/or challenge the mutual construction of race, gender, and dis/ability in the United States. The identities of the authors and characters themselves are less important for inclusion here than the ways they parse the intersections between race, gender, and dis/ability.

There are certainly limitations to this approach. Using a wide lens means touching down in various places for theoretical illustrations, without being able to attend in depth to a single genealogy of identity formation. It also means discussing representations of some identities and not others, as well as a focus on identifications I both do and do not share. This approach risks trying to cover too much ground and not being attentive to the depth of the effects of intersections of power on a specific population or community. Nevertheless, the formulation of racialized disgender is an important addition to the work currently being done that focuses on specific racial, ethnic, dis/ability, and gender formations. If we are to conceptualize useful tools for dismantling intersectional systems of power, we need ways to look at such systems in relation to one other and understand that, while able to shift over time, they have deep interlocking historical intersections. We are at a disadvantage in making any substantive social change if we cannot be simultaneously aware of both the specificities of each historical moment and each identity position and the broader ways the systems of power that construct those identities interrelate and hide their deep historical interrelations.

Throughout this book, I use the term "racialized disgender" to describe representations of bodies in a twofold manner. "Racialized disgendering" refers to (1) bodies that are physically, intellectually, or emotionally impaired or socially disabled by the process of racialized gendering and (2) bodies that are *legible* as being physically, intellectually, or emotionally impaired or socially disabled by the process of racialized gendering, often in combination with a socially designated status of illness or disability. All subjects in a U.S. context are racially disgendered in the first sense. The second category becomes important because bodies that fall into that category—those that have a disability or illness legible as outside what is considered the physical, cognitive, or emotional norm in our society—often have the epistemic and positional privilege of making the processes of racialized disgendering more legible. Thus, while all subjects are racially disgendered, representations of those subjects that experience ableism directly can be richer sites to mine for a broader understanding of how racialized disgender works. Chapters 2 and 3 of this text focus on representations of the latter category, while Chapters 1 and 4 look at speculative futures in which disability, race, and gender are used to conservative and radical ends, respectively.

Chapter 1, "White Guys in Wheelchairs: *Lost, Avatar,* and the Appropriation of Disability," analyzes the television series *Lost* (2004–2010) and the film *Avatar* (2009), to interrogate the function of whiteness within dominant narratives of disability. This chapter is specifically attentive to how visual representations of white American men in (and out) of wheelchairs figure as sites to mark the metaphorically disabled white man in a multicultural world, to appropriate the position of minoritized identity from race- and gender-based politics and political discourses, and to imagine a recuperation or rehabilitation of white masculinity via female and nonwhite bodies. Such representations of white men with mobility impairments appropriate the position of social marginality via a temporary physical disability, which can be used to identify with and gain recognition from women and people of color, to engage viewer sympathy, and then to reclaim a healed white manhood through the narrative repair of their physical disability. Both *Lost* and *Avatar* use representations of white men in wheelchairs to draw on popular cultural fears and assumptions about the loss of the patriarchal authority of able-bodied cis male white manhood. This loss is then assuaged via speculative narratives of futures or alternate presents that "give back" bodily power to white male heroes. Such narratives not only limit imaginative political possibilities for valuing disability identity and intersectional politics; they also draw on and potentially reinforce a criticism of early strains of disability studies itself—that it was focused on, written by, and tailored to the needs of white men with physical disabilities. This chapter looks at how the racial disgendering of white cis males, rather than being claimed as a disabled identity, uses disability as a prop to envision a future free of disability for white men. In this way, the chapter provides a backdrop against which to read the work of the late twentieth- to early twenty-first-century authors, engaged in Chapters 2–4, who build frameworks for understanding disability as an inherent and valued part of our shared futures.

Chapter 2, "Embodied Metaphor and Nonreproductive Futurity as Racialized Disgender in Islas and Moraga," looks at Arturo Islas and Cherríe Moraga, queer Chicanx writers who have traditionally been thought of as having radically differing politics around social identity. I argue that Islas and Moraga use metaphor in relation to representations of disabled characters (Mama Chona and Miguel in Islas, and Cerezita in Moraga) to construct similar approaches to rethinking Chicanx identity and family models in relation to disability and queer sexuality. I also begin to delve more deeply into the value of racialized disgender as a political model, particularly in relation to identity and futurity. Islas's and Moraga's literary works do not set up a straight future-oriented versus queer antifuture dichotomy but rather look at how our futures are already disabled and how that understanding can produce less restrictive futures, particularly for those with marginalized racial, ethnic, and sexual identities.

Chapter 3, "Racialized Disgender and Disruptive Futurity in Lorde's and Engelberg's Cancer Narratives," looks at intersections of race, gender, and disability in the work of Audre Lorde and Miriam Engelberg, examining how representations of disability might help us expand recent work in disability theory on the politics of what Lennard Davis calls "caring about" the body (28). A politics of caring about the body, I argue, involves attention to the rights, treatment, and oppression of disabled, nonnormative, and ill bodies, and thus would require greater attentiveness to the racially disgendering ways our bodies' histories and social narratives disable us as well as the ways these narratives contextualize and affect the experience of disability and illness. This chapter not only examines the ways in which breast cancer is a gendered and gendering disease but also provides close readings illustrating that breast cancer's social functioning and the rhetorics that have been used to make it less threatening to dominant understandings of both race and gender can reveal how racialized gender functions as a form of disability more broadly.

Chapter 4, "Speculative Disabled Futures: Octavia Butler's *Xenogenesis* Trilogy," looks to the science fiction of Octavia Butler for a narrative model that inverts that of *Lost* and *Avatar* by reconfiguring the hero as one with an alternate wounded history—that of Black motherhood that carries legacies of slavery, forced reproduction, and lack of legal agency in relation to the health of oneself and one's children. Lilith's Black womanhood is represented by Butler as embodied racialized disgender, both enabling her to survive into the future and also rooted in an inherited history of wounds. Butler's trilogy suggests that it is from the knowledge we can cull from our racially disgendered identities that we might build tools for survival and adaptability. It reveals that a sustainable ethics of caring about bodies requires that we not only accept but expect and even on some level appreciate pain, disability, and painful memories as part of our temporal future, a future that looks neither to perfectibility of bodies nor to full redemption from our social and political pasts.

I conclude with a Coda that interrogates some of my personal experiences over the course of the writing of this book to position myself as author and embodied person in relation to an intersectional understanding of race, gender, and disability and to argue that this conscious positioning is essential to framing work in disability studies as well as to narrating one's decisions in relation to both academic and medical institutional forces. I envision the sketches in the Coda as a series of situational possibilities for imagining allyship as practiced in relation to an understanding of the workings of racialized disgender as I have articulated them in my literary analyses. I look to these moments of potential allyship to experiment with ways of thinking about moving toward a more inclusive sense of futurity in which we can hold awareness of a traumatic past and its impacts alongside a revaluing of the disabilities such a past may have created.

At the center of each analysis throughout this book is a desire to unpack how disability as both a concept and a lived bodily experience has constructed race and gender and how race and gender have historically intersected (both within dominant discourses of power and within narratives of resistance) to create and define disability. My hope for this project is not that it will give us an entirely new way of thinking of the complexly intertwined structures of ableism, racism, and (cis)sexism so much as that it will help build a coalitional politics by opening up different ways of talking about some of their workings.[16] There is more to say about the intersectionality of whiteness and woundedness, disability and gender normativity, and racial nonwhiteness and the social and physical creation of nonnormative bodies than this text can address. I write with the understanding that there are gaps in my understanding and with the hope that the discourse those gaps produce will prove generative for my own and others' thinking.

1

White Guys in Wheelchairs

Lost, Avatar, *and the Appropriation of Disability*

In an international trailer for the Academy Award–winning *The Theory of Everything* (2014),[1] a film that chronicles the life of disabled cosmologist Stephen Hawking, two central tropes of the film are insistently established. The first is that male scientific genius needs an artistic, supportive, beautiful female partner to truly bring it to life. Once this "marriage" (a term used in the trailer itself) of male and female, art and science, faith and rationalism is consummated, one might be able to "wind back the clock" to the beginning of time and find a universal, whole connectedness. The second trope, which also comes second in terms of the narrative development of the trailer, is that there will be a fall away from this hopeful and perfectly balanced life in the form of a physical impairment that challenges the workings of white male privilege, the joy of heterosexual coupling, and access to a fantasized white hetero-patriarchal Edenic wholeness. This fall is figured visually halfway through the trailer, when Eddie Redmayne, playing the young Hawking, trips and falls in the Cambridge quad, violently smashing his face and glasses against the stone walkway. This scene is juxtaposed against the scene of his diagnosis—he has a degenerative neurological disease that, the trailer suggests, will change his future from one that had the potential to recapture a lost wholeness to one of "heavy defeat." Here the "marriage of time and space" that Hawking (with the support of his wife) is said to specialize in is split (as it is suggested he will be from his wife). On one side of the postfall divide is a realistic future of everyday struggle; on the other is a timeless paradise forever lost. The affective results of this loss are figured both in the trailer and in the film itself as an ongoing fantasy of recovering the ability to move one's limbs in an able-bodied manner, which is itself equated to being able to once again enact the privilege of white heterosexual masculinity that aligns with Hawking's true identity.

An instance of this fantasy is represented in a scene near the end of the film, when Hawking has established himself internationally as a scientific genius and has accessed the electric wheelchair and vocal technologies that allow him control over his mobility and verbal communication. He is sitting on an academic panel in a crowded lecture hall. Mid-discussion, a young woman drops her pen. The film shows us Hawking's internal fantasy of standing, walking to her, and holding the pen in his hand. This rather direct representation of the metaphor of recovering the lost phallus through regaining able-bodied use of one's legs and normative mobility asks for audience empathy, though not so much in relation to imagining the reality of living with ALS. Rather, it engages the audience in a shared fear of the loss of white patriarchal authority. The suffering and fear attached to this loss comes from the assumption that while someone like Hawking should, according to the hierarchies of our society, have access to the inherited privileges of white, middle-class, educated, heterosexual, cisgender manhood, that access can be unfairly denied; it can be taken as a result of tragedy outside one's control. Part of how this fear functions is that one could remain the same on the inside—that is, be neither cognitively different nor different in terms of inhabiting social identities other than whiteness and maleness—but become changed on the outside via physical disability and thereby lose access to the privileges that accompany white manhood (represented in this scene metaphorically by the social ability to woo young women and to physically dominate one's space).

The film unfolds partly as a traditional narrative of "overcoming" disability and partly as a heterosexual love story, which, though it ultimately ends in divorce, provides the female-coded strength, support, and faith needed for the disabled man to survive the traumatic loss of the physical traits that culturally represent his worth as a man. This all happens against a strikingly white, upper-middle-class backdrop. Hawking's diagnosis moment occurs in 1963 England, a time of mass postwar Commonwealth immigration and decolonization. To a mainstream American audience, however, this extraordinarily white space might register as a (fantasized) historical moment just before the broad successes of the civil rights movements of the sixties and seventies that would both create and draw attention to Black, multiracial, queer, and feminist social, political, and cultural spaces that have survived into the twenty-first century. Oxford, England, in 1963 appears in the film as the perfect time and space to wind back the clock for the indulgence of dominant fantasies of twentieth-century white manhood. This pre-Stonewall,

pre–*Roe v. Wade*, pre–Civil Rights Act space of white male prestige and progress is presented as naturally unaware of racial or class divides or of the social
oppressions of women and LGBTQ-identified people. Thus, the sole struggle
of the film can be read as overcoming disability—a struggle in which lack of
access to technologies or health care is never an issue. The only discussion of
color I found in relation to the film was, somewhat ironically, a series of In-
ternet articles noting that Eddie Redmayne is color-blind. The only mention
of blackness in the film is that of the black hole theory that figures the beginning of everything as dark, feminine, spiritual, and unobtainable. That is, it
is only in relation to a symbolic blackness/Blackness that the fantasy that one
might wind back time to an era in which white cisgender heterosexual masculinity was unaware of its privileges and oppressions and therefore unwounded and powerful can be figured.

This chapter unpacks some of ways that racial Blackness and femaleness
function narratively as prostheses in early twenty-first-century popular culture texts that figure imagined losses and fantasy rehabilitations of white
male privilege via metaphors of mobility impairment. Focusing specifically
on the popular television series *Lost* (2004–2010) and the 2009 Academy
Award–nominated film *Avatar,* this chapter investigates "the representational strategies by which white masculinity attempts to hold onto its privilege" via discourses of disability in a post–new social movement era (Carroll
17). By interrogating whiteness and maleness in narratives of mobility impairment, I am looking to lay the groundwork for later chapters that look at
how marginalized bodies mobilize disability in ways that subvert these normative intersections of whiteness, cis male identity, and physical disability
as metaphors for the perceived loss of white male privilege. I am interested
particularly in narratives that show the healing of both physical disability
and the metaphorical disability of white manhood via women and people of
color, who function as rehabilitative prosthetic devices. I examine these narratives in relation to what I am terming "racialized disgender"—a way of
naming the various linguistic, material, and ideological practices that constitute racialized gender identity in direct relation to ideas about healthy and
able bodies as well as physical, emotional, social, and psychological limitations.[2] In the narratives I examine here, it becomes clear how white cis manhood has historically intersected with various ability and disability statuses.
As is evident from a brief reading of *The Theory of Everything,* the privileges
attendant to being white and male in the United States in the twentieth and
into the twenty-first century not only include access to physical and social
spaces but also require the bodily fortitude to represent patriarchal power
and a normate bodymind that is socially constructed as desirable to women.
Such intersectional expectations have felt disabling for white men who are

poor, sick, disabled, or queer.[3] Moreover, dominant narratives of white masculinity (which have largely been reinforced rather than challenged by queer, feminist, and racial justice movements) also prevent white men from understanding the ways they are capacitated and limited by dominant narratives of race and gender, thus leading to a misunderstanding of their oppression as coming from the gains and political rhetoric of civil rights and new social movements. I explore such phenomena through *Lost* and *Avatar* for the majority of this chapter. At the end, I look briefly at potential ways the whiteness of foundational academic discourses of disability studies may have inadvertently replicated some of this logic of loss and rehabilitation.

In both *Lost* and *Avatar*, visual representations of white American men in (and out) of wheelchairs figure as sites to mark a metaphorically disabled, post–new social movements cis white manhood, to appropriate the position of marginalized identity from race- and gender-based politics and political discourses, and to imagine a recuperation or rehabilitation of white masculinity via female and nonwhite bodies. Such representations follow an appropriative prosthetic logic, according to which the positionality of white manhood can be reclaimed as a rich and complex space of broad viewer sympathy and identification. David Mitchell and Sharon Snyder have argued that, historically, disabled characters in literature often function as a kind of prosthetic metaphorical device, shoring up normalcy, bodily wholeness, and full humanity in both the text and its primary nondisabled characters. The narratives discussed in this chapter, however, utilize women and people of color as prosthetic narrative devices to rehabilitate and return wholeness to what is presented as a socially and politically wounded white manhood. And, as in the aforementioned scene in *The Theory of Everything*, this rehabilitation is also figured as turning back time, a kind of nostalgic speculative futurity.

Identity Anxiety and the Wounded White Male

The early twenty-first century was marked by an explosion of discourse about reaching a social state in which we are "beyond" identity. The widespread, if short-lived, claim that the election of President Barack Obama marked a "post-race" era as well as the political use of "post-gay" to describe dominant assimilative LGBTQ activism relate to a shift in the early millennium in thinking about social identity. Michael Millner argues, "If the 1990s were characterized by a rich and sophisticated reconceptualization of identity . . . the new millennium has been frequently marked by a sense of exhaustion around the whole project of identity" (541). However, with the election of Donald Trump we meet with rhetoric that evidences not so much an exhaustion around identity, but a heightened anxiety, particularly by those in positions of dominance. A study conducted from 2012 to 2016 by Diana C. Mutz, political scientist at the University of Pennsylvania, concludes that "the status threat felt by [a] dwindling proportion of traditionally high-status Americans (i.e., whites, Christians, and men) as well as by those who perceive America's global dominance as threatened combined to increase support for the candidate who emphasized reestablishing status hierarchies of the past" (1). My readings in this chapter suggest that this "status threat" backlash to minority-empowering critical identity politics produced a national anxiety that was legible in popular narratives of the early twenty-first century. These narratives figured that threat as a disability to be overcome not only by reestablishing status hierarchies but also, and perhaps more importantly, by making space in which white cis male racialized disgender could take its place as a wounded identity alongside the minority identities around which the identity politics of the new social movements of the 1960s and 1970s and their 1990s ideological counterparts were constructed.

Lost and Avatar utilize a narrative logic that allegorizes and soothes fears around the social disabling of white cis manhood (which is both a threat of the loss of privilege and the threat of not being relevant to current discourses and politics) at the end of the twentieth century by presenting it as a recoupable position of privilege that must now be accessed via the narrative appropriation of minority positionality, accessible metaphorically to white men specifically via physical disability. The spectacularization of white manhood via the use of mobility impairment and the signifying function of the wheelchair both foreground the metaphorical impairment of white men and enable narrative rehabilitation of them to full social agency and a rightful place of leadership within their respective fictional communities. Symbolic representations of wounded white cis manhood such as those found in Lost and Avatar work against the epistemic and politicized value of disabled perspectives and political attachments to minority identity positions. In such representations, the disabled body that works in the service of reconsolidating the hegemony of white manhood undermines a socially constructed and a complexly embodied model of disability, race, and gender and makes it difficult to perceive and further build the coalitional politics that exist between disability rights, feminist, and racial justice movements.[4]

"All the Best Cowboys Have Daddy Issues": White Masculinity Lost and Found

Lost, described by Time magazine as "a stunningly original, mass-culture hit," was an Emmy-winning television drama that aired from 2004 to 2010 (Poniewozik). Lost tells the story of the survivors from a transpacific flight

(Sydney to Los Angeles) that crashes on an unknown island with strange magnetic properties. On the island the survivors discover a monster made of black smoke, the remnants of the "Dharma Initiative" (a research group from the 1970s and 1980s), and a group of people identified simply as "the others." Though there is, at least initially, a standard shipwreck narrative in which all the characters try to survive and/or escape, the show is primarily invested in exploring ways that the characters are "lost" in other aspects of their lives. Many have strained or broken relationships with family members and secret histories of crime, addiction, deceit, or physical or mental illness. The show interrogates how people become lost to themselves and others as a result of personal histories, the effects on individuals when their social groups and communities are altered, and speculates on how any single difference in one's experience or history might change their life via the introduction of alternate life narratives that play out in a parallel reality. Ultimately, the characters are not freed so much as they are found by each other and themselves, culminating in a series finale in which they enter a shared afterlife together, suggesting that the entire series may have been the story of each individual moving toward personal spiritual resolution.

Part of the intrigue of the show comes from its representation of time as unstable and nonlinear. Over the course of the series there is actual time travel on the island as well as narrative flashbacks to characters' previous lives and intermittent "flash-sideways" to the alternate-life timelines. While one might initially think this extensive playing with time could open up a kind of Halberstamian queer temporality, the flash-sideways tends to work more as a rehabilitative temporality, a narrative that recenters the importance of bonding between white men and in which the characters come to self-understandings that fit dominant heteronormative and ableist models of mental and physical health.

In season 3, we are given the history of one of the plane crash survivors, John Locke (Terry O'Quinn), in a series of flashbacks. Locke is a white man in his late fifties, whom we know has incurred a physical injury—visually signified by his use of a wheelchair—as a result of violence perpetrated against him by his father. We also know that Locke is consistently frustrated by people who believe he cannot do what able-bodied men can do. His refrain is "don't tell me what I can't do." At this point in the series, Locke has recovered full use of his legs via an unexplained physical change that happened immediately after the plane crash. Locke interprets the recovered use of his legs as a gift bestowed on him by the island and uses this interpretation to appoint himself a spiritual and tribal leader to the other survivors.

Episode 13 of this Locke-centric season, "The Man from Tallahassee," begins with Locke sitting behind a desk across from his social worker, who is a Black woman. She asks him his name, followed by a series of personal questions, including what is his marital status, whether he has a girlfriend, and whether he has ever thought about seeking out his biological parents. We slowly realize that he is being evaluated as to whether or not he qualifies for disability benefits. When he reveals he is not seeing a therapist, she stamps a big red "BENEFITS SUSPENDED" on his paperwork, indicating both that he cannot receive disability payments and that his social benefits as a fully able-bodied white male have been suspended as he is now at the mercy of a Black woman who is allowed to access formerly private details of his life and use them to deny him access, income, and control over his own narrative. The twist in the scene comes when Locke stands up and walks out, revealing that he had been receiving disability benefits not for paraplegia—the disability that viewers associate with his pre-island life—but for depression after being conned into giving away his kidney by the man claiming to be his father, the man who also later causes his paraplegia. Narratologically this suggests that Locke's impending physical disability is almost an inevitable side effect of his inability to inherit the phallic power of his father. He is figured here as both dependent on and denied by the government and its nonwhite, nonmale representatives.

Vincent Brook includes *Lost* in a list of postnetwork shows that embrace the representation of "a multicultural and transnational universe in which not only everything is interconnected but also interconnectedness provides the key to salvation" (346).[5] Yet despite the complexity of the narrative and the multiracial cast, the central focus of the series is the conflict between fathers and sons and the difficulties faced in becoming "a man" in a world in which white manhood has become a damaged identity.[6] The narrative of *Lost* is driven by what Richard Dyer calls the "compelling paradoxes" of whiteness that, when coupled with stories of disabled masculinity, "provide the instabilities" that engage the viewer and "generate . . . attempts to find resolution" (40). The interconnectedness that is represented as ultimately most necessary is not between people of different races, genders, or nationalities, but between white American men who have lost a meaningful connection to their predecessors and to each other.

While arguments such as Aris Mousoutzanis's that "*Lost* exemplifies [the way] that trauma creates new identities based on shared experiences of victimhood and suffering" using "discourse[s] of grief, suffering, and trauma" to build a sense of "political community" may resonate with many reviews of and audience reactions to the series (56), my argument here aligns more with David Magill's suggestion that *Lost* "resolves the narrative of wounded white masculinity by restoring white manhood through a progressive ethical stance while retaining its traditional characteristics of authority" (145). The global discourses of trauma referenced by Mousoutzanis function in the series to make a space for white masculinity first as a wounded identity that has become more ethical through that wounding (made legible via a metaphorical use of physical disability that enables identification with minority positions), and second through a full recovery and rehabilitation of authority that must still to some extent bury the histories that create and continue to reinforce the wounds of other social identity positions—including enslavement, the oppression of women, genocide, and colonization.

Lost's narrative is structured largely as a struggle between the main character, Jack Shepherd (Matthew Fox)—a straight, white cisgender male doctor, leader, caretaker, and rational and ethical decision maker who before the crash had reported his widely respected physician father for performing surgery under the influence of alcohol—and the island itself, which represents mystery, chaos, the natural world, the irrational, and the supernatural. The character of John Locke connects and illuminates what is at stake on both sides of this struggle. His disability and its narrative overcoming (first physically by the supernatural powers of the island, then internally psychologically and emotionally, then by the surgical cure offered him by Jack) come to link rational and mysterious, light and dark, primitive and scientific, and ultimately serve to recreate a sense of white male lineage that becomes central to the healing of this multiracial, multiethnic, and mixed-gender microcosm of a global society. Though Locke is also a straight, white cis man in search of the liberal individualist identity that his namesake suggests, he is figured as the opposite of Jack: a working-class orphan who becomes not a surgeon who "fixes" people but a "broken" man with a disability. His paraplegia comes to visually mark all of these nondominant social positions. The linking of disability with lack of social power is reinforced by the fact that his paraplegia was created by his father—who thus withheld rather than passed on the phallus—as well as by the fact that Locke lacks the professional skill and economic resources to access potentially rehabilitative spinal surgery. Both of these instances of lack of access to masculine and medicalized power are highlighted by their contrast to Jack's status as an able-bodied, highly successful surgeon specializing in spinal injuries. Locke's off-island self has a low-paying office job at a box company, is single (his girlfriend left him after he let his emotional reaction to his rejection by his father drive him to obsessive behaviors), is frequently shown being ridiculed by his coworkers, and has been conned and injured by a man claiming to be his father. Thus, he becomes a representation of numerous ways a white, straight American cisgender man might not have access to privilege—particularly the privileges imagined to inhere in the combination of social positions embodied by Jack. This logic makes space for white manhood within discourses of identity politics and reveals how intersections between whiteness and cis manhood can also be affectively experienced as social disability, even before the intersecting identity of disability. It also reinforces an ableist connection between disability and lack, as Locke's physical disability is a materialization of his social marginalization, thus obscuring the epistemic and political possibility of marginalized and disabled experiences.

Locke's character represents a post–new social movements anxiety influenced by the success of identity-based politics, that white male authority might not be passed down from father to son via white middle-class heteronormative reproduction of gender, sexual, and racial identities. As a person with a disability, Locke represents someone who can claim access to minority status with its attendant woundedness and thus find a place within a post–new social movements narrative that on a surface level validates and commodifies marginalized identities. Locke embodies what Hamilton Carroll has termed the "so-called crisis of masculinity"—a claim emerging at the end of the twentieth century "that white men, whose franchise on opportunity in the United States has putatively been revoked, are those most adversely affected by the social transformations of the post–civil rights era" (2). "No longer able . . . to rely on its status as unremarkable or normative," states Carroll, "white masculinity attempts to manage the stakes of its own fragmentations by co-opting the forms of representational meaning secured by women, gays, and people of color over the preceding decades" (7).

Historically, white cis masculinity has retained its hegemony when faced with various historical challenges and threats, by reconstructing ideologies of masculinity that retain power and authority. Such reconstructive narratives have shifted over time, depending on the nature of the perceived threats. Gail Bederman suggests that in the Progressive Era, economic changes, working-class and immigrant labor organizing, and the women's suffrage movement were perceived as challenges to the authority and hegemony of white men. Bederman reads this as a moment when middle-class white men "adopted a number of strategies in order to remake manhood" as tough, athletic, able bodied, spectacular, and white (16)—a new masculinity opposed to effeminate Victorian manhood, womanhood, and racial Blackness. Susan Jeffords similarly argues that the Vietnam War era, which coincided with civil rights and second wave feminism, produced not more open-minded and less-dominating forms of manhood, but rather a "remasculinization of America." Though this remasculinization came in part as an appropriation of woundedness, specifically class woundedness as represented in the figure of the (usually white) Vietnam vet, the response was a reconsolidation of a separate sphere of masculinity as defined against and independent from women and femininity (168–169). Historically, then, white manhood when read through the lens of racialized disgender reveals specific intersections between access to a consolidated sphere of white cis masculinity and disability status that has shifted over time but consistently reveals gender, race, and disability status to be mutually constituted as part of preserving the privileges of white manhood.

Early twenty-first-century "crises" of white masculinity are distinct from these earlier versions in that rather than consolidating white male power by disenfranchising, doing violence to, isolating itself from, or repressing the voices of women and people of color, this post–new social movement reconstruction of white male authority must incorporate, identify with, be validated by, and find a place among those minority positions in order to then recenter white manhood. This crisis requires a temporary identification through disability that can then be rehabilitated—both allowing white men a place within identity politics discourse and preserving their privilege of unfractured universal status. Turn-of-the-twentieth-century middle-class white males felt their political and economic power threatened, and they adapted by proving that they had not lost their primal virility, which most commonly took the form of "aggressiveness, physical force, and male sexuality" and differentiated them from women and people of color (Bederman 19). The turn-of-the-twenty-first-century logic that *Lost* articulates, however, is not so much worried that white men will lose material authority as it is that either they will take it from those in marginalized positions by destructive and no longer acceptable ways, as their fathers did, or that they will become culturally and socially impotent and irrelevant, like the pre-island John Locke. If the white men in *Lost* cannot connect with or utilize the forms of power their fathers did, if they cannot become the kind of fathers to their sons that have something meaningful and authoritative to pass on, if they cannot make a space for themselves in their careers in which they are special or venerated while still being capable of forming meaningful human connections with the women in their lives, then they have no social value—no place in a global, multicultural narrative.

Thus, rather than finding value in social and individual wounds (which might look like true empathy and equity across racial, gender, and disability identities), our central white male characters insist on "fixing" them (a term Jack uses repeatedly to describe successful spinal surgeries). Where one might hope for a study of and reckoning with histories of racial and gender expectations that have put white cis men in a relationship to power that feels disempowering, that limits access to a sense of belonging and legitimacy, and thus reveals structures of racialized disgender that might be used to build allyship with women, queer people, and people of color, we find instead a narrative push to deny such allyship models and use the appropriation of a marginal-

ized status to regain a normate body, secure the property of white male privilege, and repress any knowledge of the histories of oppressions on which
both ableist and white male power have been built. Ultimately, *Lost*'s narrative reveals a desire to enter an imagined future in which white cis men have
social authority that is not taken by force or by economic or political hegemony, but rather is given to them by women and racial minorities who recognize white male leadership, identify and value white men's sense of personal
woundedness, and give their blessing to a rehabilitated white manhood separable from the systemic social oppressions that created a white supremacist,
hetero-patriarchal, and ableist society.

"Because You're in a Wheelchair and I'm Not": Overcoming the Sins of the White Father

In the section that follows, I look at two Locke-centric episodes that illuminate the logic of prosthetic rehabilitation and discuss the binary outcomes
for Locke in his central and alternate story lines. In his central story line
Locke is consumed by histories of white male violence, and in his alternate
or flash-sideways story line he is able to bond with other white men of his
generation to fix their shared historical wounds and thereby physically rehabilitate himself. Episode 4 of season 1, "Walkabout," is the first Locke-cen-
tered episode of the series, and it opens to a flashback scene of the plane
crash on the island. While the general tenor of this scene is one of trauma
and chaos, Locke is framed in the foreground of one shot lying calmly on his
back, looking down at his feet. The camera shot is from ground level—his
feet in focus in close-up and the rest of his body (smaller and blurry) behind
him. His foot, positioned phallically in this shot, begins to move as the rest
of his body comes back into focus. Locke looks to the sky, and the episode
begins, inviting us to interpret the crash for Locke as a moment of recovered
virility and unified selfhood, which we are signaled to read as having been
granted by a higher power, at least from Locke's perspective.

Later in the episode, when the crash survivors fight over food, Locke kills
a boar with the knives he had brought for the walkabout to which he was
denied access because of his disability. Locke thus regains his status as a man
deserving of participation in the "authentic aboriginal walkabout," which
has been internalized by Locke as communing with the natural world, individual autonomy and strength, and a non-Western, nonwhite form of mas-
culinized spirituality. Locke calls it "a journey of spiritual renewal, where
one derives strength from the earth, becomes inseparable from it." While he
is likely repeating the tourist pitch from the brochure, what he finds on the
island seems to be precisely this journey of appropriative twenty-first-centu-

Locke's phallic foot. (From the television series *Lost*, season one, episode four. Copyright 2004, Touchstone Television.)

ry Lockean individualism, where he is returned to an imagined state in which he relies on no one and is validated via a natural connection to a natural space free of civilization as he knows it. Additionally, the absence of a father from whom to inherit both a familial identity and its burdens (in contrast to the experience of Jack, who says of his work as a doctor, "I was born into it; kind of a family business") allows Locke, when he regains able-bodied status and escapes the metaphorical wounding that using a wheel-chair marks, to further claim an identification with his Enlightenment namesake—a textual inheritance of a theoretical liberal individualism that would under other circumstances be impossible to inhabit because of the systems of interpersonal and technological dependence built into our con-temporary lives. On the island, Locke can (at least in the initial seasons) stand literally and figuratively as an independent white man, unencumbered by dependence on (particularly Black and female) others or the weight of the inheritance of his white masculinity. This inheritance entails both the sins of his father who represents an earlier, unapologetic form of white male privilege, and his father's ejection of Locke from that genealogy of privilege. Locke's on-island physical independence is highlighted by being juxtaposed to his physical dependence when getting onto the plane, where he needed to be carried by a white woman and a Black man because the gateway was too narrow for his wheelchair. At the end of the episode, this same wheelchair burns in the funeral pyre of everyone who died in the crash, symbolically killing off that version of Locke and allowing him to emerge phoenix-like into a new seemingly unencumbered and nondependent white masculinity that can be claimed by associating himself with tribal or indigenous knowl-edge and abilities.

Despite the rugged ableist independence on which Locke's transformation is based, it comes representationally from Locke's relationality to female and nonwhite characters and is highly dependent on the presence, physical and metaphorical, of Black characters in particular. The presentation of Locke as a man of faith who is more in touch with the natural world and with himself than other characters is frequently reinforced by his association with Black characters on the show. Walt (Malcolm David Kelley), who is the only child and one of a handful of Black characters on the show, and who appears to have psychic abilities, becomes attached to Locke as a father figure when his own father (who has been absent in his life up until this trip) is struggling to maintain a relationship with him. Locke's role in Walt's life validates Locke as different from his racist forefathers and as having a legitimate place in a new construction of masculinity as passed down through men.

The authenticity of Locke's faith is also echoed and thus narratively reinforced by Rose (L. Scott Caldwell), a Black woman who was cured of cancer by the island and loses her husband in the crash but has unshakable faith that he is not dead and turns out to be right. Rose and Locke first meet in the airport in Sydney. Rose sees Locke in his wheelchair and Locke picks up a pill bottle that Rose has dropped. Rose and Locke thus share insider knowledge about their secret histories of disability and marginalization. Rose's faith in things that no one else believes in but turn out to be true also lends credibility to Locke's belief that the island is sending him a message about his value and importance as a leader on the island by giving back use of his legs.

Via Locke's relationships to Rose and Walt, and their approval (at least initially) of him, Locke is authenticated as a rehabilitated white man who becomes validated because he can share in the epistemic privilege of the oppressed, while shedding his minoritizing disabled status. The network of dependence on and caretaking by women and people of color that Locke experiences off-island (his physical therapist, social worker, the people who carry him on the plane) transforms on the island into a network of recognition and reinforcement of his worth. It seems that Locke emerges from this rehabilitative support structure of youth, femaleness, and racial nonwhiteness as a newly reborn white man, with the stereotypical knowledge and strength of an Australian aboriginal, faith and calm of the religious African American woman, and intuitions of the preternaturally gifted child. Locke, however, has not yet resolved his relationship to other white men or to contemporary (2004–2010) white cis manhood more broadly. Most importantly, he has not resolved his relationship to his father, and there continues to be no place for him in the off-island world or a sense of personal resolution—he becomes dependent on validation both by minority characters and by the island itself, and thus the rehabilitation of his white manhood and its attendant social privilege is constantly under threat of being once again denied.

A later Locke-centric episode, which I mentioned above, "The Man from Tallahassee" (season 3, episode 13), helps us understand why the connection to the island and support by those whom white men have historically oppressed is not enough to secure Locke's privileged position in the contemporary world. He also needs to establish a meaningful relationship with other white men and reconstruct a functional inheritance of white manhood. In this episode, Locke is surprised to see Ben (Michael Emerson), the leader of "the others," newly using a wheelchair. Locke tells Ben he wants to destroy the submarine that can take people off the island because Locke believes that if he leaves the island, he will be unable to walk again—reinforcing that Locke's relationship to white manhood has not been socially rehabilitated in the off-island world. Ben then interrogates Locke, asking him why the island "healed" him, while Ben remains unable to walk, despite the island's powers. Ben complains to Locke: "You've been here eighty days, John. I've been here my entire life! So how is it that you think you know this island better than I do?" To which Locke says, "Because you're in a wheelchair and I'm not," a phrase later repeated by Ben to reinforce the correlation between white male patriarchal power, able-bodiedness, and an authentic, preordained connection to the land. Both men express a faith in a mystical nature that endows Locke with strength, ability, leadership, and worth that he innately deserves, for which he competes with other white men, and which is visually registered in his positionality out of the wheelchair and the alternating low-to-high camera angles looking up at Locke from below and down on Ben from above.

Locke's precarious position of authority arises from his historical (pre-island) failure to inherit the white male power of his father, continually placing him socially on par with or below Black men and women and unable to win the love of a white woman. Locke's structural appropriation of the intuitions and knowledges of as well as his validation by racial minorities on the island is not enough to trump the effects of a broken lineage with other white men. What Locke ultimately needs to confront and overcome is not only the perceived disempowerment of white men by those who benefit from new social movements but, moreover, and possibly more importantly, the guilt and shame of the historical oppressive racist and sexist power of white masculinity made more visible by these movements.

Ultimately Locke is presented as taking two paths. After Locke sacrifices himself in an attempt to save the island, his storyline is split. In one reality, the violence of the inheritance of white manhood turns him into a monster. In the other alternate flash-sideways reality, Locke is able to rehabilitate himself via reestablishing a meaningful lineage and network between white men in the contemporary world. In the latter alternate and successfully rehabilitative reality, Locke has caused both his own and his father's paraplegia, and he refuses to have surgery because of his guilt. His guilt is also a symbolic one over inheriting the authority of white masculinity, as presumably would have happened if he had had a good relationship with his father. Locke is convinced by Jack to let go of this guilt and let himself be surgically "fixed." Letting go of the guilt of white male privilege and the historical violence it comes with allows for his rehabilitation by another white man in power. Once Locke accepts this medical and psychological intervention, he is able to walk again and becomes ready to leave purgatory and enter the afterlife with the others.

In contrast to and interspersed with this storyline is the Locke who has been embodied by a monster—the Man in Black, also referred to as the Black Smoke or the Smoke Monster—associated with racial Blackness and the histories of trauma and loss that have occurred on the island and then been buried or built over, much like the histories of race- and gender-based oppression to which the series alludes. Such histories include colonization, referenced both by the series of "others" on the island and the story of Mr. Eko (Adewale Akinnuoye-Agbaje), an African drug smuggler negotiating postcolonial national and international spaces; slavery, referenced most directly by the slave ship *Black Rock*, which crashed on the island in the nineteenth century, destroying the fertility statue and marking a rupture of white futurity;[7] domestic violence represented by several characters whose mothers were abused or killed; and controlling the bodies of pregnant women, a continued theme on the island involving the abduction of several women who are given medical treatment without consent. This on-island Locke that does not find internal, personal resolution with his father and does not learn to work with other white men to let go of the historical violence they have inherited is fated to be controlled by the dark monster. Without the psychological and symbolic physical rehabilitation shown in the alternate reality story line, the histories of violence and oppression contained by the island literally overtake white men, claiming not only their social power but also agency over their bodies. This ending suggests that the fear driving Locke's narrative is not primarily that white men will lose privilege or status, but that their reckoning with their own racialized disgender, the histories of power and oppression that have intersected to create white masculinity, might be more traumatic than the bodies conscripted into white manhood can survive.

In the final scene of the series, Locke walks into a church with the rest of the characters, healed of his wounds of white manhood, reinstated into its lineage, and guided by Jack's father. It is a white, patriarchal, medical model of care that makes Locke ostensibly whole again and thus able to both claim and overcome his wounded status, thereby symbolically embodying a rehabilitated able-bodied white masculinity. Celeste-Marie Bernier argues that the Africanist presence in *Lost* is an insistent "denied testimony" that re-emerges despite "illusory attempts by white men of reason . . . to erase histories which leads to national amnesia, racial terrorism and the resurfacing of trauma" (258). In 2009, when Bernier's essay was published, Bernier could not know that the ultimate resolution of the show would represent a resolution of the tensions of these histories in which white manhood, in spite of the histories of violence against others that haunt it, is revalued and recentered. The use of the metaphor of paraplegia as wounded white masculinity and the hyperableist ideologies its narrative logic requires obscure the histories of racialized disgender that have constructed white manhood, rehabilitate white cis masculinity, use women and people of color as prosthetics that are ultimately no longer needed, and leave no room for people with disabilities as a group that might use their own discourses of grief, suffering, and trauma to build strong political communities.

"Roll This Piece of Meat Out of Here": White Men and *Avatars* of Color

James Cameron's 2009 Academy Award–nominated blockbuster film, *Avatar,* tells the story of Jake Sully (Sam Worthington), a paraplegic Marine who is asked to take over as the pilot of his nonparaplegic brother's avatar after his brother's death. In the future setting of this science fiction film, the earth's resources have been depleted by capitalist greed and military-backed colonization. The Resources Development Administration (RDA) Corporation, a nongovernmental for-profit company, is attempting to mine "unobtanium" from the planet Pandora, which is inhabited by the Na'vi—tall, blue, humanoid creatures who worship the land and in particular an ancestral tree that grows over the source of the unobtanium. The RDA (a company that alludes both to Halliburton and, because it functions primarily via military force, to the U.S. military presence in oil-rich countries) works with scientists who have developed the avatar technology to allow humans to enter the atmosphere of Pandora by transferring their consciousness into hybrid human-alien bodies and thereby to pass as and interact with the Na'vi. The scientists working for RDA (including Dr. Grace Augustine, played by Sigourney Weaver) perceive the avatar technology as a way to communicate with the native population—a mode of communication that functions to some extent as culturally imperialist but does not have the explicit intent of exploitation. The RDA executives, on the other hand, understand the avatars to be a means of aggressively infiltrating enemy territory for the purpose of securing the valuable unobtanium. To this end, they use the scientists' anthropological and biological research as a gateway to cultural infiltration.

In the hypermasculine militarized context of the film, physical ability is figured primarily as a commodity. We are told that current technology could "fix" Jake's legs if he had the money to access the procedure. As a working-class veteran, he does not. Disability, by contrast, is figured as lost property, which functions symbolically as a loss of access to a simultaneously ethical and powerful white masculinity. In the world of *Avatar*, the white, imperialist, military-industrial capitalist power of the RDA is figured as a bad guy version of powerful white masculinity. Racist, colonialist, and sexist expectations that powerful whiteness includes the property rights to land and possessions that others live on and use are presented to the audience explicitly as both unethical and unnatural. To figure this power dynamic as a futuristic dystopia is also to erase the historical construction of whiteness as property. According to critical race theorists such as Cheryl Harris, out of the histories of slavery and colonization that constructed racial whiteness as the legal right to claim land and to have ownership over your own body, your children's bodies, and potentially another's body and their children's bodies has come a legal and social system in which whiteness has become a form of social property. This is also to say that the histories of disablement, gendering, hypergendering, and ungendering that slavery entailed all contribute to the value of whiteness.[8] Thus, the film's figuration as a dystopian fall away from a less violent version of white masculinity obscures its historical construction in and as racialized disgender.

The critique of white masculinity in the film is also confined to a particular sort of white male villain who consciously harms others and represents Western economic, governmental, and military powers. The film's narrative logic uses Jake's disability to present him in contrast to the allegorical figures of violent hypermasculinity—the capitalist imperialist, Parker Selfridge (Giovanni Ribisi), and the military imperialist, Colonel Miles Quaritch (Stephen Lang). Juxtaposed against these two forms of white male power, the everyman Jake is figured as disabled, lacking access to white male power because of his class status. His participation in colonizing acts occurs at the level of a powerless foot soldier. He is figured as a disabled innocent who does not know how to fully lay claim to an older version of able-bodied, white supremacy and male dominance and thus appears wounded, which registers visually in the film primarily via his mobility impairment.

Jake's disability, associated with his wounded white manhood, is in part what enables him to be a successful avatar pilot. In response to a comment from the Na'vi that "it is hard to fill a cup that's already full," Jake says, "My cup is empty. Just ask Dr. Augustine," figuring his disability and his social identity as a relatively powerless white male as constituting a lack and thus presenting himself as an empty vessel ready to be filled by the technology and purpose of the RDA, even as he himself fills the skin of a Na'vi via his avatar. Jake embodies the imagined loss of the economic and social hegemony of white masculinity for the everyman, which becomes his wounded identity and puts him in the position to be able to have his white masculinity rehabilitated in this post–new social movements world. Like John Locke of *Lost,* the normatively able-bodied use of Jake's legs is restored in the literal space of a prelapsarian setting and via identification with women and people of color, but it is figured not as an inborn right that requires rebuilding connections between white men, but as a commodity Jake has to prove he is worthy of accessing. In both *Avatar* and *Lost,* it is by means of white male-controlled technology that a physical "wholeness" is returned to Jake and Locke as they use an identification with marginalized others to make a space for a reemergence of a respectable and benignly powerful white masculinity. The ability to walk is equated with the ability to stand one's ground, with vitality, with an innocence that saves one from being associated with the historical violence of white masculinity, and with the ability to rehabilitate oneself both physically and ethically.

Avatar opens with a high-angle shot panning over a beautiful rainforest-like landscape. In the voice-over we hear Jake say, "When I was lying there in the VA hospital with a big hole blown through my life, I started to have dreams about flying. I was free." From the opening moments of the film, then, freedom and disability are figured as antithetical, while freedom and ability are linked via a fantasy of escaping lower-class and physically wounded positions of white manhood. The viewer is not yet aware of this connection, as there is no indication that Jake has a physical impairment until after the introductory sequence. In the scene following the opening sequence, Jake's disability is merely suggested via contextualization in other people's responses to him, which we as the audience do not know are related to his paraplegia until several scenes later. This technique allows viewers to associate Jake with a general sense of limitation, oppression, and woundedness, and also to transfer those assumptions to the visual representation of his paraplegia and the presence of the wheelchair itself, once the camera begins to frame him in medium shots.

The visual confirmation of Jake's disability first happens in the scene in which Jake arrives on Pandora via military transport vehicle. Jake exits the vehicle last, moving distinctly more slowly than the rest of his cohort, highlighting his bodily and social difference. On the base a commander calls him "Special K," while the other new recruits are called "ladies" and "fresh meat"—this both conflates femininity, queerness, and disability and signifies the way able-bodied heterosexual manhood is constructed specifically in contrast to these identities. While the other recruits are hazed by these terms and expected to come out more masculine, straight, and physically powerful, Jake is positioned as more feminine, more confined by his body, and permanently lower in status than other men.[9]

In the scenes on the base in which Jake is using his wheelchair, everything towers over him in brown- and gray-toned shots, reinforcing the smallness of his body in relation to the industrial, militarized culture. Jake in his Na'vi avatar, however, towers over the physical landscape in scenes in which vivid colors return, Oz-like, to the screen. The scenes in which Jake first enters his avatar and negotiates the world as a strong, tall, able-bodied Na'vi also indicate to the audience that full enjoyment of life is available to Jake only when he is using his legs to walk and run. Once in the able-bodied avatar, the ever-serious Jake begins to act like a child, evidencing a kind of joy in rebirth—running, jumping, and playfully ignoring orders. He has apparently regained a sense of his former self, despite the fact that he is in a body not his own. This suggests that disabled bodies are hindrances to freedom, happiness, and certain types of male gender performativity. In fact, when Jake first wakes up in the avatar body, the camera frames him similarly to the way it framed Locke in *Lost* when he first awakens with the feeling returned to his legs—with feet in the foreground and framed to suggest a phallus. It suggests that the nonwhite, racialized body can provide a reconnection to a virile and joyful white male self that the seriousness and emotional weight of white masculinity have hindered.

Jake's newly found other-embodied freedom, however, does not provide him independence or autonomy in the Pandoran landscape, which is described by the colonel as similar to the "mean bush" of Venezuela, figuring it as untamed, racially and culturally other, and female. The first night Jake spends alone on Pandora off the RDA base he is attacked by a wild animal. Even though he is in the stronger avatar body, he does not have the native knowledge of the landscape and needs one of the native women, Neytiri (Zoë Saldaña), to save him from the attack and then to train him to survive in the Pandoran jungle. This training requires unlearning his bodily stiffness, awkwardness, and lack of control (each signifying his racial whiteness) and training himself to use his body as the natives do. He is ironically brought into the "natural" world—where even human-made fire is forbidden and there is certainly no technology for physical accessibility such as wheelchairs, ramps, or crutches—via a technologically constructed avatar body in a filmic scene it-

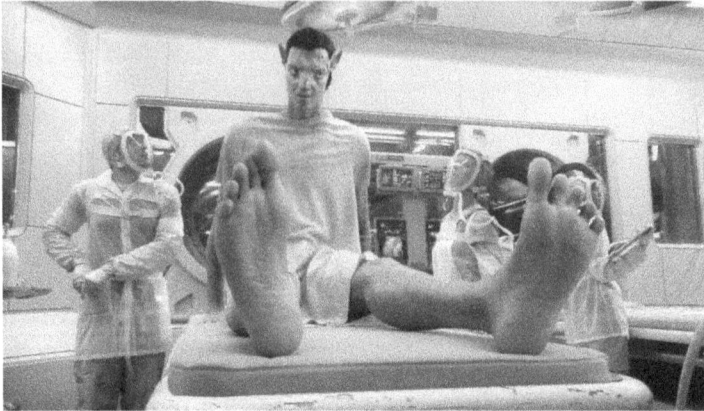

Jake's avatar's phallic foot. (From the film *Avatar*.
Copyright 2009, 20th Century Fox.)

self created with advanced digital imaging and facial- and motion-capture technology. Jake's avatar body, like Locke's supernaturally healed body, becomes a bridge between the technological, the natural, and the supernatural, which functions in both narratives as a bridge between white Western identities and nonwhite bodies. For Jake and Locke, the fantasy narrative of rebirth into a hyperable body allows them recognition as having a type of native status while maintaining their internal sense of whiteness and allows them to use their embodiment of nonwhiteness to rehabilitate their white manhood. The technologies that enable that rebirth render disability irrelevant in this white-led and androcentric utopian future.

Such recognition and rehabilitation come both through the physical embodiment of the racial other (and thus continued appropriation of their bodies and social identity) and through recognition and approval from these same racial others—an approval that goes so far in the case of *Avatar* as to allow Jake to become their leader. How recognition across difference works in this rehabilitative structure appropriates many of the generic tropes of sentimental fiction in the service of sympathy for white men. For example, it is Jake's disability and resulting minority status that allow him to initially inhabit a space of sentimental identification with another's suffering—that is, the audience is initially asked not to sympathize with or feel for Jake's wounded status as a white man, but for his position as a person with a disability in an otherwise highly ableist world. As the plot unfolds, however, we realize this is not a story about identification between able-bodied and disabled people, or a film that asks those without disabilities to understand or become allies to people with mobility impairments. Rather, it reveals how contemporary positions of white cis manhood might be sympathized with, understood, and aided by people of color via tropes not of disability, but of hyperableist embodiment.

Jake's body is presented, as disabled bodies often are, as both too much and never quite enough, even after he regains able-bodied status through use of the avatar. In the avatar, it is Jake's whiteness that disables him in the context of Pandora—a whiteness that is too loud and clumsy, and lacks strength and control. Thus, his physical disability again becomes a metaphor for white masculinity that is trained, repaired, and strengthened via the labor of the racial other. Jake has to learn from the natives, in the tradition of Natty Bumppo, how to fully inhabit his body. Ultimately Neytiri, the daughter of the patriarch of the clan of Na'vi directly under attack from the RDA, needs to validate him by seeing his true self (the disabled white human) and loving him, thus legitimating his post–new social movements white masculinity and validating his historical power as a white man to create the kind of structural change that could save the oppressed. Rebecca Wanzo describes "sentimental texts in the U.S." as "uncritically treat[ing] the representation of suffering bodies as a means for accomplishing political and social change." In such texts, "identification with 'pain' is thus an organizing principle of citizenship" and "empathy and sympathy are treated as central to the concept of universal humanity" (72). In *Avatar* we are asked to sympathize with the Na'vi in their experience of colonization and exploitation. But the truly emotionally identificatory moments in the film are with Jake—as he "frees" himself from his disabled body (both paraplegic and white) and regains an unwounded and respected body and self through the use of the bodies and sympathies of the Na'vi.

It is worth taking a moment to note the multiple racial significations of the Na'vi and the histories of racial otherness they suggest. While the Na'vi are in actual hue blue, they signify global racial nonwhiteness, including specifically people of African heritage as well as the nonwhiteness of colonized and tribally organized people more generally. This is evident (1) through their stereotypically native attire and weaponry (e.g., feathers, beads, braided hair, leather jewelry, bows and arrows) and (2) through the character types they reference. As Silva Martínez Falquina notes:

The cinematic Indian roles that are recovered in *Avatar* include the expected types: the Pocahontas-like Indian princess Neytiri, who starts by saving the hero and is the helper at the service of the white man; the warrior chief . . . who follows in the dying Indian tradition; the spiritual mother . . . who immediately recognizes the value of the human hero; and the young rival . . . who takes time but ultimately accepts Jake's leadership, and who also dies in a courageous fight. (122)

Additionally, all the main Na'vi characters are played by people of color, whereas the only humans who are played by nonwhite actors are part of the supporting cast of military personnel and scientists who help Jake escape—centrally, Michelle Rodriguez (a military pilot, who incidentally also plays a defiant woman of color in *Lost*) and Dileep Rao (the "xenobiologist" responsible for transferring human brains into avatar bodies). Both of these roles reinforce the legitimacy of Jake's appropriation of the Na'vi body as well as his role in liberating them, by showing the audience that this role is supported by human people of color who themselves distrust the aims of the RDA. The Na'vi are voiced and face-captured for animation by actors who mark a range of racial nonwhiteness. Neytiri is played by Zoë Saldaña, who was born in New Jersey to Dominican and Puerto Rican parents. Though she lived in the Dominican Republic for several years, she does not usually speak with a Dominican accent. In the film, however, Saldaña employs a heavy accent, indicating the film's need for her to orally represent not only Blackness but also a postcolonial non-U.S. space. Wes Studi, who is Cherokee, plays Neytiri's father, the tribal chief Eytukan (Studi also culturally signifies a dying or at-risk nativeness because of his role as Magua in Michael Mann's 1992 *Last of the Mohicans*). Laz Alanzo, an actor of Afro-Cuban descent, plays Tsu'tey, the original heir to the tribal chieftainship and betrothed to Neytiri before she falls in love with Jake. And C. C. H. Pounder plays Mo'at, Neytiri's mother and the chief's wife. Pounder, who is from Guyana, has also only a very slight Guyanese accent in interviews but exaggerates it for the film. These casting choices, along with the oral direction and costuming ensure that the Na'vi will be read not only as associated with the natural world but also as colonized, tribal, and, most importantly, nonwhite bodies against which Jake's white disabled body (and Sam Worthington's white and nondisabled body) can be read as both wounded and rehabilitated.[10]

The Na'vi are also presented as hyper-able-bodied, particularly as compared to the majority-white humans, who are reliant on multiple devices of extra-bodily technology to survive. The reason there are no prosthetic limbs on Pandora, no wheelchairs (and no paved surfaces or ramps to use even if there were) is, we assume, because the Na'vi have "naturally occurring carbon fiber" in their bones to make them stronger. They are also supposed to be taller and stronger because of the lighter gravity on Pandora, in addition, of course, to their "natural," active lifestyle and lack of any kind of processed food consumption. These factors create the fantasy scenario in which there is a population with no appreciable or long-term disability. Here we might note the ways histories of racialized disgender function to separate the white male characters from the characters of color. Historically, Black people in the United States, though a population systemically disabled by racial violence,

Jake's sentimental blackface. (From the film *Avatar*.
Copyright 2009, 20th Century Fox.)

have had their bodies constructed in opposition to culturally understood disablement. Black men are frequently stereotyped as hyperable, as in the stereotype of the superhuman athlete, the "thug," or the physically threatening criminal. Conversely, Black people who experience disabling working or living conditions are often not considered disabled as it applies to an individual bodily impairment that one is either born with or acquires through accident. As Jasbir Puar notes, "what counts as disability" in a rights-based and mainstream sense of the term, "is already overdetermined by 'white fragility' on one side and the racialization of bodies that are expected to endure pain, suffering, and injury on the other" (*Right to Maim*, xiv). The ways Jake is figured as still "white," even while inhabiting a nonwhite racialized Na'vi body, highlight that white maleness can be defined in part by its potential to be disabled as well as its right to able-bodied masculinity. Jake here has less become a person of color than engaged in a kind of sentimental blackface—a reading suggested visually in the scene in which Jake learns to ride the Mountain Banshee, a feat that will ultimately gain him leadership status among the Na'vi—when he falls and his face is covered in a mask of dark mud.

When Jake enters his avatar, his brain is "plugged in" to a racially other body. However, it is suggested that his brain is already one that belongs to a normative able body, despite Jake's paraplegia—race here trumping disability, or revealing it to be a temporary state for white men. It also suggests that in identifying with the Na'vi, Jake is able to escape the wounds of his white masculinity, which were, like his paraplegia, never truly a part of him but rather unnecessary historical psychological baggage. Thus, Jake as racial other can keep his personality, mind, and history of racial and gender privilege intact. The way the white man's mind can enter the racially other body is a metaphor for what Christiane König calls "the whole seemingly 'biological-natural' environment" of Pandora for Jake, which is a landscape "unmarked from the scars, the cruelties, the inequities and the deaths of the (social, political, historical) real" (3). König also notes that it is only the face of the avatar that really takes on the human brain—just as in the film the voice actors are captured in facial, though not bodily difference. It is the face that links these blue alien–animated creatures to their identities in the extra-filmic world and allows us to read their racial status via that of the humans playing them. It also links Jake and Augustine to the human minds behind the avatars that otherwise might be disabled by what König describes as the histories of the real. The way the face-to-body relation works here replicates histories of erasure of the wounds of those oppressed by white narratives, continuing to place the white mind, face, and authority at the center of even the bodies of people of color. As König suggests, this is "imperialism/colonialism on [the] deepest level of interface-technology" (11). It is also a colonization of the body allowed by the use of disability as a metaphor for white men's racial wounds—here both the wound of guilt over past violences and the related wound of not being seen or appreciated by women and people of color and thus losing a rightful place in Eden. It is this woundedness that is healed for Jake by his relation with Neytiri, thus allowing him to escape the damaged history of his white maleness as well as his disabled human body.

The Na'vi give Jake back his manhood by taking him from the able-bodied boy that human technology and appropriation of nonwhiteness have given him, and teaching him to be a better man. Ultimately Jake must be trained as a warrior in the avatar body and prove himself to be Toruk Makto, a legendary leader who can unite the tribes of the Na'vi. David Brooks refers to this role as belonging to the "white messiah fable," in which a white man joins and then becomes the hero of a community of nonwhite others.[11] Distinct to this iteration of the white messiah fable is that the white man is disabled and must wear the body of the racial other in order to fulfill the messiah role. Additionally, Jake relies on not only the support and knowledge of but also the physical salvation by a woman of color. It is Neytiri who ultimately kills the colonel and saves Jake when, back in his human body, he cannot reach the oxygen he needs to breathe on Pandora. This scene again equates Jake's paraplegia with his white-coded humanity. We are asked to assume that it is Jake's disability and white masculinity that cause him to become vulnerable—without the use of his legs he cannot access the oxygen he needs to breathe, which he would not need if he were not dealing with the fallout of the imperialist white supremacy and male dominance that has disabled him socially/environmentally in the first place.

Jake is seen. (From the film *Avatar.* Copyright 2009, 20th Century Fox.)

When Neytiri finds Jake near the end of the film struggling in his human body to breathe, she holds him like a child. Physically, he is very small compared to her. She puts the oxygen mask over his face in a gesture echoing a parent feeding a child. "I see you," Neytiri says to Jake. In the Na'vi culture "I see you" is a common greeting that indicates not just recognition but, as Augustine's scientists tell Jake, something more akin to "I see into you, I understand you." This has been connected by critics to a version of the Sanskrit "Namaste,"[12] often translated in English as "the God in me sees the God in you" (Michaelson), as well as to the Samburu greeting meaning "I see you," as in "I see into your soul through your eyes," and indicates being present in the moment for another (Tillman). Lisa Hatton Sideris notes that the Samburu phrase refers to "seeing through another's eyes, and seeing oneself through the other's eyes, both of which are important dimensions of empathy" (466).

I would suggest that this particular "I see you" incorporates all of those meanings into Jake's ability to be seen and recognized both as a white man and as one of the natives, thereby allowing him to be his authentic self, and to be recognized in his whiteness and continue to use the avatar Na'vi body as if it were his own.[13] Once he has been truly seen, he can become Na'vi as well, all histories of violence and privilege aside. The phrase indicates that his whiteness and its accompanying woundedness have been validated by the racial other, which is why the climactic romantic scene takes place between Jake in his disabled human body and Neytiri, even though ultimately he permanently assumes his Na'vi body. In order to become the leader of the Na'vi his white manhood must be seen and loved in its woundedness, after which he can let go of any relationship he had to the violent aspects of that identity, become bodily Na'vi, and still always "be seen" for who he is—a white guy who is ultimately better at being Na'vi than the Na'vi.

The film ends on Jake's "birthday," when he is reborn permanently into the avatar body. The disabled older version of white masculinity can be discarded and transcended, like an imperfect body, with no perception of loss. Jake is figured as complete in his rebirth, a combination of white male experience and historical privilege in a nonwhite, hyperable body. While it performs a slight twist on *Lost*'s conclusion that white men must work in conjunction with one another to reclaim an ableist white masculinity from a social history of its disablement, *Avatar* similarly illuminates and sympathizes with a story of the rehabilitation of an externally limited white masculinity. Jake, like Locke, says he was sick of being told "what [he] can't do," and both narratives reveal not what people with mobility impairments can do but what white cis men can still do even in a multicultural post–new social movements era. In both films, the wounded but also (and implicitly consequently) open to personal and political change white cis man is chosen by an Edenic, spiritual space inhabited by racial and gender others, and led by and in relation to this othered space to let go of the wounded aspects of white cis manhood and rehabilitate himself by rehabilitating a social place of central importance for white men within multicultural and nonwhite spaces.

Both *Avatar* and *Lost* draw on the sense that the disabled status of the everyday straight, white cisgender man will be one that audiences will sympathize with and read as both worthy of rehabilitation and possible to rehabilitate. Both narratives suggest that the recognition and forgiveness of women and people of color along with access to scientific and medical technology can cure white manhood without returning it to the shadow of historically violent forms of white male power. Through this rehabilitation, both men can reenter reproductive futurity. The rehabilitated Locke has a successful relationship with Katy Segal's character—thus referencing a possible alternate future of marriage and children, and Jake marries Neytiri presumably to raise the next generation of clan leaders. Thus, both men find a way as rehabilitated able-bodied men to reassume a central position in relation to a heterosexual political future.

Both *Avatar* and *Lost* represent a cultural desire to erase the pain caused by the advent of identity politics—that is, the surfacing of the preexisting disablement of historically oppressed minorities into the larger national consciousness—by fantasizing how white manhood, figured as the villain by certain culturally dominant identity politics models, can leave the violent history of white cis manhood behind by embodying its own fetish: the infinitely able-bodied and physically and ethically perfectible racial and gendered other. Both narratives reject a traditional medical model of treatment and rehabilitation (doctors represent another model of professional white masculinity, a hierarchical class model, dictating what they can and can't do), but not in favor of a social model of disability activism and identity pride, nor in favor of a more complexly embodied or political/relational model of disability that would value the care of disabled and ill bodies while still critiquing the assumption that the only solution to disability is medical intervention rather than shifting environments, ideologies, and patterns that exclude or stigmatize people with disabilities.[14] Rather, these narratives figure a fantastic transcendence of history that would remake white manhood as a kind of superhuman white subjectivity with native bodily traits, in the process erasing the histories of minority social identities as well as possibilities for cultural coalitions between disability activism and other minority identity politics.

While both narratives turn away from a recognition of the histories of racialized disgender that construct white cis masculinity and the intersecting systems of power and oppression behind them, the tensions and fears they seek to soothe also reveal these interlocking historical power structures and allow us to think through what alternate endings or alternate futures might look like that harness the knowledge of racialized disgender. One might use this knowledge to recognize the fantasy of a white cis manhood rehabilitated out of the histories of violence that created it and to build stronger allyship models that continue the work of identity politics in a way that does not shy away from histories of disability nor create a false dichotomy between the disabling of the marginalized and the ableing of the dominant. Such a perspective understands all subjects under racist, ableist, cis-normative hetero-patriarchy to be differently and differentially disabled by these histories and all positions as having valuable lenses into the working of oppressive power.

Disability Studies' Racial and Gender Inheritance

Popular cultural representations of white male disability like those in *Lost* and *Avatar* echo a concern within disability studies about the privileging of disability (particularly physical disability) over other identities and the way such a privileging might reinforce a white, straight cisgender male perspective. Disability studies as a field must be careful to distinguish the politically powerful and disruptive aspect of the fluidity of disability identity from that same fluidity's possibility to become all-encompassing, thus potentially conflating and equating all bodily differences and social identities. That is, disability theory's premise that everyone could potentially become disabled and most people will runs the risk of appearing to be the ultimate and uni-

versal minority identity, thereby trumping or absorbing other minority identities or figuring able-bodied versus disabled as the foundational power im-
balance on which all other social oppressions are built. This potential
universalizing tendency becomes dangerous to the extent that it could
muddy the insights and precision of thinking that valuing the differences,
difficulties, and specific knowledges gained from particular histories of oppression can give us. This is a risk within disability studies because of not
only the fluid nature of the identity "disabled" but also disability theory's
history of dominance by white men. As Joan Corbett O'Toole has noted, the
disability movement has a sexist and racist inheritance to overcome, historically constructing the universal image of disability as the "myth of the
white, straight man in a wheelchair" (295).[15]

Thomas J. Gerschick points out that "for men with physical disabilities,
masculine gender privilege collides with the stigmatized status of having a
disability, thereby causing status inconsistency, as having a disability erodes
much, but not all, masculine privilege" (1265). This collision or inconsistency
symbolically equates the disabled white male body with the positionality of
the female, queer, or nonwhite body. It does not, however, actually erase white
male privilege and, depending on its context and implications, can actually
allow the white, straight American cisgender man to access a professed loss
of authenticity of identity as a white man via his association with minority
status as a person with a disability. Robert McRuer and Abby L. Wilkerson
have pointed out that the "previously able-bodied white middle-class heterosexual who dominates the genre" of disability narratives tends to reinforce
the able-bodied/disabled binary more than work to open accessible spaces for
all types of bodies and identifications (12–14).

Disability theory, as it gains prominence in the academy and takes its
place alongside gender, sexuality, and critical race studies, may ironically be
at risk of working to rehabilitate a space for white masculinity to claim equal
injury, thereby inadvertently undermining the powerful work of feminist,
queer, and critical race critiques. Even Tobin Siebers, who critiques the white
male–centered, postidentity approach to disability studies so incisively, runs
into some logical fallacies when it comes to thinking of disability intersectionally. One of his foundational assumptions is that disability is exceptional because is it "less stable than identities associated with gender, race, sexuality, nation, and class" (5). The example he gives is that "as a white man" he
knows "that [he] will not wake up in the morning as a Black woman, but [he]
could wake up as a quadriplegic" (5). This line of thinking appears in many
works of disability studies. The assumption is that race and gender are fixed
over time, which does not acknowledge many trans and gender queer identities that figure gender as fluid and nonbinary, narratives of people who pass

(racially or otherwise) at certain times in their lives, or people who find out something unknown about their background, such as the existence of a Black grandparent or having intersex characteristics previously unknown to them. People are destabilized from and destabilize the race, gender, sexuality, class, and nationality positions within which they are socially inscribed all the time.

Rather than looking at a particular intersectionality between multiple identities, including disability, this project uses disability studies as a central theoretical framework because it provides narratives that resist an attachment to a reified, wounded identity, while also valuing disabled positionality and wounded histories as constituting legitimate sites from which to organize politically and build a common sense of political futurity. In the chapters that follow, I explore texts written in the wake of new social movements that explore valuable and complex connections between disability, other socially marginalized identities, and relations to wounded and disabled histories—narratives that resist the hegemonic drive to appropriate the political wound for a rehabilitation of white masculinity. I suggest that we can use the potential for disabled futures as a way to hold on to what has always been valuable, fluid, and challenging about social identity–based theory and knowledge—futures that highlight and form their politics around the epistemic privileges of multiple and intersecting experiences of marginalization and inherited historical disablement. My hope is that such an approach might help us parse the paradoxical relation between minoritized social identity politics and the fact of being historically and socially—and possibly also physically, mentally, and emotionally—disabled, and thereby to revalue histories of disablement endemic to disability, gender, sexual, and racial identities.

2

Embodied Metaphor and Nonreproductive
Futurity as Racialized Disgender
in Islas and Moraga

The relationship between metaphor and disability has long been central to disability studies and disability rights critiques. A central critique of early disability studies was how disability is used primarily as a metaphor in dominant cultural texts, rather than represented as a complex, lived, and valuable aspect of a character's identity. Hollywood has been repeatedly criticized by disability activists for casting actors without disabilities in stigmatizing and often Oscar- and Emmy-winning disabled roles.[1] David T. Mitchell and Sharon Snyder famously named the ways "physical and cognitive anomalies promise to lend a 'tangible' body to textual abstractions" the "materiality of metaphor" (48). Susan Sontag has critiqued the ways that cancer and AIDS are used as metaphors for social crises and are described through distancing metaphors that mythologize disease and prevent patients from seeking and receiving the best treatment. The ways that linguistic theories of metaphors are themselves ableist have been explored by Amy Vidali, while Sami Schalk has looked at the use of ableist metaphors in feminist theory and politics.[2]

The disability and/as metaphor problem is a complex one. Metaphor is intrinsic to our cultural forms of communication, and thus we cannot do away with metaphor in literature, cultural narratives, or our everyday language. And disability itself functions not only at the level of material bodymind impairment but also as a cultural and linguistic signifier and as a status that intersects with and makes meaning in relation to other social identity markers. As Rosemarie Garland-Thomson frames the problem, it is not metaphor itself that is the problem but rather the fact that "disability is so strongly stigmatized and is countered by so few mitigating narratives," which results in "the literary traffic in metaphors often misrepresent[ing] or flatten[ing] the experience real people have of their own or others' disabilities" (10).

This chapter examines the work of Arturo Islas and Cherríe Moraga to complicate the dichotomy between metaphorical narrative and literal lived experience by interrogating representations of disability that are simultaneously and inseparably both literal and metaphorical, and whose embodied metaphoricity is most pronounced as disability intersects with and illuminates the workings of race, gender, and sexuality. Here I follow similar logic to Schalk, who argues that "disability can take on both metaphorical and material meaning in a text. . . . Reading for both metaphorical and material significance of disability in a text allows us to trace the ways discourses of (dis)ability, race, and gender do not merely intersect at the site of multiply marginalized people, but also how these systems collude or work in place of one another" (*Bodyminds* 34). Whereas it may be clearly problematic to use disability only as a metaphor for race or gender, many texts, including those I examine here, allow disability to register on both metaphorical and material levels and in so doing help us to perceive how race, disability, and gender work as interlocking systems at the site of individual bodies and as semiotic tropes that circulate and make meaning in relation to one another. The disabled futures constructed in Islas's and Moraga's texts are built on not only a revaluing of disabled bodies but also the ability to view race and gender constructs and experiences in terms of and in relation to disability, highlighting both how race and gender themselves can disable bodies and how disabilities can allow for queerer and more flexible and enabling embodiments and conceptions of race and gender, a process I term "racialized dis-gendering."[3] This chapter forwards the argument that close readings of disability metaphors that straddle literal/metaphorical discursive boundaries can reveal how disability and all social identities are created and lived through dynamic and interconnected physical, material, linguistic, and tropological instantiations.

In Arturo Islas's novel *The Rain God* (1984) and Cherríe Moraga's play *Heroes and Saints* (1994), characters who are or conceptualize themselves to be bodiless from the neck down are vehicles for exploring narrative and political relations between gender identity, queer sexuality, Chicano/a/x identity, and the effects of racially based colonization and its resultant ongoing systemic oppressions. *Heroes and Saints* is a play about environmental racism that tells the story of a Chicanx community living in California's Central Valley.[4] The community members' primary form of employment is working in the local agricultural fields, which are being treated with a pesticide that is poisoning their water and affecting the health of the children in particular. The play's main character, Cerezita, is a disabled young woman who uses a platform on wheels for mobility (her *raite* [ride] as she calls it). She is confined for the majority of the play to the house by her mother, and ultimately inspires and organizes the communal burning of the agricultural fields in protest. While it is arguable that Cerezita may have simply been born without limbs, she is described on the play's cast page as *"the head,"* and is frequently portrayed on stage by an actor with their body hidden inside the platform and only their head showing (Moraga, *Heroes and Saints* 90). *The Rain God* is an exploration of the multigenerational family dynamics of the Angel family, a Chicanx family living on the Mexico-U.S. border. It is focalized through Miguel Chico, a semiautobiographical character, as he wrestles with the internalized racism and homophobia of the family matriarch, Mama Chona; the experiences of the family's various "sinners"; and his openly acknowledged disability and alluded-to queer sexuality. Mama Chona is a character who "den[ies] the existence of all parts of the body below the neck" (Islas 164). This trait is inherited to a large extent by Miguel Chico, who, after a colostomy, believes he might almost be able to achieve Mama Chona's ideal of becoming "a perfect astronaut"—"pure, bodiless intellect. No shit, no piss, no blood" (8). Each of the characters—Cerezita, Miguel Chico, and Mama Chona—functions figuratively (and at points literally) as "just a head." The metaphorical use of amelia (the medical condition of missing one or more limbs) in Islas's and Moraga's texts is potentially politically problematic from a disability studies perspective in that it presents disability as a symbol or sign; thus it may risk drawing attention away from the lived experiences of disabled bodies by using them to figuratively represent other social identities or systems of oppression. Islas's and Moraga's use of metaphor is also, however, precisely what is most narratively interesting and politically radical about their representations of disability and what helps us to perceive the ways that disability as a culturally constructed and internalized material reality contributes to and can help us expand our understandings of racialized gender identity.

Moraga's and Islas's disabled characters may at first appear as different as these writers' forms of political engagement. Moraga has been an outspoken political activist, tending toward a critical queer cultural nationalism and pushing for more Chicanos and Chicanas to publically embrace their queerness, while Islas was an introverted academic, whom Moraga critiqued as an author whose writing "boldly begged to announce his gayness" but did not ("Queer" 234). While Cerezita is the most outspoken and politically effective character in *Heroes and Saints,* Miguel Chico and Mama Chona from Islas's

The Rain God use their physical impairments to disengage from external politics and internal awarenesses related to their racially and sexually marked bodies. Moreover, the ways in which metaphor can circulate in Moraga's drama are different from the ways it can circulate in Islas's novel. For example, even if we interpret Moraga's stage directions to make Cerezita "a head" literally, there is no way to cast a live actor with that disability. While Moraga's staged metaphor is more material—in that Cerezita is at the very least literally limbless and her disability is embodied in the performance of the play—the staging of her as "a head" highlights the tropological and performative aspect of disability identity. No living human is just a head, and thus one must create the performance of a representation of disability in the play's performance rather than assuming a mimetic relation between actor and character. In Islas's novel, we can never see nor are we asked to see a material instantiation of amelia. Islas's characters function as extended textual metaphors for the ways their racial and gender identities have interrupted and complicated their mental and physiological relation to their bodies. However, there is a literalness to this disability in that this interruption does, in fact, change their material relation to their bodies and functions as the lens through which they experience the other disabilities they have or acquire throughout the novel. Though some of this internal relationality might be captured in dialogue or stage direction, the ability to narrate characters' internal states in the novel form allows Islas's extended metaphor, though less material in its instantiation, to be potentially more fully understood as a lived reality than Moraga's physically impossible "head."

These differences aside, I find these texts extremely useful to read alongside each other in their mutual investment in the overlaps and intersections of both race/gender/disability and their use of disability as a metaphor and simultaneous lived reality as a framework for building more radical inclusion within Chicanx communities. As Julie Avril Minich has noted, Islas's use of representations of disability in his novels offers an "early instantiation" of Moraga's "Queer Aztlán" in that they "produce a vision of Chicano/a community that circumvents the exclusions upon which cultural nationalisms are often predicated" (32). Both authors' works use disability in ways that resist normative ableist ideas about bodily and communal wholeness and theorize more inclusive racial politics. Here I read Islas's and Moraga's mobilizations of representations of disability as consciously and inseparably both literal and metaphorical, as a literary device for figuring racialized disgender as both a historically disabling and contemporarily valuable identity. I address the literal and metaphorical uses of disability in the texts first and then turn to and further define racialized disgender as it circulates in both texts. Racialized disgender and the complex embodiment of disability, as it circulates as a culturally defined and tropologically reinforced position, provide a conceptual framework that challenges the intersections of whiteness, maleness, and physical disability as loss that contribute to the more restrictive and less historically aware oppressive representational intersections of race, gender, and disability discussed in Chapter 1.

The literal and tropological is a combination that to some extent informs any representation or experience of social identity, in that all social identities are constructed through circulating symbolic meanings that have literal impacts on the way people inhabit material bodies. In the case of disability, the tropological can become highly limiting to the acknowledgment of the complex experiences of living with a disability because in dominant cultural narratives disability has historically functioned as what Mitchell and Snyder refer to as a "narrative prosthesis"—a presence that incites disruption in or interpretation of a story and/or functions as a way of grounding larger cultural and linguistic abstractions in material bodies. In the narratives Mitchell and Snyder discuss, this proliferation of representational disability ultimately limits the realities, experiences, and full humanity of persons with disabilities. In the narratives of Islas and Moraga, however, the combination of metaphorical and literal representation of disability opens up queer and crip narratives of minority social identity that resist liberal individualist notions of political "progress" via assimilation, fantasies of wholeness and health, and heterosexual reproduction, thus potentially allowing more narratives of different bodily experiences that are politically useful for people with nonnormative bodies and oppressed social identities. Both authors also complicate understandings of minority racial and sexual identity as they arise from and relate to histories of oppression and injury and intersect with gender expectations, exemplifying disability theory's insights that an ethical politics of identification can ameliorate historical and contemporary pain without erasing it from existence or memory as a complex site of identity and identification.

Nirmala Erevelles reminds us that a truly transformative politics, rather than ignoring histories of wounds or deconstructing the binaries that enable and are reinforced by social oppression, must foreground "the materiality of structural constraints that actually give rise to [those] oppressive binaries" (129). Michelle Jarman is similarly invested in examining the material structures of social wounding and the ways racist and ableist ideologies worked in conjunction with each other to produce rationales for lynching and the castration of disabled men. Both Jarman and Erevelles insist on exploring the material conditions that lead to the violence toward and impairment of certain bodies so as to challenge their continued workings in the present. In this chapter I aim to remain rooted in a knowledge of the material realities of oppression and marginalization of disabled and nonwhite bodies, while also exploring moments in the texts of Islas and Moraga where one cannot easily separate a discursive potential from a lived limitation and in which one must question the drive to heal or move toward normalcy at the cost of acknowledging and even valuing impaired bodies and historically disabled social identities. I take seriously the materialist critiques of theorists like Erevelles and Jarman, but I also suggest that in addition to questioning the binaries wounded versus healthy or impaired versus normal, as disability studies theorists have historically done, we might push more on the binaries often taken for granted by those same theorists, including material versus discursive and literal versus tropological. As Therí Pickens suggests, rather than deconstructing the binary impairment versus normalcy, we might consider whether it is possible that "healing and belonging are neither desirable nor necessary" (*New Body* 12). Islas's and Moraga's texts allow us a way into reading the complicated relations between the tropological aspects of social identity and their literal embodiments by keeping intersectionalities of lived minority social identities and their attendant historical constructions—material and discursive—at the center of their narratives while also reclaiming the abjection of historical wounds as sites of potential aesthetic, political, and psychological value.

Mitchell and Snyder suggest that many narratives that rely on disability as part of their structure often do not end with a focus on disability as a lived experience but rather rehabilitate or fix "deviance in some manner. This . . . may involve an obliteration of the difference through a 'cure,' the rescue of the despised object from social censure, the extermination of the deviant as a purification of the social body, or the revaluation of an alternative mode of being" (53–54). Islas's and Moraga's texts resignify the rehabilitative stage of narrative, allowing for narrative conclusion without rehabilitation, purification, rescue, or revaluation, thereby inviting interpretation of the narrative and social identities' (including disability's) role in it, while resisting authoritative interpretations of disability. They do this not by getting outside of our cultural scripts and assumptions about disability, nor by refusing to use disability as metaphor, but by constructing metaphors that create emergent meanings that challenge the ideological authorization for cultural metaphorical interpretation of disability as well as marginalized gender, sexual, and racial/ethnic identities. Islas's and Moraga's use of disability as metaphor is not a denial of the bodily reality of disability, or a sign of individual or narrative deviance, but rather a way of using disability to stand in for and to help explore the experience of disabled social identities—metonymically for disability identity and metaphorically for racial, ethnic, and sexual identity.

Though cognitive linguistic approaches to metaphor—often called "conceptual metaphor theory" because they look at how metaphor use reflects the ways we organize concepts in our brains—have been critiqued for their underlying ableist assumptions,[5] they can provide useful insights into how a representation can work simultaneously on literal and metaphorical levels, particularly representations related to the body, which conceptual metaphor theory suggests is the foundational source for primary metaphors in our culture. Whether biologically determined or simply a function of the way we culturally conceive of the body, the conclusions of conceptual metaphor theory point to the body itself as a primary site for the source of metaphorical language that can also have the effect of rhetorically grounding the abstract/linguistic nature of metaphor in a physical object. This is precisely one of the narrative uses of disability that Mitchell and Snyder critique and that they refer to as "the materiality of metaphor" (48).

Islas's and Moraga's texts draw attention to and make use of the disabled body's impacts on culturally shared language and the assumptions that language relies on and reproduces in relation to bodily norms and expectations. At the same time, their focus on the body as body and not solely as metaphor helps us understand how physicality matters to our construction of the metaphors that shape the ways we conceptualize and inhabit our bodies. Their texts illuminate the ways that illness is already embroiled in metaphor in that we think our bodies conceptually through shared cultural metaphors that gather their power through a largely unquestioned belief that they are rooted in shared bodily metonymic experience. Our cultural metaphors tell us repeatedly that illness equates to pain, negativity, incompetence, and weakness. Yet the body and its experiences of health *and* illness constitute the primary metaphors by which we conceptualize the world. As Vidali points out, "While metaphoric representations of disability are often criticized, there has been little engagement with theories of metaphor, which seek to explain how metaphors are created and proliferate. A re-evaluation of these theories is necessary to better understand problematic disability metaphors at theoretical and methodological levels, and to resist them in ways that go beyond 'policing' language" (34). In the analyses that follow, I explore how Islas and Moraga make use of our cultural metaphors of disability as loss or lack; create emergent meanings of disability by blending gender, sexual, racial, and ethnic identity with representation of wounds and impairments; and create representations of bodies that are racially disgendered as a challenge to ideologies of normative futurity, assimilation, and belonging.

"What Biznis You Got with the Body?"
Moraga's *Heroes and Saints*

In Moraga's *Heroes and Saints,* Cerezita, the child born without a body as a result of a systemically racist economic system that allows planters to dust crops with a substance poisonous to the Chicanx people who work the fields and live in nearby housing developments, is both a metaphor for the injury of her community and a full and complex character in the play who has a real physical impairment. Cerezita represents the hidden pain of her community metaphorically in that her disability was caused by the poisoning of their water and her mother will not allow her to be seen outside or to become politically active. Cerezita also deals with practical effects of her impairment in that it is very difficult for her to disobey her mother and leave her home without someone physically helping her, particularly because of the way the controls on her *raite* are configured.

Telory W. Davies argues that while Moraga's play represents disability as a metaphor for race, the staging of the production, including its stage directions, keeps disability from remaining metaphorical only, thus allowing disability to function, "simultaneously as a lived reality and a metaphor for oppression" (31). Moraga's stage directions describe Cerezita as "*a head of human dimension, but one who possesses such dignity of bearing and classical Indian beauty she can, at times, assume nearly religious proportions. . . . This image, however, should be contrasted with the very real 'humanness' she exhibits on a daily functioning level. Her mobility and its limits are critical aspects of her character*" (90, italics in original). In these opening directions, Moraga establishes that Cerezita's character should function neither on a wholly symbolic nor a wholly literal level. This combination of symbolic and literal is reinforced by the dramatic genre, in which real material bodies need to perform this (at least in part) metaphorical disability.[6] Moraga's stage directions also indicate that Cerezita's "*classical Indian beauty*" makes her appear like "*the pre-Columbian Olmecas*," thus connecting her disabled status as "just a head" to religious symbology and to an ethnic lineage from the pre-European-colonization civilizations of Mesoamerica. Including a character who is a head only is also a reference to Luis Valdez's first full-length play, "The Shrunken Head of Pancho Villa," in which a child is born with just a head and no body the same year that Pancho Villa's body is disinterred and found to be headless. The bodiless head in Valdez's play is meant to symbolize not only the ongoing spirit of Villa but also the inability to ignore the wounded history of Chicanx identity. Thus, Cerezita as literary reference functions figuratively as a link to a Chicanx sociopolitical heritage. The use of Cerezita's disability as metaphor is about her connection to a history of racial and ethnic oppression as well as a rich cultural history of artistic and symbolic representation. Thus, we are invited to read Cerezita as a metaphorical figure for a larger history of racialized and nationalistic oppression and pride—a symbolism she will utilize to promote political affiliations across her community. Cerezita also functions metonymically as a stand-in for all the children born with illnesses or disabilities in her community. She is one of few survivors of a generation of children born in similar circumstances. Her visibility marks the material conditions of global capitalism, including class inequity and environmental racism, that create higher death, illness, and impairment rates in her community.

In addition to functioning metaphorically and metonymically, Cerezita is a literal figure showing that lack of access to social spaces and marked bodily difference carry limits to both action and mobility at the same time that they provide certain political and epistemic privileges.[7] On this literal level, Cerezita's mother's reactions can be read as a critique of the social infantilization of people with mobility and other physical impairments as well as of the responsibility our culture puts on women, particularly mothers, to provide unpaid care to family members who might not need it if those family members' needs were not considered extraneous to socially and communally provided support.

All three of these functions of Cerezita's character rewrite and undermine our cultural metaphors that associate disability with weakness or obstacles to overcome. In Cerezita's role as symbol of systemic oppression, disability represents a wound that both oppressor and oppressed want to hide but cannot. As a metonym for a community living with a history of social oppression, Cerezita's disability becomes an exposed wound that functions as a site for political organizing. And as a disabled person negotiating lack of autonomous mobility and control by her caretaker, Cerezita embodies a disabled subjectivity that resists metaphorical meaning altogether and reveals connections between the oppression of bodies marked as disabled with a failure of radical revolt, and, as Minich suggests, possibilities for more "radical inclusivity" in nationalist movements (73). The particular bodily violences done to the community via poisoning the only workplaces and living spaces its members have access to give metaphorical rise to an association between illness and racial/ethnic oppression, which then opens up metaphorical meanings that abstract neither from actual bodies and their material circumstances nor from functional political activism.

Moraga also uses Cerezita to prompt her audience to think through the ways we experience our bodies as they are shaped by cultural metaphor. In Act I, Scene 8, Cerezita verbally draws attention to her hair and tongue, both as a way of flirting with Father Juan (whom her mother has invited to visit Cerezita—it is unclear whether as a representative of the church or as a man with whom to socialize) and as a way of refiguring our literal understandings of how these body parts function, what roles they can play, and how they are valued and perceived. She tells Juan, "Touch my hair, Father," contextually making her hair a sexualized body part. She also describes her hair as a "curtain" and compares it to "the veils" of "Arab women," imagining it like "all those soft cloths secretly caressing their bodies" (107). This reference both sensualizes her hair and draws attention to the agency, sexuality, and bodily pleasure of covered women, and it suggests a parallel between women whose societies tell them to hide their female bodies and her society, which tells her to hide her disabled body. This parallel disrupts the cultural perception dividing the sexually exoticized Brown female body from the desexualized disabled body. It also draws attention to how gender is always already at work to hide/limit/restrict and draw attention to the sexual legibility and general freedoms of all socialized bodies.

It is not her veil of hair but her tongue that Cerezita most powerfully resignifies by recircuiting and signifying on definitions and cultural metaphors already available to her. She uses the ways tongues signify linguistically, culturally, and metaphorically to draw attention to the ways the tongue can register as a powerful, essential, and sexual body part—more so even than the limbs, genitalia, and breasts that she does not have. She first claims that her tongue has "the best definition . . . in the world unless there's some other vegetable heads like me who survived" (107). Cerezita here establishes her physical strength and sexual skill—her disability having the effect of making one of her muscles stronger (and one already associated with a queer female sexuality) than anyone else's in the world.

More important is the phrase "best definition," which she first uses in the literal physical sense—that is, as a muscle that has clearly carved contours. Yet even this seemingly literal use of the word "definition" begins to lean toward the linguistic/abstract rather than the physical/material, as the tongue is an organ many people use for speaking. When "tongue" and "define" are juxtaposed they also call to mind the meaning of "tongue" as speech or language—she is also referencing the sharp contours of meaning she can make with that tongue through her use of language. This then also calls attention to the material metaphorical origins of the word "define" in relation to language, which comes from the Latin *de finire,* "to put limits or boundaries to."

Cerezita proceeds to perform this linguistic definition of definition, defining "tongue" by reading its meaning as given by her dictionary and using these official cultural significations (which are themselves a mixture of physical and metaphorical description) to redefine herself, all the while using her strong physical tongue and not losing the audience's focus on it as a powerful bodily tool. The first definition she reads is physical: "a fleshly movable process of the floor of the mouths of most vertebrates." The second is linguistic: "the power of communication through speech." The third is again physical: "the flesh of the tongue used as food." The forth is linguistic: "language, especially a spoken language." These second and fourth linguistic definitions are literal, but their etymology is figurative, a dead metonymy in which the body part with which something is associated stands in for it. Cerezita's use of these official and presumably universal meanings highlights the irony of the assumption of universal bodily experience as Cerezita does not herself have a body (reminding the audience indirectly that it is far from true that everyone communicates with their tongue). Yet in other ways she inevitably shares the universal condition of living in a body defined by cultural metaphors and expectations. The last few definitions are based in this primary cultural metaphor, including figurative phrases such as "tongue in cheek," "tongue-lash," "tongueless," and "tongue tied" (108–109). These metaphorical uses of the tongue highlight ways that the body is part of our cognitive systems of figurative meaning making, and they make a space for Cerezita's head as a culturally legible body by figuring it within the linguistic and cognitive tropes through which we already culturally construct bodies' meanings, uses, and boundaries. These metaphorical uses of "tongue" also reference Gloria Anzaldúa's "How to Tame a Wild Tongue," from *Borderlands*, in which she uses the idea of an untamed tongue to represent what it means to speak as a queer Chicana. Anzaldúa writes, "I will no longer be made to feel ashamed of existing. . . . I will have my serpent's tongue—my woman's voice, my sexual voice, my poet's voice. I will overcome the tradition of silence" (81). Moraga, in effect, provides a character that could speak with the wild tongue that Anzaldúa's radical Chicana feminism theorizes, thus both grounding an abstract political goal in a disabled character and reclaiming her disability as precisely that which allows the tongue to grow strong enough so that, in fact, it is not tamed by traditions of silencing disabled, female, queer, Brown bodies.

Her definitions also call attention to the sexual uses of the tongue and the ways that (female/queer) sexuality is already a part of our meaning-making systems in relation to particular uses of body parts and legible gender identity. The phrases she mentions, including "to give tongue," "to touch or lick with," and "to articulate by tonguing," are flirtatious and suggest to Juan ways she might make sexual use of her tongue. Cerezita tells Juan she once played the trumpet, an instrument for which there is "no fingering needed . . . just a good strong tongue" (108–109). This set of definitions connects Cerezita's physical disability (which is the figurative and material reason for her strong tongue) and sexual acts often coded as queer or nonnormative. Cerezita creates emergent tropological meanings via euphemism and sexual wordplay that signify on deeply ingrained culturally coded cognitive understandings of bodies (many of them disabled) that we already have.

By putting all these definitions—literal, figurative, physical, and linguistic—into play, Moraga strips disability of its paradoxical inverse metaphorical functioning, in which symbolic interpretive readings of disability limit a realistic and politicized representation of disabled bodies. She does this not by producing more positive metaphors and only partially by including the "technology previously hidden in the corners of homes and institutions . . . in the drama of disability as lived experience" (Mitchell and Snyder 24). Rather, Moraga integrates the rhetorical power of metaphorical meaning with a representation of lived disability by complicating our cultural distinctions between the literal and metaphorical body, between the body as material object and the body as linguistic construct. For Cerezita, the power of her tongue comes from a range of literal and figurative uses. It also comes from the physical state of her body, which is what makes her tongue her "most faithful organ" (108). It is her disability that sharpens her use of spoken language, her sexual prowess, and her ability to be tongue in cheek. The way she is treated by her mother and community because of her disability also causes her to be publically tongueless or tongue-tied—ironically since her ability to use language is one of the most normatively able-bodied aspects of her character, a fact she proves here through her use of her tongue to highlight existing definitions and to reappropriate meanings for her body. In so doing she also reappropriates metaphorical uses of the body more generally that might otherwise reinforce cultural narratives of the disabled body that present it as inherently limited.

Despite the play's highlighting of the inextricability of the physical from the metaphorical, it is also very much aware of the political and ethical importance of continuing to differentiate lived embodied experience from the body's use as metaphor or symbol. Speaking to a coffin holding an infant's corpse that will be hung on a cross by protesters to draw attention to the abuses of the farming industry, Cerezita says, "Before the grown ones come to put you in the ground, they'll untie the ropes around your wrists and ankles. By then you are no longer in your body. The child's flesh hanging from that wood makes no difference to you. It is . . . you are a symbol. Nada más" (138). Here Cerezita equates becoming a symbol with death, with being removed from one's body. The dead children can become symbols of oppression because they are *nada más,* nothing but dead flesh that might become a conduit of change for the living, existing on a linguistic border between "you" and "it." Cerezita's comment about the dead children suggests that she herself cannot be such a symbol for change and a living present person at the same time. Her metaphoricity, in other words, does violence to her if it makes her a symbolic body only.

Cerezita's metaphoricity expands beyond a state of simply being a symbolic signifier. In fact, although Cerezita's disability can be read as a material symbol for the abstract oppression of the Chicanx community, the play suggests that it is the history of her lived experience as a disabled Chicana that allows her to understand the metaphorical and symbolic nature of bodies and to develop a well-defined tongue to articulate ways that bodies can be used politically. This use of epistemic privilege does not extend to all characters in the play. In fact, some embody a form of internalized racism, ableism, and sexism that suggests how historical oppressions can be internalized as victim subjectivity, in which a continued attachment to that marginalized identity continues to replicate harm. Dolores, Cerezita's mother, blames herself and her husband for Cerezita's physical disability, she is angry that her son is gay because he will "suffer like a woman," and, rather than supporting Cerezita, she prevents her from being seen for fear she will be hurt. Dolores's attachment to historical and present minority identities of victimhood keeps her in a state of suffering and also prevents her from perceiving the material circumstances and actual sources of her community's wounds, which are the agricultural industry and the government-funded housing that exploit her community members' labor and treat them as disposable resources. Her attachment to her history of oppression replicates dominant power structures by individualizing her suffering and remaining faithful to dominant narratives that have been constructed to marginalize her. We might assume Dolores's inability to take advantage of her epistemic privilege as a working-class Chicana is due to her position as not only female and Chicana but also a mother who has experienced the death of her children and the caretaker for a disabled daughter whom she fears will also be taken from her. Unlike their family friend and community activist Amparo, who is biologically childless, and Cerezita, who we assume cannot have biological children, Dolores appears unable to hold up under the weight of the ideologies that position her as both victim and failed caretaker. In response to these pressures and histories of loss, she preemptively thinks of her daughter as already half-dead and takes the blame for Cerezita's disability onto herself as a last attempt at controlling an overwhelming sense of limited agency to protect those she loves.

Cerezita is presented in contrast to Dolores's victimized sense of identity in that she manipulates her disabled position and the cultural narratives that make it legible so as to make herself appear more powerful and less vulnerable. Her final act is to dress as La Virgen de Guadalupe in order to get into the fields and burn them down, sacrificing herself in the act of destroying the economic system that has caused not only her disability but also the deaths of children in her family and wider community and the suffering of those in her community from poisoned water and exposure to harmful chemicals. Cerezita's death might be read as an instance of what Mitchell and Snyder identify as the too-common trope of the disabled character who must be sacrificed to bring a narrative to its conclusion and reconsolidate or purify the social body. What differentiates it from the standard narrative prosthesis that uses then disposes of the disabled body is the way that Cerezita's disability is figured as providing access to the political knowledge, strength, and effectiveness to change the ongoing abuses that are happening to her community. She uses her understanding of how disability as it intersects with femininity and Chicanx culture could work symbolically to signify on her disabled, racialized, and female-gendered body to gain access to a public political realm and effect change there.

In her guise as the Virgin, Cerezita plays on cultural narratives that associate disability with saintliness, sacrifice, innocence, and overcoming. This guise also allows Dolores to see Cerezita differently because of the role of the Virgin in Roman Catholicism and Mexican culture in particular. The image of the Virgin combines womanhood with revolution and cultural identity in a symbol that is legible to Dolores, and it allows her to hear Cerezita when she says, "Let me go, ámá. . . . I know about death. I know how to stop death. . . . You tie my tongue, ámá. How can I heal without my tongue?" (147). Here again, Cerezita's physical disability and her disabled social position work *for* her, both in terms of being able to use her disabled status to present herself as blessed and powerful and in terms of the epistemic privilege that comes with it—that is, "I know death" and "how to stop it." Cerezita is in a sense speaking in tongues—using a religious structure and the assumptions it carries about certain bodies in order to be heard via its cultural power of legitimation. She also calls on all the definitions of tongue, literal and metaphorical, that she has established throughout the play and ultimately uses her tongue's physical and linguistic strengths to get her mother to help her metaphorically untie her tongue. Finally Dolores concedes and *"pushes the raite with la virgin out the door"* (147, italics in original).

Cerezita's final act is to use her tongue to speak to *"el pueblo"* (the people of her community and the play's audience). She frames this speech entirely in relation to wounds both literal and metaphorical, connecting the wound not to a politically ineffectual attachment to anger and hurt, but to political power, hope, land rights, and access to social and material freedom. "Put your hand inside my wound," Cerezita says; "inside the valley of my wound, there is a people" (148), thereby connecting her own physical and emotional hurt to the others in her community. She calls on not the pain itself to call people to political action, but their knowledge and memory of pain: "The river runs red with blood; but they are not afraid because they are used to the color red. It is the same color as the river that runs through their veins, the same color as the sun setting into the sierras, the same color of the pool of liquid they were born into. They remember this in order to understand why their fields, like the rags of the wounded, have soaked up the color and still bear no fruit" (148). Cerezita suggests that in reclaiming ownership of wounds the community is also reclaiming rights to the land. She relates this memory of woundedness to cultural identity and cultural memory, also suggesting that the people "are Guatemala, El Salvador . . . the Kuna y Tarahumara. You are the miracle people too, for like them the same blood runs through your veins. The same memory of a time when your deaths were cause for reverence and celebration, not shock and mourning" (148). She connects *el pueblo* to a wounded history and notes explicitly that this does not mean that their collective identity is itself ill or wounded. At the same time, Cerezita resignifies the value of illness and death as states that are inevitable in life and can be cause for "reverence and celebration." In other words, there is nothing inherently negative about death, illness, or inhabiting a minority cultural identity. In fact, each of these inevitable parts of being alive for her audience can reconnect them to a strength in their history, community, and bodies via the shared wound that Cerezita symbolizes and is now consciously embodying for them. In tying this sense of shared cultural history to a shared history of woundedness, Cerezita is able to suggest that it is in part the interdependence, knowledge, and sense of identity that has come from these histories that can create spaces for political and social change to happen. She mines the intersectional metaphorical meanings attached to disability, minority racial, ethnic, and gender identity (in the form of direct references to her physical wound and Chicanx ethnicity, and indirectly to female sexuality—"inside the valley of my wound") to create emergent and politically useful meanings that move beyond our dominant historical cultural narratives that use disability as a metaphor for weakness, negativity, obstacles to be overcome, and wounded minority social identity positions. Rather, the wound here is the source of "that red memory [that] will spill out from inside you and flood this valley con coraje. And you will be free" (148). It is this bloody memory of social and physical disability that allows the political action of the burning of the fields to become a communal action with deep personal and political meaning. It is the wound, in other words, that enables organized communal political action.

A Perfect Astronaut: Islas's *The Rain God*

In Arturo Islas's *The Rain God,* a similar intersectionality of the physical and metaphorical is used to subvert standard narrative tropes of disability via less overtly radical and politically active characters, who nonetheless challenge dominant modes of figuring disability and complicate ways disability is used to metaphorically reference other minority social identities. Miguel Chico, our main character and the story's focalizer, is a member of the Angel family who has moved from El Paso to San Francisco to escape the family and to become a college professor. It is implied that he is gay, though his sexuality is never overtly discussed. His physical disabilities—which include polio acquired in childhood that resulted in a limp, as well as a history of intestinal illness that is retriggered when a doctor prescribes him medication for a bladder infection resulting in a colostomy, sutured anus, and use of a colostomy bag—can be read as a metaphor for Miguel Chico's closeted status or, as some critics have argued,[8] for the HIV-positive body of Islas himself or for both Miguel Chico's and Mama Chona's wounded identities as Chicano/ as inheriting all the bodily directed racist, sexist, and homophobic self-hatred of their minority ethnic and dominant U.S. cultures. At the same time, like Cerezita, Miguel Chico is represented as a character with a real lived disability, and he is autobiographically based on Islas, who himself had polio, a colostomy, and AIDS.

Immediately following his colostomy surgery, Miguel Chico thinks, "perhaps he had survived—albeit in an altered form, like a plant onto which has been grafted an altogether different strain of which the smelly rose at his side, that tip of gut that would always require his care and attention, was only a symbol" (28). The representation of Miguel Chico's most prominent physical wound, the opening in his side where his colostomy bag is attached, as "the smelly rose at his side," is both a visceral description of the body and a metaphorical abstraction from it (28). In fact, even in its visceral imagery, it not only is described figuratively—the "tip of the gut" described metaphorically as "a smelly rose"—but is itself a metaphor for something else: It is "a symbol" for his postoperative self, described again metaphorically as a grafted hybrid plant. Instead of an abstraction being materialized in the metaphor of a wounded body, metaphor is used to even further materialize the reality of the body. That bodily reality is then experienced as a symbol that Miguel uses to narrate the more emotional and abstract changes in his life directly related to his disabled status and the intersections between his disability and his race, gender, and sexuality.

The physicality of Miguel Chico's disability is experienced as both a ritual connection to and distancing from bodily experience, which is captured by the novel's representation of Miguel Chico's weekly changing of his colostomy bag. This is a ritual connected to music and food, both sensual bodily pleasures. But it is also a solitary bodily experience that reminds Miguel Chico of and distances him from the shame his impairment evokes in relation to his sexuality. During the procedure, he thinks about how "he had forgotten what it was like to be able to hold someone, naked, without having a plastic device between them" (25). This "forgotten" memory functions both literally and metaphorically in that negotiating a colostomy bag in bed is a real lived experience (and indicates that he might be sexually active if he knows what this experience feels like), while it also suggests that Miguel Chico uses his disability and its attendant shame to distance himself from an acknowledgment of his queer shame and from physical and romantic closeness with other men. One might also read this not as a longing to re-member but as a simple forgetting. Either he is not sexually active now and has not been for a while, or he is, and he has gotten used to it involving a plastic device attached to his side. I do not push for a reading of Miguel Chico as explicitly asexual, but I point out that I am not aware of any inter-pretations of the novel that explore this option, possibly because, as Eunjung Kim points out, "following the corrective claims launched after their long history of desexualization and the pronounced challenge by disability rights movements against the presumption of asexuality, asexual individuals with a disability are often erased" (481). Without making a claim that a fictional character has or does not have any particular identity, I do want to suggest that the normative reading is to assume Miguel Chico is gay and ashamed rather than that he is not interested in sexual activity at the present. One might then read his lack of discussion of his sexuality not as a closeting, but as a revealing of an at least in part asexual queer identity.

Islas's layering of physical and figurative has several intersecting layers to it. The most immediately legible metaphorical construction here is "smelly rose" as source mapped onto visual wound as target. Initially, then, the met-aphor appears quite visceral, highlighting the shape, color, and smell of the wound. However, roses also carry cultural symbolic meaning in that they evoke themes of love, romance, beauty, and delicacy. "Smelly" is an adjective that aesthetically clashes with those meanings. In this dissonance, germina-tion and decay, pleasure and disgust are suggested in equal amounts. Addi-tionally, the fact that Miguel Chico is comparing his wound to a flower con-nects to the extended metaphor of Miguel Chico himself as a grafted hybrid plant, thus linking his wound and his identity as live, natural, growing things. Dominant cultural metaphors that present disability as obstacle or weakness and are figured in opposition to an idealized able body are resigni-fied here in that the wound and the body are inseparable and both are as-sociated with life and growth. At the same time, the physicality of the smelly rose and the association with decay does not deny the bodily, painful, un-pleasant aspects of Miguel Chico's wound. Germination and growth are not separated from decay or dependence in this tropological rendering of the body, thereby refiguring illness and disability as normative and part of life rather than in opposition to it. Moreover, even in its aspects of decay this wound is not presented as something to reject or recoil from in that as readers we are sensually provoked by and drawn to the scent and visual beauty of the image of a smelly rose, an image that, considering Miguel Chico's queer sexuality and the physiological function of the smelly rose, also evokes an eroticized anus.

This complex wound as rose metaphor, which is then itself a symbol for the extended grafted plant image that is used to describe Miguel Chico's postoperative body, connects disability not only to the natural but also to the prosthetic and artificial. The hybrid plant and the stoma are both human-cultivated combinations of natural and artificial, which suggest that Miguel Chico's post-op self (both in terms of physical body and social identity) is similarly prosthetic. The disabled post-op self is metaphorically represented via the grafted plant as unnatural, singular, nonreproductive, and a new variety that is not the same as either of its origins but is not yet a new species. These associations with hybridity all reinforce Miguel Chico's disability and his doubly or triply queer sexuality (as gay, a gay male bottom with a sutured anus, and as potentially currently asexual) and evoke the bodily markers that make him other, outsider, unnatural. At the same time, grafted plants are created specifically to have aesthetic qualities unavailable in their previous forms, to heal plants that have been damaged, or often to make existing species denser, hardier, or more productive. The post-op body as grafted plant creates a space of metaphorical signification in which the singularity, uniqueness, and cultivated nature of the hybrid body that is joined inseparably to a medical device evoke creativity, growth, aesthetic pleasure, and strength.

These emergent meanings for the disabled and queer body stand in rich opposition to the starkness of Miguel Chico's inherited understanding that he should separate himself from his physical self, particularly from its shame-inducing raced and gendered stigmas. Miguel Chico's internalized figurative disability—the fact that he conceptualizes himself as ideally bodiless—originates from his relationship to the family matriarch, Mama Chona, from whom he inherits racist, sexist, and homophobic wounding in the form of a desire to separate himself from his "sinning" physicality and his social identities. Miguel's wish to be "a perfect astronaut," "no shit, no piss, no blood," reflects learned ideologies from Mama Chona about the dirtiness of the body—particularly the Brown, queer, feminized, or female body (8). Mama Chona's perspective is understood by her family as an unconscious internalization of racist ideology, which causes her to strive to be as white as possible via a set of affectations for which she is both humored and gently chided by the younger, post–Chicano Movement era family members who describe her as dark skinned with "Indian cheekbones" (28). It is not until the end of the novel that we learn about the more direct violences done to Mama Chona that have caused her to "den[y] the existence of all parts of the body below the neck" (164). Her first child was shot in the street during the Mexican Revolution, and she lost twin daughters to drowning. Some of the desire to separate herself from her body, as was the case for Dolores, comes from the traumatic loss of the children her body (particularly its sexual acts and female-coded organs) created. "In her mind, she conceived [her other children] immaculately . . . blotting out the act which caused her to become distended like a pig bladder full of air" (164). To an extent, then, Mama Chona is utilizing white racist and sexist discourse to distance herself from a pain related to her sexed and gendered body and to her personal histories of motherhood. This increasing denial of her body—particularly the parts of it that mark her as female, sexualized, a possible site of reproduction and therefore also vulnerable to loss—culminates in the "bath incident" (173) in which it is discovered that Mama Chona has a prolapsed uterus, which she refers to as "the monster" (175).

Mama Chona's partial internalization of and partial manipulation of racist and sexist bodily ideals to make her own body into a metaphorical monster from which she must escape are precisely what drives Miguel Chico's astronaut metaphor. It is the embodied social and cultural experience of the world that marks women's sexuality, queer sexuality, disabled sexuality, and disabled masculinity and femininity as monstrous. The astronaut metaphor is one that is not bodiless so much as without context. The perfect pure intellect is a body floating in space with no social or cultural context. Not existing in the social and physical world is what rids the body of its abject qualities—piss, shit, blood, race, sexuality, gender. The perfect astronaut is the impossible scenario of escaping the reality of the body with its pain and waste figured metaphorically as the impossible scenario of escaping the social identity categories and their oppressive effects and painful histories that give us subjectivity in the world.

This complex relation to the body in social context and the drive to escape it is addressed in the opening scene of the novel, in which Miguel Chico is prescribed medication potentially lethal for someone with a history of intestinal problems, resulting in a colostomy. Here the novel highlights the importance of attending to histories of illness and injury, both to histories of the physical body by medical professionals and metaphorically in terms of the novel's broader project of mining the Angel family's histories of injury (including deaths, affairs, murders, and psychological and physical illnesses) to make sense of Mama Chona's influence on the family and Miguel Chico's place within it. At the point Miguel Chico enters surgery, he says he felt people touching him "as if he were a person in pain" (6). His disembodied state, interestingly, allows Miguel Chico to present his literal physical condition as a metaphor—to be touched *as if* he were a person in pain. The "as if" does not connect "person in pain" to his body, the current state of which he still cannot feel. It connects the touches he sees directed toward himself to touches he has seen directed toward others. It is a metaphor that tells us how he perceives others to perceive his body, but nothing about what he actually feels. And instead of enjoying the separation from his bodily sensations as we might expect, given Mama Chona's influence, Miguel Chico "longed to escape from the drugged and disembodied state of twilight in which he had lived for weeks" (6). Here disembodiment becomes a kind of torture that turns metaphors into tautologies: He longs to escape from a state of disembodiment caused by the body from which he longs to escape. In part, the pain of literal disembodiment here disrupts its metaphorical signification. Additionally, without the body as the foundation for the metaphor of disembodiment, Miguel Chico loses primary source material for metaphorical meaning. Rather than longing to inhabit the metaphoricity of being bodiless, he wants to escape the bodilessness that he physically experiences. Miguel Chico's illness and his experience of it as both disembodiment and excessive embodiment interrupt the metaphorical disappearance of the body and present the representation of the body in the novel itself as constantly and simultaneously both literal and metaphorical, and social identity as both stemming from bodily experience and being filtered and experienced through external ideological narratives, imposed bodily significations, and cultural metaphors of bodily health and ideals.

Nonreproductive Crip Futurities

One of the most interesting things about the ways metaphor functions in both Islas's and Moraga's texts is the interpretive frameworks it offers for critiquing normative gender and the racist, heteronormative, and ableist ideologies of futurity that normative understandings of gender subtend. The disabled perspectives constructed through representations of disability as both literal and metaphorical highlight how, as Alison Kafer suggests, "one's assumptions about the experience of disability create one's conception of a better future" (2). Whereas our dominant cultural imaginary posits the able-bodied white female child as the symbol of innocence who must be protected to ensure a better future and the "disabled fetus or child" as the symbol of an "undesired future" (Kafer 2), Moraga and Islas offer narratives of disability that present the experience of living with disability and the ways that can reconfigure and expand ideas about race and gender as valuable models for building alternate and more radical conceptions of futurity.

Mama Chona, though a matriarch, does not promote a belief in a better future for her children, à la Lee Edelman's "reproductive futurity"—a phrase Edelman uses as shorthand for conservative ideological narratives that place the safety of the (white, middle-class American female) child above all else to justify racist, homophobic, nationalistic and transphobic acts and systems. Mama Chona is more closely associated with a kind of death drive—not dissimilar to Edelman's "antifuture queer," whom he figures as a possible site of resistance to the logic of reproductive futurity. In fact, she instills a kind of death-drive ethics, teaching Miguel Chico "to suffer and, if necessary, to die" (Islas 7). Edelman suggests a disability-resonant alternative to heteronormative conservative ideologies of futurity when he suggests that "rather than expanding the reach of the human," we might "insist on enlarging the *inhuman* instead—or enlarging what, in its excesses, in its unintelligibility, exposes the human itself as always misrecognized catachresis [semantic misuse]" (152). For Edelman, the burden of queerness is also its political power. It is "the agency of disfiguration that punctures the fictions of the symbolic," "the gap or wound of the real that insists . . . within the symbolic" (22). Not only does Edelman employ metaphors of disability to describe the position of the queer but, as Anna Mollow has pointed out, the position of queerness in his work "could also be understood as disability" (302), since both sex and disability in this reading "serve as signifiers for the same self-disintegrating force" (305). Here I would like to use Islas and Moraga as test cases for expanding this linguistic parallel between queerness and disability, particularly as it relates to understandings of race; gender; and white, heteronormative, ableist models of futurity, and to explore the possibilities and limitations of thinking of social identity in terms of woundedness and disability.

Mama Chona and Dolores function in Islas's and Moraga's texts, respectively, as representational limitations to a politics of wounded social identity. Focalized through Miguel Chico, Islas's narrator tells us that "after the deaths of her first three children, Mama Chona resigned herself to Christ and His holy Mother with a fervor she would never have admitted was born of rage, and she accepted suffering in this life without question or any sense of rebellion" (164). At the same time, she remains very protective of her family, trying to prevent their present suffering and to keep them connected to one another. Miguel Chico finds strength in this aspect of her character, but it is also for him associated with a political and social apathy, an acceptance of suffering in the world. Moraga's Dolores offers a similar perspective of depoliticized resignation. She is also a mother whose strength has been worn down by her own lack of power and the social expectations of motherhood and caretaking she finds it impossible to meet on her own. Via these characters, both texts critique the social institution of motherhood by demonstrating the ways it has turned both women's desire to protect into a static suffering that neither betters their understanding of structures of oppression nor allows them to connect to and recognize interdependence with other oppressed people. A history of physical and emotional wounds and social disablement, then, is certainly not inevitably a politically useful tool. Nevertheless, both texts suggest, via the disabled bodies of Cerezita and Miguel Chico, that it can be. In the representation of these characters' histories, acts, and desires, histories of woundedness help construct futures that resist both the raced and gendered expectations for womanhood, manhood, and family structure, and ideas about who is considered to have healthy and whole bodies and therefore whose bodies matter to and in that future.

Edelman's theory of reproductive futurity, while it does not treat illness as inherently negative, does not address nonheteronormative ways of experiencing parenthood or the experiences of actual bodies with actual disabilities—as opposed to the figurative "disfiguration," "gap," or "wound" of the queer. His theory continues to rely on the primary metaphors "disability is lack" and "disability is other" (Edelman 24, 22). Theoretically this may not be a problem according to Edelman—for him lack and otherness are sites of political potential—but in terms of the lived experiences of those with disabilities such metaphors continue to reinforce social and material exclusions of their bodyminds. Islas and Moraga negotiate this double-bind of social identity as metaphor, which functions along the lines of what Judith Butler has referred to as "the quandary of autonomy," which she describes in the context of trans people needing medical diagnoses to get access to hormones and surgery as "learning how to present yourself in a discourse that is not yours, a discourse that effaces you in the act of representing you" (91). I would suggest that this quandary of autonomy occurs not only in many instances of individualized diagnoses of disability but also in the negotiation of gender identity more broadly—that is, not just for people who are physically transitioning. In *The Rain God* and *Heroes and Saints,* part of the need to balance the literal and metaphorical use of disability is to negotiate having to represent disabled characters in an inherently metaphorical discourse that could potentially efface them as fully human, complex, and whole persons. Moreover, it starts to let us perceive how other discourses of social identity function in similar ways, particularly how race and gender are constantly reproduced discourses that rely on the same conservative narrative of individual and social health, and in relation to the social values placed on people's futures in relation to those ideas of health. These discourses of ableism and racialized gender normativity are dominant enough that one often needs to find a place within them in order to claim autonomy and be heard as fully human, but finding that place often involves being diagnosed by others and potentially creating other limitations to social access that can silence or shrink, if not completely efface, one's sense of autonomous selfhood in the process.

Cerezita is a character who challenges the ideologies of reproductive futurity in the sense that she is a child whose sustained innocence or protection does not represent a better future for anyone. Dolores attempts to protect her, thereby preventing change from occurring within the community that might improve their future chances of survival. If Cerezita does function in relation to a better or different future, it is via her own sacrifice, which she freely chooses in pursuit of community-based political goals. She is also a challenge to the ableist ideology that presents life with severe physical impairment as a life not worth living—that is, a life with "no future." In fact, Moraga, throughout the text, challenges dominant cultural assumptions and expectations for motherhood and femininity that arise from narratives supporting the apolitical cult of the child, assumptions and expectations that often rely on cultural metaphors that reproduce ideas about certain forms of embodiment, such as "children are innocence," "whiteness is purity," and "queerness is threat." The community organizer, Amparo, says at one point, "Our children are flesh and bone. They weigh mucho. You put them all together and they make hunerds and hunerds a pounds of Razita. . . . Yesterday the school board refuse the gift of clean water for our chil'rend's already poisoned throats. . . . Look into your children's faces. They tell you the truth. They are our future" (111). The language here might appear to be drawing on the logics of reproductive futurity in which the innocence and safety of children must be protected no matter how much violence that does to marginalized adults. But Amparo's metaphor of "children are future" here resists the abstraction of the white child's innocence as a treasure that will ensure the purity of society's future. The children are "flesh and bone," heavy, and already poisoned. To protect the children in this instance is not to remain in a conservative regime but to become radicalized. It is not to protect white children from change or from loss of innocence, but rather to use the deaths of children of color as a way to publicize the oppression of the entire community.

The dead children's bodies are crucified in the fields to make visible a set of broadly unrecognized violences. This act, which is itself performed by children who act on behalf of Cerezita when she is confined to the house, is read as scandalous and immoral by Ana Perez, the local news reporter. "Why would someone be so cruel, to hang a child up like that? To steal him from his deathbed?" Perez asks (94). Amparo answers, "They always dead first. If you put the children in the ground the world forgets about them" (94). Amparo here reveals part of the cultural work of the practice of burial—to cover over the dead, to keep death (and the injury, illness, disability, the fragility of our bodies that it signifies) confined to spaces of mourning and out of public sight. Moraga thus connects ableist ideologies, reproductive futurity, and the silencing of women via dominant ideals of motherhood. By resurrecting the dead children's bodies as a political act, the community is resisting the cult of the child, which uses the idealized imagined future of innocent children as a reason not to engage in political action as well as the logic that says a good mother/parent/protector would never use the body of their child to improve life for marginalized adults. The heteronormative, white ideology that Perez expresses in her statement reads this as cruel precisely because the pressure on parents, especially mothers, to treat children (dead and alive) as pure, innocent, nonpoliticized treasures is always working in the service of a white, heteronormative conservatism. It is the same cultural pressure to silence and make invisible the suffering of women and people of color that leads Perez to say that they will "edit [Amparo] out" (94) after she speaks these words on camera. Perez's criticism and editing out of Amparo represent official public discourses and reinforce Dolores's need to keep Cerezita in the house for fear that if she is seen and judged, it makes Dolores a bad mother who has failed to protect her innocent child.

Amparo's edited-out speech about the future of the children ends with the phrase "Pero no tendremos ningún futuro si seguimos siendo víctimas" (But we will not have any future if we remain victims) (111). Here again the text relies on a metaphorical and literal blurring in relation to the wounded body. Figuratively the community has no productive, sustainable future if they do not act to change the ways they are violated by broader economic and social systems. And if their bodies fall victim to the poisons in the field, they will die, thereby literally depriving each of them of a future. Accessing a sustainable future entails having a fighting chance to live, and it requires the metaphorical and literal sacrifice of children to make the kinds of changes that could create that possibility. This future is not about making a community of those literally and figuratively disabled healthy, able-bodied, or pure, but rather about the opportunity to live without the unnecessary pain caused by broader systemic inequalities and the understanding that those who are disabled deserve access to full humanity without redrawing limiting ableist and heteronormative boundaries around the idea of what it means to be fully human. The metaphorical use of the child here symbolically undoes dominant narratives of fear, racism, sexism, and ableism, while the literal use of the child makes oppressed bodies into sites of political power and activism. In this metaphorical and literal political futurity, the category of human is queered and disabled and finds strength in the social identities and shared oppressions of being Chicanx and female. Structurally, the final two acts of the play involve the actions of mothers offering up their children resulting in group political action. Cerezita's sister, Yolanda, offers the body of her dead child to be crucified in the fields and Dolores allows Cerezita to take the cross into the fields where she will be shot. This then prompts Cerezita's brother, Mario, who before had used his masculine woundedness as an excuse to leave his family, to lead the people in burning the fields, an act through which they collectively refuse to remain victims to the racist economic system in which they currently exist.

Resistance to the ideology of reproductive futurity and to our cultural metaphors that use healthy, able, white bodies to represent political and social well-being appears in more subtle ways in *The Rain God*. It is Mama Chona's literal ability to reproduce that she perceives as her disability, understanding her own uterus as a monster. As readers, however, we understand the social and physical power of reproduction as necessary to the survival of the entire family. We also understand that it was the internalization of a racism directed against her body and her family, represented by the eruption of political violence that killed her son and thereby disrupted the literal future of her children, which caused Mama Chona to reject her body and its sexualized/reproductive organs as monstrous. Miguel Chico too represents a kind of queer lens for reproductive futurity. He is not a sexually reproducing body, but he is highly invested in himself and his family members as part of a lineage: "He felt he was still a child of these women, an extension of them, the way a seed continues to be a part of a plant after it has assumed its own form which does not at all resemble its origin, but which, nevertheless, is determined by it" (25–26). This metaphor echoes the body as hybrid plant metaphor discussed earlier and also resignifies heteronormative reproductive futurity into a generation-based futurity that is about emotional and psychological reproduction of female influence rather than (hetero)sexual reproduction of bodies.

Additionally, the movement of the novel as a whole is cyclical rather than teleological. It begins with Miguel Chico's sickness and a description of Mama Chona's deathbed scene, in which she whispers to Miguel Chico, "*la familia*." It then moves through the stories of several of the family's "sinners." And it ends with Mama Chona again in the hospital, Miguel Chico having survived his operation but still living with the prosthesis of the colostomy bag. This cyclical narrative structure allows readers to achieve an understanding of how the family's cohesion and reproduction happen not via the creation of a metaphorically pure, white, or able-bodied familial body directed toward a teleological future, but via physical and mental illness, sexual deviance from culturally inscribed norms, self-delusion, and very messy and sometimes harmful forms of love. The idea of a future that would be perfect for a new generation of children is never presented as a possibility in the narrative, nor is the future ever fully separable from the site of a wounded past. Survival, or as Miguel's aunt Nina puts it, "endurance," is the closest thing to a future presented for the Angel family and for Miguel Chico himself.

Reading *Heroes and Saints* and *The Rain God* through an intersectional disability studies lens yields readings that revalue histories of woundedness and potentially point to ways of imagining queer futurity that not only do not rely on assimilation to homonormativity but also allow for more interdependent, disabled, nonwhite, and woman/femme-oriented positions within queer politics. This approach might also help us parse the paradoxical relation between minoritized social identity politics that push for the health and independence of women, queer and trans people, people of color, and people with disabilities and the fact of inhabiting one of these positions and being historically, socially, physically, and/or cognitively disabled and interdependent. Moraga's and Islas's texts utilize metaphorical and literal representations of disability to begin the linguistic and ideological practices of such a parsing and revaluing leading to what I address more fully in this last section as a highlighting of the racialized disgender of their characters.

The Racially Disgendered Body as Embodied Catachresis

The blurring of literally and metaphorically disabled bodies in Islas's and Moraga's works creates representations of "the human" as, following Edelman's formulation, a kind of "catachresis." These authors move disability beyond metaphor for rhetorical flourish to metaphor as that which points out the limitations of language to access what it is trying to describe. Patricia Parker suggests catachresis differs from metaphor in that it is "the practice of adapting the nearest available term to describe something for which no actual [i.e., proper] term exists" (60). Islas's and Moraga's intersectional and literal/metaphorical representations of disability help us to conceptualize how race, gender, disability, and sexuality function in such a way all the time. Though linguistically we have socially understood and to some extent culturally shared names for varying minority positions—for example, Black, woman, physically disabled, gay—none of these actually capture a lived subject position. Each social identity position also relies on metaphor to fill it out and structure its social meanings in our everyday lives and particularly in literary narratives that strive to access a closer representation of the lived reality of the complex experiences of inhabiting these identity categories. Racialized disgender, as I extrapolate below in further readings of these texts, is a term that attempts to capture how this sort of catachresis functions in relation to gender as it is inevitably structured through and intersects with race, and race as it is inevitably structured through and intersects with gender. It is a name for how race and gender are always a misrepresentation, a disability, a dissonance, a use of terms and tropes that are the nearest available to construct a complex, intersectional, context-dependent, lived reality based on complex histories of oppressions and resistances.

The metaphor to "suffer like a woman" is used by Dolores to describe Mario's wounded gender position as a gay man. The assumption behind this metaphor is that there is an able-bodied, unwounded maleness that women cannot access but men can, if and only if they perform heteronormative roles and traditionally masculine affects. The play, however, flips the idea of what it means to "suffer like a woman" via an exchange between Father Juan and Mario, after Mario returns from San Francisco HIV-positive. Mario frames queer sex as something he believed was so powerful it could cure "whatever [he] had crippled or bent up inside [him] . . . that sex could straighten twisted limbs" (Moraga, Heroes 141). Mario here uses physical disability as a metaphor for his own feelings of woundedness and assumes that this "crippling" is something inherently negative, something that can be made better only by a "cure." Interestingly, this scene directly follows the sex scene in which Father Juan refuses to help Cerezita use sex to be able to feel herself in her disabled body—to feel herself "fully of fine flesh filled to the bones in my toes" (144). In Cerezita's case she does not mean this as a metaphor. To be treated as a sexualized body creates the sensation of body, which is denied her within normative models of able-bodiedness, sexuality, and gender. Mario, while able-bodied, was also unable to feel like he fully inhabited his body without the use of queer sexuality. However, he is not cured of disability; in fact, he returns with a body marked as ill and highlighted as more queer than before he left.

The play ties the difference between Mario's use of sex and Cerezita's not to their disability status (though that difference is clear through the use of metaphorical disability to describe one body versus literal disability to describe the other), but rather to their racialized gender positions. When Father Juan asks Mario about taking care of his biological family, Mario responds: "I'm not strong enough, I'm not a woman. I'm not suited for despair. I'm not suited to carry a burden greater than the weight of my own balls" (141–142). While this comment is on one level misogynistic, on another it does speak to what it means to "suffer like a woman" in this community, which is not only to be given the responsibility for (frequently ill or disabled) family care but also to have the strength to make structural changes at home rather than leaving and to focus on interdependence, community, and shared responsibility and thereby to take pride in and use what others perceive as the social and sometimes physical disability of Chicana womanhood.[9] Here the play points to gender as disability but not as useless, even in its nonwhite and female form. Mario can't suffer like a woman because he does not have the social history of being wounded as a woman—a particular kind of racialized wounding as a Chicana that could lead to the strength of a Cerezita or an Amparo. Dolores makes an interpretive mistake about female wounding because she has internalized a victimized attachment to her own identity, believing the rhetoric of her own oppression and its attendant linguistic and metaphorical constructs. Mario and Cerezita are racially disgendered in that their intersectional identities—queer Chicano and disabled Chicana, respectively—highlight the limiting and disabling nature of gender norms. At the same time it is their disabilities, metaphorical and literal, that enable them to move beyond the confines of normative racialized gender roles and thus to become racially disgendered in an empowering way—to claim a queering of normative roles to allow more space and strength for bodies with a range of desires, physiognomies, and identities.

Mama Chona's distancing from and even denial of her body is rooted in her reactions to her raced and sexualized gender identity. The reason her dark skin is to be rejected is largely because it is associated with what she perceives as an impure working-class womanhood. In this sense Mama Chona is racially disgendered in that she experiences her body as a form of wounded nonwhite womanhood. Miguel Chico similarly experiences his body as carrying and signifying a wounded or disabled Chicano manhood. This disabled (in a cultural sense) manhood is made clear via his father, the macho Miguel Grande, in his reaction to both Miguel Chico's disabilities and his queerness. As a child, Miguel Chico was told by his father not to play with dolls because he didn't "want [his] son brought up like a girl" (Islas 15). Miguel Chico's polio, which he acquired as a child, could be argued is a result of his gendering as a Chicano male. Miguel Grande refused to let Miguel Chico's mother, Juanita, take Miguel Chico to the doctor at the first signs of illness, fearing that Juanita was "spoil[ing] him" and "tak[ing] him away" from his father. Miguel Grande's need to replicate Miguel Chico as a little version of himself through instilling a racialized machismo literally causes Miguel Chico's limp. The limp only reinforces the distance between Miguel Grande's internalization of gender norms and his son's resistance to performing them: "It pained [Miguel Grande] to see his son walk, and eventually he invented ways to make a man of the adolescent boy. One device had been to ask Miguel Chico's school friends to engage him in fistfights so that he might learn to defend himself" (96). Miguel Chico's Chicano identity is informed by the expectations for certain gender performances; his queerness is informed by having already been marginalized by this racial nonwhiteness; his disability informs a fall away from gender expectations; and gender expectations as filtered through Chicano machismo contribute to his physical disability.

According to idealized notions of racialized masculinity both Miguel Chico's physical disabilities and his gender queerness read as disabled gender. And his disabilities disgender and queer him as well. Miguel Chico himself conflates the wearing of his colostomy bag with his queer sexuality. When someone would ask why he was not married, he would say, "'Well, I had this operation,' stop there, and let them guess the rest" (5). The non-hetero/macho/able male Chicano body is racially disgendered by the limiting expectation of normative manhood. At the same time, Miguel Chico is able, through his more aware embodiment of racialized disgender, to resist the ways normative racialized gender expectations have wounded, traumatized, or limited Miguel Grande. The reason Miguel Grande pushes normative gender on Miguel Chico is in part because he feels guilty for having caused his illness and its resultant limp in the first place: "If later he made excuses to himself and others for his behavior toward his son, Miguel Grande never forgave himself" (95). Miguel Grande is also unable to experience physical affection outside of heterosexual sex: his "physical contact" with his son "had been limited to a slap in the face or a bone-crushing hug that lacked affection" (96). Ultimately, Miguel Grande finds himself lonely, unable to connect to his wife sexually and unable to be emotionally close to his lover, Lola. The inheritance of racialized disgender, while appearing to disable Miguel Chico more than his father, actually allows him the perspective to gain some awareness of the intersections of his social identities and to reflect on ways of embodying them other than the ways modeled for him, thereby not only becoming more aware of but also resisting co-optation into more harmful forms of racialized disgender.

The metaphor of body as monster is also a trope used by both Mama Chona and Miguel Chico as a way of representing the racially disgendered body. Through complex intersections between physical disability and wounded gender identity, the monster metaphor is used to both reject the characters' sexuality and to some extent inform it. For Mama Chona the monster is a metaphor for her uterus during her uterine prolapse. It is when she loses her uterus—that is, when illness or bodily disability is aligned with one of her reproductive organs—that that organ becomes fully monstrous. This is also a sexualized metaphor. The term "monster" is used as slang for penis and is something associated by Mama Chona with nudity: "By not allowing herself to be naked, [Mama Chona] had successfully denied the existence of the monster" (175). Mama Chona's fears about her racialized and gendered sexuality as monstrous echo Leo Bersani's arguments about the masochistic nature of all sexuality as "a radical disintegration" linked to "the terrifying appeal of a loss of the ego, of a self-debasement" (217, 220). But in *The Rain God* Islas makes clear that it is, in fact, the intersectionality of femaleness and racial Brownness that creates a self-debasement that would not otherwise exist in the same way—Mama Chona uses discourses of white womanhood and purity to deny the body that she feels has not protected her children and become the site of a history of racial violence and woundedness.

Similarly, Miguel Chico's disability is not only a metaphor for his queer sexuality but also part of what constitutes it. In a scene near the end of the novel, Miguel Chico dreams that the monster that killed Mama Chona comes for him, asks him "into [his] cave," and holds him from behind saying, "I am the manipulator and the manipulated." The monster puts "its velvet paw in Miguel Chico's hand and force[s] him to hold it tightly against his gut right below the appliance at his side" (159). As Ricardo L. Ortíz has pointed out, the colostomy bag metonymically stands in for the other results of a colostomy like the one Islas himself had, including a sutured anus. I would suggest that it also metonymically stands in for the nonsutured anus in that it represents his queer sexuality, which has functioned as a disability for him in that it disables his phallocentric power and is treated as an illness by this father and to some extent causes his mobility impairment. The monster appears for Miguel, as it does for Mama Chona, as a manifestation of the racially disgendered body. However, for Miguel Chico, unlike Mama Chona, this metaphor also sexualizes his literal disability, thus providing alternate ways of experiencing a raced and gendered body. The "monster," then, for Miguel Chico is, in part, as it was for Mama Chona, a signifier of a traumatized, wounded, or, as Ortíz puts it, "phantom" part of the body. It is also part of his current erotic life. Miguel's monster, again like Mama Chona's, is the site of internalized shame and self-hatred and the agency with which both M.C.s negotiate the ideological bodily restrictions and narratives in which they find themselves in the service of protecting their own mental and physical well-being. While Minich argues of this connection between M.C. and M.C. that "the novel links Miguel Chico's survival with Mama Chona's death and suggests that the demise of Mama Chona's repressive ideology is causally linked to Miguel Chico's acceptance of his embodiment" (44), I would suggest that while Mama Chona and Miguel Chico both struggle with embodiment, there is also a more empathetic reading that interprets Mama Chona's raced, gendered, disabled, and sexualized experiences as parallel contexts to Miguel Chico's and that both characters manipulate the narratives available to them in order to inhabit their racially disgendered bodies.

Each of these racially disgendered characters functions something like Garland-Thomson's description of the disabled woman of color as a "cultural third term" in the gender binary. She sites "[Audre] Lorde's 'third designation'" as "a figure whose body bears the marks we think of as 'disabilities'" and whose "extraordinary body disqualifies her from the restrictions and benefits of conventional womanhood, freeing her to create an identity that incorporates a body distinguished by the markings—some painfully inflicted, some congenital—of her individual and cultural history" (105). The following chapter turns to a reading of Lorde herself, pairing her *Cancer Journals* with Miriam Engelberg's *Cancer Made Me a Shallower Person* to explore ways that representations of disability might help us expand on this idea of racialized disgender beyond the notion of a third term, such that racialized disgender is a state that all raced and gendered individuals inhabit, though it may appear more pronounced in bodies that are not read as able, white, or cis male.

3

Racialized Disgender and Disruptive Futurity in Lorde's and Engelberg's Cancer Narratives

On being diagnosed with breast cancer, Eve Sedgwick famously responded, "Shit, now I must really be a woman" (262). While Sedgwick is certainly being humorous, playing on her queer identity and its resistance to dominant modes of gendering,[1] she is also drawing attention to how medical diagnoses actively gender bodies. It is, in fact, often in medical settings that many of our bodies are first read and subsequently assigned a legal gender identity. It is not only a gender identity that is being assigned here, however, but also, and more subtly, a racial identity. Sedgwick notes that one of the dominant cultural narratives around breast cancer is that it is *the* woman's disease and that it is often posited in contrast to AIDS as *the* gay man's disease. This use of AIDS as comparative illness posits all women as "not only the thing defined by breasts, but also that-thing-that-is-not-man, that is not the male labeled queer, that thing not vulnerable through poverty or racism, through an injection, through an insertive or hot and rubbed-raw sexuality to the bad luck of viral transmission" (263). Narratives of breast cancer here not only define women in relation to specific secondary sex characteristics; they also reinforce a strict gender binary, heteronormativity, and white middle-class understandings of whose bodies matter, whose suffering matters, and who can still imagine themselves as, while sick, still not socially and economically vulnerable. Medical and social narratives of breast cancer actively gender, race, and assign certain levels of disability/vulnerability to sick bodies.

Such practices of racing and gendering through medicalized discourses of breast cancer cures are apparent in what has come to be known as "pink-ribbon culture." The media has recently taken a critical eye to Komen for the Cure, the foundation responsible for the image of the pink ribbon to represent breast cancer awareness, for multiple reasons, including its affiliation with Baker Hughes, a hydraulic fracturing company. Not only are the chemicals used in "fracking" linked with breast cancer, but fracking is also more likely to occur in impoverished areas and areas with higher numbers of people of color.[2] While a number of critics have taken "pink-washing" to task, fewer have looked at how, precisely because the body with breast cancer is clearly and actively raced and gendered, the narratives of people with breast cancer, particularly those who take a critical view of mainstream narratives of the disease, are rich sources for understanding how bodies are intersectionally raced, gendered, and dis/abled on a broader cultural level. Diane Price Herndl notes of Sedgwick's comment that it draws attention to notions of biology as community as well as identity questions, such as "Who am I now that I am a person with breast cancer?" ("Our Breasts" 221). While in this chapter I look at questions of community and identity, I suggest that there is a more specific meaning to Sedgwick's phrasing, which is connected to the ways illnesses are experienced and narrated through our lived understanding of social identity and function to inscribe and describe our raced, gendered, classed, and sexualized bodies. In this chapter I use Audre Lorde's and Miriam Engelberg's representations of gendered and raced experiences of breast cancer to further explore the concept I call "racialized disgender"—that is, how race and gender are constructed via symbolic, social, and material disabilities and how the ability status of the body intersects with and co-constructs racial and gender identities.[3]

Narratives of breast cancer can be productive sites to explore the concept of racialized disgender not only because they focus on a disease that is considered a woman's illness but also because highly gendered narratives of and around breast cancer have entered mainstream cultural discourses to the extent that breast cancer has its own month and pink ribbons have become a legible form of marketing, fund-raising, and self-identifying across class, gender, race, region, and ability status. Mary K. DeShazer and Anita Helle suggest that postmillennial cancer narratives "differ from their twentieth-century counterparts" in that they address "environmental carcinogens," "question the medical establishment," and "challenge mainstream cancer culture" (8). At the same time, many breast cancer autopathographies replicate normative ideologies of (white) womanhood, gender conformity, and ableism in relation to a medicalized and heteronormative understanding of the normate body.

In the analyses that follow, I examine two cancer narratives that resist dominant narratives of womanhood and illness not only via the critiques mentioned by DeShazer and Helle but also by highlighting relations between mainstream ways of representing breast cancer and broader modes of racialized disgender. Engelberg and Lorde both write narratives of what Lisa Diedrich calls "politicized patienthood" (41), in that they recognize, criticize, and resist normative reactions to breast cancer and breast cancer patients. Lorde is consciously politicized by her involvement in feminist politics and the feminist health movements of the 1970s and in *The Cancer Journals* (1980) explores how breast cancer fits into larger systems of social oppressions through a collection of nonfiction essays and journal entries. Miriam Engelberg's comic memoir, *Cancer Made Me a Shallower Person* (2006), is a humorous and understated critique of the ways breast cancer intersects race, gender, and what we consider normative perceptions and behaviors from the perspective of a white, straight, relatively economically privileged Jewish woman.

Both texts reveal not only the ways that breast cancer narratives are gendered but also the ways that experiences of gendered illness are haunted by racial trauma. Both authors' narratives speak to how illness can highlight our social racialization and disgendering as well as the cultural and intergenerational ways we receive our racially disgendered selves, which are affected by histories of political disabling, impairment, and death. Formational histories of violence and the negative affects often experienced by those who are ill, impaired, or socially marginalized are also systematically revalued by both authors, particularly in contrast to dominant medical and rehabilitative discourses and their potential to stifle access to knowledge about the ideological structuring of race, gender, and disability.

Dominant medical and rehabilitative industries work within a broader consumer capitalist system as ideological state apparatuses, enforcing an institutionalized surveillance that predominantly disciplines itself along normative gendered lines. Lennard Davis terms the work of these industries "care of" and "care for"—as opposed to "caring about"—the body (27–29). A politics of caring about the body involves attention to the rights, treatment, and oppression of disabled, nonnormative, and ill bodies, and thus would require greater attentiveness to the racially disgendering ways our bodies' histories and social narratives disable us as well as the ways these narratives contextualize and affect the experience of disability and illness. Lorde's and Engelberg's autobiographical personas' bodies are represented as racially disgendered not because they are cancerous, amputated, or undergoing chemotherapy but, rather, because the ways their bodies are marked by breast cancer reveal how various social forms of racialized womanhood are not constructed to care about women. The remainder of this chapter explores the ways that breast cancer is a gendered and gendering disease and suggests that a close reading of its social functioning and the rhetorics that have been used to make it less threatening to dominant understandings of both race and gender can also reveal more clearly ways that racialized gender functions as a form of disability more broadly.

Audre Lorde: Diagnosing Patterns and Responses

Lorde opens *The Cancer Journals* by stating that "every woman responds to the crisis that breast cancer brings to her life out of a whole pattern, which is the design of who she is and how her life has been lived" (7). This means not only that each person brings to illness their own experiences but also that the ways women have learned to be women, the patterns and designs of their gender identities, are intimately related to the ways women experience breast cancer. Female-coded illness in general is experienced through the same affective and responsive lenses that gender bodies marked as female more broadly. Particularly in the case of breast cancer, expectations associated with recovery and rehabilitation reflect expectations for ideal womanhood in dominant cultural constructions such as self-sacrifice (sometimes in the form of painful and disruptive treatments to save one's breasts, sometimes in the physical removal of one's breasts), making oneself an unobtrusive presence to others (the prosthetic and social/emotional covering of that loss), and making space for and attending to others' needs before one's own (to appear as a physiologically "normal" woman becomes more important than dealing with one's own emotional and physical needs). While this does not mean that women who chose to have mastectomies or reconstructive surgery are making those decisions in order to sacrifice their needs or to appear normal (in fact, it may be a way of reclaiming access to a body that feels inhabitable or a way to have some agency in a scenario that is threatening to one's very existence), both medical and cultural discourses often construct such decisions in this way. As Diedrich puts it, via a reading of Carole Colbourn, breast cancer is associated with the loss of body parts that matter in a patriarchal culture because they are "objects to be desired by heterosexual men and as symbols of motherhood" (65).

These are not the only dominant discourses of female worth that Lorde is negotiating. Dominant expectations for Black womanhood involve self-reliance, hyper- or de-sexualization, and social caretaking beyond the immediate family. These expectations, which might otherwise register strength, power, visibility, and influence, have historically been used instead to reinforce Black women's social invisibility and lack of power.[4] The figure of the Black woman has, in fact, historically functioned as a kind of "supercrip," whether physically disabled or not—constructed through what Therí Pickens refers to as "the discourse of the superhuman survival" (*New Body* 142). From historical mythologies about Black women's bodies being able to handle what white women's could not, thereby marking them as other than true women, to more contemporary stereotypes about strong Black womanhood,[5] the body of the Black woman has often been figured as both disabled in relation to true womanhood and simultaneously superhuman in its ability to overcome hardship.

Lorde identifies a significant portion of the "patterns and designs" of her own experience of Black female identity as having been learned through the internalization of fear and vulnerability—affects associated both with dominant figurations of the sick female body and with Lorde's marginalized queer, Black womanhood. Here her experience as a queer, Black woman echoes and reinforces the way she is read and treated as a sick body. In response to her diagnosis of breast cancer, Lorde fears most "that [she] was not really in control" of her body and "that it might already be too late to halt the spread of cancer," thus highlighting how illness contributes to feelings of fear and vulnerability (33). Yet she also tells us that "as women we were raised to fear" (13). And she is constantly aware of the ways her body is constructed as a particularly vulnerable object in her society by being marked Black, female, and queer. Thus, the experience of cancer augments the affective experiences of fear and vulnerability, but it also draws attention to the ways these emotions are socially constructed and projected onto certain bodies to be processed and experienced by the culture more broadly. Lorde suggests that if she can become aware of how as a Black woman she is taught to fear, she might then become more able to be attentive to and aware of the ways that as medically diagnosed bodies, sick women are also taught to fear. And in that recognition she might potentially find a place to be less fearful, despite the real bodily vulnerabilities that exist for women of color and people with chronic or terminal illness.

When Lorde is taken into surgery, she describes her body as a vulnerable object in a white-dominated medical complex. "The clanging of disembodied noises . . . ha[s] no context nor relationship to me. . . . I have ceased being a person who is myself and become a thing upon a Gurney cart to be delivered up to Moloch, a dark living sacrifice in a white place" (35). This scene highlights the ways her body becomes vulnerable in terms of the power dynamics involved in marking bodies as ill, Black, and female. She will lose her Black breast (for her and her society, a physical marker of her race and gender) to the white place, as a sacrifice to its success (in curing her) and its continued functioning (bringing in more patients to do the same to). Lorde asks us to attend to all of what must be sacrificed of oneself as a Black woman in order for her to gain access to medical care. Not only is she losing her breast, but the white place itself co-opts even the space of injury—it is the place that produces "disemboweled noises"—while her body, which should be the subject at the center of care, becomes a passive "thing" offered up to the injured white space. She is disallowed claim to her own illness, as it is instead claimed by the medical institution, her self becoming a sort of prosthetic used in the process of keeping the body of the white place intact. And yet the figurative body of that white place registers its presence via disemboweled noises, implying a violence or sickness even inherent in the structure and practices of the sites of medical power that would ideally be working toward healing or wholeness. Her function as a prosthetic, like the false breast she will be asked to wear after her surgery, is nonfunctional in the sense of actually bringing any sense of healing.

She is also metaphorically positioned as a child, in that the sacrifices offered to Moloch were often children. Barbara Ehrenreich has argued that infantilization is a part of breast cancer rhetorics more broadly, and specifically in breast cancer awareness products such as teddy bears and the relentless "it's-a-girl" pink theming. "You are encouraged to regress to a little-girl state, to suspend critical judgment, and to accept whatever measures the doctors, as parent surrogates, choose to impose" (52). This regression is specifically encouraged for patients with "women's illnesses," such as breast cancer. Ehrenreich implicitly notes the function of racialized disgendering here when she suggests that perhaps, "in some versions of the prevailing gender ideology, femininity [i.e., idealized white femininity] is by its nature incompatible with full adulthood" (46). The way the medical industry produces vulnerability, then, is a form of created dependency that is both new for recently diagnosed patients and an extension of the kind of social diagnoses that many women have been living with their entire lives.[6] This includes the stereotype and expectation of social dependency for Black and poor women as well as patriarchal male dependency for middle-class and wealthy white women.

It is in this heightened and gendered state of vulnerability, Lorde suggests, that "many patterns and networks are started for women after breast surgery that encourage us to deny the reality of our bodies which have just been driven home to us so graphically" (41). It is Lorde's illness that reconnects her to a sense of the reality of her body—a reality that normative gendering itself has had the effect of undoing and that is undone again after breast surgery. While all gendering involves social pressures and expectations that can disconnect people from a sense of the needs and reality of their bodies, women—who have historically been represented as objects of the male gaze; caretakers for men and children; and ideally small, silent, and confined—are often particularly distanced from an embodied exploration of themselves that would attend to and privilege a physical and psychological connection to themselves. One value of the experience of illness, as Lorde represents it, is an awakening to bodily awareness that distances one from one's own gendered positioning—that is, it legibly disgenders one enough to become aware of the gendered teachings that have separated one from a sense of bodily autonomy, agency, and general comfortable embodiment.

In *The Cancer Journals,* as Lorde becomes more aware of this pattern of disgendering, the medical and rehabilitative industries augment their ideological pressures to reinforce normative gender (i.e., compliant, white-centric, and heteronormative) performativity from her. For Lorde, they find their ultimate objective correlative in the prosthetic breast, which, Lorde believes, "encourages [women] not to deal with [themselves] as physically and emotionally real, even though altered and traumatized" (58). In my reading of Lorde's protest of the prosthetic breast, the false breast functions as both a tie to and a repression of a wounded past. The prosthetic breast ties the female patient not to the actual physical wounds of cancer or surgery, nor to the awareness of being socially and politically oppressed, but rather to the ideological wound that reproduces womanhood as a state of vulnerability and fear, and Black womanhood as never fully meeting the standards for successfully embodying that feminine vulnerability. The prosthesis, Lorde says, "encourages women to dwell in the past rather than a future . . . and to focus [their] energies upon the mastectomy as a cosmetic occurrence, to the exclusion of other factors in a constellation that could include her own death" (58). The prosthesis functions as a reinterpellating of women, including the historical ungendering of Black women through a white supremacist ideal (represented by the "grotesquely pale" lamb's wool Lorde is given to pad her bra), to repress traumatic histories rather than attempt to engage and process them. It encourages women to dwell in a surface history of their oppression, shame, and lack of power, rather than to engage the deep history of physical violence and trauma that constituted this oppressed position and to incorporate that into their current understanding of themselves. For Lorde, the prosthesis represents a sick (disemboweled) medical environment that prefers quick fixes that reinforce the hegemonic control of institutionalized medicine and encourage individual protective (rather than group political) responses to fear and vulnerability. Lorde's point is not about the individual women who choose to wear prosthetics or get reconstructive surgery, but about how these are assumed to be the only viable options. The individualized medical approach limits access to others' experiences as well as time to consider options, and privileges professional knowledge. This reading of the prosthetic breast as a reattachment to the disabling ideologies of womanhood at the expense of processing actual wounds gives us another lens for thinking the risks and value of attaching to and identifying with disabled and wounded histories. The risk, as discussed in relation to the characters Dolores and Mama Chona in Chapter 2, is the possibility that it will keep one trapped in a victimized relationship to an identity formed via oppression and a concomitant inability to disengage oneself from that oppressed position. However, if we think of the history of oppression as having both valuable and disabling effects in the current moment, we can start to perceive how hegemonic discourses encourage an attachment to the more limiting forms of that historical knowledge, while other types of understandings of historical wounds can actually help one become more aware of, and therefore potentially resist, the disabling aspects of those discourses. The victimized attachment in Lorde's narrative is the attachment to hiding or covering the pain caused by inhabiting the position of womanhood. "The terror and silent loneliness of women attempting to replace the ghost of a breast," says Lorde, "leads to yet another victimization" (68). Covering the wound that marks the lost breast is a form of covering access to the knowledges that the histories of wounds and the visible markers of what one has lost can provide. The values of looking at wounds include the creation of group experience and knowledge and the prioritization of "psychic time and space to examine what our true feelings are, to make them our own," thereby incorporating the knowledge of loss and traumatic experience rather than avoiding it (58).

The repression of pain and trauma that the prosthetic breast represents not only encourages a return to fear and vulnerability; it also reinforces expectations inherent in the ideology of the "strong Black woman." Tamara Beauboeuf-Lafontant describes the ideology of the strong Black woman as an internalized stereotype that prevents Black women from complaining about systemic oppression and often takes the physical form of ill health. "The discourse of strength," argues Beauboeuf-Lafontant, "renders the material and relational aspects of oppression into realities Black women should endure rather than injustices worthy of their outrage and challenge" (108). Black women, in order to maintain an image of strength, might take on others' obligations, and not sleep enough, not eat well, nor get enough exercise. They might also, Beauboeuf-Lafontant argues, deal with the anger and exhaustion they cannot overtly express (because of the expectations of strong Black womanhood) by "engaging in compensatory behaviors such as excess in eating, drinking or shopping" (108). These forms of self-medication can allow Black women to "register and attend to some of their needs without disrupting the fiction of strength"—eating, drinking, or shopping become a way of both keeping oneself silent and providing some quiet time to oneself to feed one's own needs (114).

In *The Cancer Journals,* dominant discourses of strong womanhood, strong Black womanhood, and medical rehabilitation reinforce one another, producing a situation in which, to meet the expectations of being good patients and strong women, the time and energy of sick women become focused on care *of* and *for* their bodies (which is often ultimately other-directed), rather than prioritizing time to care *about* them and the histories inscribed onto and within them (which would be more self-directed). They collude to encourage an attachment to historical racialized disgendering that undoes the self rather than allowing for a recognition of and reckoning with one's racialized disgender that might offer fuller integration. As Jennifer C. James points out, our cultural obsession with a "perfected female form" and the rehabilitation of disabled bodies both allow "us to suppress the effects of the violent and violating objectification of women" and the extreme fragmentation of Black women in particular (154). The ideological power of normative "female" forms is at work when the woman from Reach for Recovery brings Lorde lamb's wool and a bra (part of her aesthetic rehabilitation) and also gives her physical exercises to do (part of her physiological rehabilitation), presenting them as equally important tools in regaining her strength and getting past the painful experience of surgery (Lorde, *Cancer Journals* 43). Even the group's name, "Reach for Recovery," implies that it is through being active and physically and emotionally "strong"—that is, positive and compliant—that one heals, not by processing or acknowledging the experience of one's pain.

Lorde's use of the phrase the "fantasy of reconstruction" to refer to immediate surgery to "replace" one's lost breast(s) alludes historically to the national failure of post–Civil War Reconstruction—a time period in which, as Jim Downs has argued, African Americans were exposed to more illnesses and physically threatening circumstances than ever before in the nation's history and during which a newly defined population of "dependents" was created against the category of Black workers (Downs 14). The Freedman's Bureau utilized the category of "able-bodied" to recruit men for agricultural labor and to reject from the labor population "single freedwomen, elderly, disabled, and orphaned former slaves" (Downs 127). This historical allusion grounds Lorde's argument about her contemporary experience as a Black body under the care of a white-dominated medical industry in a history of medical models designed to reconstruct and rehabilitate that have actively and aggressively prevented cohesive community for women, African Americans, and people with disabilities; undermined social changes and access to the resources that might benefit and allow healthy lives for those groups, in favor of hegemonic ideas about communal or national health; and devalued the worth and autonomy of those bodies marked female, dependent, and non-able-bodied.

Contemporary ideologies of medical reconstruction and rehabilitation that do similar work by putting those who might gain access to such knowledge under surveillance with the aim of preventing their attempts at shared knowledge creation are reflected in the practices of the hospital and associated medical sites. Lorde demonstrates how a woman who does not wear a prosthetic breast is perceived as a threat to the "morale" of a breast surgeon's office and asked to hide the very wound she is there to treat (61). Here the amputated, disabled body is the cultural construction of the female body itself in that the normate female body is expected to reveal itself by visibly registering certain fetishized body parts such as breasts and buttocks even as they are ostensibly hidden. The line between a tight shirt or push-up bra and the prosthetic breast Lorde is pressured to wear is a difference of degree rather than kind. Gendered and able-bodied norms work together to hide women's bodies both before and after they are diagnosed as ill via idealized images of the female body. This hiding actually, then, reinforces a normatively disabled female-coded body (one that already needs certain prostheses to register as properly female) and simultaneously hides that disabled status. The prosthetic breast functions in the same way, here doing potentially even more harm by hiding one's history of immediate suffering and experiences with both illness and the infantilizing structures of the medical industry from others in one's position, limiting possibilities for a more powerful feminist disability community and thereby more powerful feminist disability activism.

Elizabeth Alexander argues that Lorde points out the frequent incompatibility of the descriptors "woman" and "powerful" in our society via representations of her mother (706). Alexander quotes Lorde's description of her mother in her biomythography, *Zami:* "This was in a time when that word-combination of *woman* and *powerful* was almost unexpressable in the white american common tongue, except or unless it was accompanied by some aberrant explaining adjective like blind, or hunchback, or crazy, or Black" (Lorde 15). Alexander further argues that from her powerful mother, Lorde learns to change the linguistic forms she inherits to fit her own needs, to "make a physical space for herself in a hybrid and composite language wherein what she knows is frequently at odds with what the world tells her to see" (Alexander 696). Certainly, Lorde does use language in this way. However, I would suggest that Lorde is also pointing out here, in relation to her mother, that "woman" as a category is already both racialized and disabled to the extent that one cannot be a woman and be powerful/strong/able unless they are already disabled either physically (blind, hunchback), mentally (crazy), or racially (Black). Each of these qualifiers, which redoubles the racialized disgendering of the female body, also allows that racialized disgendering process to become more perceptible. It can also trump its dominant limitations (in this case that you cannot be powerful and a woman) and thereby allow a space for alternate womanhoods to be conceptualized, albeit ones that are disabled and modified via other minority identifications.

A closer look at Lorde's response to being given the pink prosthetic can help us understand how racialized disgender registers for Lorde and her readers and how that allows alternative perspectives on the Black, female, wounded self. The woman from Reach for Recovery is posited as the voice of a harmful, racially disgendering culture that expects Lorde to cover her experience and reproduce white heterosexual femininity by basically putting a fake white breast on her body. The disjuncture between the "blush-pink nylon" form that she is supposed to stuff into her bra and her sense of her Brown, lesbian, breast-loving self allows Lorde and the reader to understand the limiting and restricting narratives of idealized, white-centric womanhood that have already been at work on bodies marked as female, long before their cancer diagnoses. For Lorde, nothing could be further from the "area of feeling and pleasure" that her right breast represented than "the thing" that "perched on [her] chest askew, awkwardly inert and lifeless, and having nothing to do with any me I could possibly conceive of" (43, 44). The overlay of racialized gender norms onto her amputated body reveals that the norms themselves are more wounding, lifeless, and inassimilable aspects of this experience than the loss of her breast. Looking down at herself without the prosthetic afterward, she says, "I looked strange and uneven and peculiar to myself, but somehow, ever so much more myself . . . than I had looked with that thing stuck inside my clothes" (44). Lorde's racialized disgendering, acquired through her illness and amputation, allows her, following Hortense Spillers's suggestion discussed in this book's Introduction, to claim the monstrosity of racially disgendered Black womanhood. It is in claiming this gender that is not gender in our dominant cultural narratives—one breasted, queer, Black womanhood—that Lorde is able to come back to a love for herself.

We are also given some insight into the ways that white-centered, idealized, cis femininity is disabling for those who are not able to come to an awareness of a relationship to their racialized disgendering. The woman from Reach for Recovery becomes a salesperson for her own oppression. She is full of "admirable energies," but they are all directed toward her own objectification. She suggests that if one looks the same on the outside and can pass as a two-breasted woman for men, then one can be "just like anybody else" (42, 43). Lorde is able to perceive what has been lost in this drive to be like anybody else, a "normal" woman, able to please men: "Her grip was firm and friendly and her hair smelled a little like sun. I thought, what a shame such a gutsy woman wasn't a dyke, but they had gotten to her too early, and her grey hair was dyed blond and heavily teased" (43). It is, in fact, the straight, white woman who has been most disabled, most covered and shaded from herself, through her racialized disgendering.

I would argue that, in *The Cancer Journals,* Lorde is less, as Alexander suggests, making a physical space for herself via language than she is inhabiting an already racially disgendered space while actively and attentively describing it as such. She not only "chooses to wear breast cancer," in Herndl's terms, by not wearing the pink prosthetic, but also wears her Black, queer, sick, and disgendered female identity legibly when the world is asking her to hide it because of its threat to the normative racialized structures of gender ("Reconstructing" 147). These structures otherwise work to recreate white womanhood as self-objectification and Black womanhood as a shameful monstrosity to be covered by trying to be more like racially disgendered white women.

Miriam Engelberg: Inherited Patterns, Racially Disgendered Responses

Miriam Engelberg similarly critiques the discourses and expectations of the health-care industry and engages a history of inherited trauma and identity formation, experienced through her cancer as a form of racially gendered embodiment. Engelberg begins her comic memoir, *Cancer Made Me a Shallower Person,* with a set of four panels entitled "Personal," in which she, like Lorde, plays with the idea of choosing to wear her cancer. She jokes that breast cancer, unlike more "internal forms of cancer," brings with it the social awkwardness of people trying not to look at the person with cancer's chest or think about their breasts. To resolve this awkwardness, she suggests creating a line of T-shirts that say "cancer inside" and point to one breast.

What is represented as "personal" in this strip is information that is not just private or revealed to only certain people but also personal in that it refers to Miriam's person and the way that person is already vulnerable and sexualized because of her female identity and the politics of visuality surrounding bodies marked as female. When Engelberg jokes that more "internal" forms of cancer wouldn't provoke the same response as breast cancer, she associates women's illness with a surface performativity of bodily health and gender normativity. The reason that a breast is considered less internal than a liver or a lung is because of the way the secondary sex characteristics of bodies read as female are understood to belong to the person (part of the breasted person's insides) but are also available for consumption, particularly by bodies marked as male (and thus as something the breasted person

"Personal," from Miriam Engelberg's *Cancer Made Me a Shallower Person*.
("Personal" [four panels] from CANCER MADE ME A SHALLOWER PERSON: A MEMOIR IN
COMICS by MIRIAM ENGELBERG. Copyright © 2006 by Miriam Engelberg.
Reprinted by permission of HarperCollins Publishers.)

wears, projects, or gives to others). Breast cancer focuses attention on these
internal/external sexualized body parts and specifically on the primary sexualized body parts that our culture asks people marked as female to partially cover but also to make present and visible. In fact, breasts must inhabit this contradictory space of hiding and revealing at all times. To be read
as healthy and normatively bodied, our culture constructs the category of
woman as legible specifically by asking those who identify as women to have

breasts and to reveal that they have breasts via clothing choices and bodily presentation, even as they are also expected to cover them. It is acceptable to notice breasts, but not to touch them or refer explicitly to them in public spaces. Women's breasts represent the dichotomy of forbidden/private and accessible/public that figures many of women's daily experiences in terms of how their bodies are read and treated by others.[7]

Engelberg captures the ways such contradictory expectations of what should be private and public in relation to bodies read as female are reproduced in relation to illnesses marked as "women's" such as breast cancer, which is often considered something that is expected to be hidden but also licenses people to cross personal boundaries, drawing attention to that which is usually treated as the unseen seen. In the final panel of this first strip, in which Engelberg draws herself with a shirt that says "Cancer Inside" accompanied by an arrow pointing to her right breast, she draws explicit attention to the surface/depth and hiding/revealing paradoxes that women must negotiate in their self-presentation. Thus, it performs disgender by representing Miriam as dissociated or decentered from her gender identity not because she has cancer, but because of the ways public presentations of cancer create frictions with our normative modes of reinforcing gender embodiment norms, thereby revealing socially disabling aspects of womanhood (i.e., "personal" belongings are also available for public consumption). It also suggests, like Lorde's memoir, that women's breast cancer is treated as an aesthetic, superficial, or topical problem, rather than a matter of overall mental and physical health, or a matter of life and death. Finally, the shirt is ironic because it does what a great deal of women's fashion does already—that is, draw attention to breasts via covering them. In fact, the shirt might as well say "Breasts Inside." But the disjuncture between "breasts" and "cancer" also does the critical disgendering work of drawing attention to the illness itself, thereby disrupting habitual ways of looking at women's bodies and the normate expectations for them by making disability and its intersections with gendered expectations more legible.

The drive to reproduce normatively gendered racial whiteness is also at work in such expectations for hiding/revealing the female body. White women have historically had access to the, albeit constricting, double expectation of hiding/revealing, whereas the bodies of women of color, particularly but not exclusively African American women's bodies, have often been either commodified, hypersexualized, made unsafe, or stripped of legible femaleness as circulated in dominant culture. This comic can also be read as racially alluding to Engelberg's Jewishness and her family's history as Holocaust survivors, though the reader would need to have read the rest of the comics to make that connection. The words "Cancer Inside" with the arrow, though marked on the right side of her chest, evoke the Stars of David and other triangle-based camp badges that Jewish and other people marked by the Nazi regime were forced to wear on their left breasts. The arrow includes an upside-down triangle, also used in Nazi camps to denote, among other things, asocial or gender deviant (later reclaimed by lesbian feminists), mentally ill, and sexually deviant (later reclaimed by the gay rights movement). Thus, the image reveals both the privilege of access to racial whiteness and the ways this access is complicated and in certain ways denied by Engelberg's inheritance of racial, gender, and disability trauma through her Jewish heritage.

Engelberg suggests in several comics that she was already living with a certain amount of depression and anxiety before being diagnosed with cancer, which she implicitly connects to her Jewish identity and inheritance of the trauma of genocide. Gabriele Schwab argues that "the damages of violent histories can hibernate in the unconscious, only to be transmitted to the next generation like an undetected disease" (3). Schwab's language is telling here, as she associates unprocessed transgenerational trauma with an illness not yet diagnosed. In both Engelberg's and Lorde's texts, cancer diagnosis and treatment call to the fore a processing of other inherited traumas. Engelberg's representation of Jewish identity in part as an inheritance of somatic trauma echoes Lorde's reading of the medicalized experiences of the Black female body under white-dominated social and economic systems as an inheritance of vulnerability. For Lorde, this vulnerability is a positional trauma related to a loss of subjectivity—becoming an object on a table. For Engelberg, it relates to inherited fears and anxieties in everyday life that trigger fears of death or illness. For example, Miriam tells us that her parents are "the two most health-conscious people in the entire western world," constantly mailing her articles about illnesses linked to poor diet, lack of exercise, stress, and so on. Thus, both authors connect inherited racial trauma to a sense of loss of control over the body. This giving over of control is in part an actual loss—being under anesthesia or not being able to physically do things because of pain or fatigue. It is also a loss of the perception of control—historically as subjects whose health or illness is determined by larger social forces, and in the contemporary moment by becoming aware of the ways their gendered bodies are read by and expected to perform in certain ways for others.

Engelberg's comics make us aware of the way the normate gaze genders women and reads female-identified bodies as healthy or ill by the approximation to normative aesthetics in their gender performativity. Miriam, after her first round of chemo, is watching a detective show about a doctor who helps sick patients kill themselves. She imagines the detective coming into her house and seeing her lying there bald, watching bad TV and assuming she would be better off dead. "No wait a minute," she imagines saying. "For all you know I'm just a bald woman watching TV!" Part of the joke here is that there is no broad cultural signification of bald women watching TV except illness—particularly for a white, middle-class, professional woman. Her bald head already racially disgenders her body, the illness and assumption that her life is worthless is both an assumption about the worthlessness of the futures of people with disabilities and about a racialized, gender-non-conforming aesthetic having no other cultural meaning than disability, which then also equates to a future without value. The joke that she could just be a bald woman watching TV is also juxtaposed against earlier references to her parents fleeing Nazi Germany, in which context the idea of a bald woman that a person in authority wants to help kill takes on another set of meanings involving racially, sexually, gender-, and disability-coded eugenic ideas about whose lives are worth continuing and reproducing. The history of racialized disgendering that Miriam has inherited appears throughout her comics in these uncanny moments of dark humor.

Laura S. Brown argues for a feminist analysis of trauma, which "rather than desensitizing survivors to symptom triggers," would help people to "reconstruct their world views" such that they can integrate "their painful new knowledge" (109–110). Engelberg uses humor and suggestion to move toward such a feminist reintegration in the face of additional trauma, though Miriam as a character remains highly ambivalent about her relation to both her gender identity and its history of woundedness as well as that of her Jewish identity as a history of violence. Engelberg's larger project is attentive to the numerous social identity–based traumas and disabilities that inform Miriam's experience, and what those experiences allow her to critique in the present as well as what they open up or foreclose in terms of conceptions of the future. Cathy Caruth argues that trauma is not only history oriented but also future oriented, in that what remains unassimilable in the past directly affects the ways we imagine possible futures (xiv). Engelberg's comic series as a whole links aspects of ethnic, gender, and disability identity that have been unconscious or unassimilable to the possibility for other kinds of futures—futures that are less certain but in which Miriam can become more aware of (and possibly more able to integrate) many of the disabling narratives of her broader culture, including the repression of the knowledge of women's oppression and the devastating effects on Jewish people of the history of anti-Semitism, including the Holocaust.

Miriam's ambivalent relation to and at times seemingly unconscious articulation of historical and contemporary trauma are ways of negotiating a recognition of historical woundedness without inhabiting a victimized identity or equating disability or impairment with an irredeemably negative state of being. One "danger of emphasizing memory and mourning lies in using trauma as the foundation of identity," Schwab writes. "Such attachment to injury is problematic, especially in a 'wound culture' oversaturated with stories and studies of trauma. An excessive emphasis on mourning may indeed contribute to an identitarian definition of cultural belonging by tying identity to victimization" (19). This logic of an oversaturation of trauma, however, can reinforce dominant narratives that suggest that women's everyday experiences of fear and oppression are not traumatic because they are a normalized part of our culture. We may not be oversaturated with stories of trauma, but with trauma itself. As Laura Brown points out, many of the traumatic experiences of women in our society are not uncommon; in fact, the threat of trauma is a daily, or what is now commonly referred to as insidious, trauma. Insidious trauma "shapes a worldview rather than shatters assumptions about the world," but nevertheless may result in "symptomology similar to that of direct or indirect trauma" (Root 240). Using Brown's lens of normative cultural traumas and Engelberg's references to a more commonly acknowledged social and cultural trauma—the Holocaust—we can begin to read Engelberg's presentation of gender itself as disabling in terms of not only access to income, authority, and freedoms but also mental health. Racialized disgendering is itself an ongoing set of culturally acceptable microaggressions as well as a "lifetime risk of exposure to certain trauma" (Brown 108). Miriam's desire not to present an "excessive emphasis" on mourning or victimization leads to ambivalence over her minority social positions and self-critiquing of her thoughts and feelings around her illness. It is only in relation to her inhabiting of a potentially physically and emotionally traumatizing position— that of the body diagnosed with what is likely a terminal illness—that the text becomes more able to articulate the traumatic aspects underlying gender itself, thereby making the reader more aware of gender as racialized disgender.

Looking on the Dark Side of Things: Racialized Disgender and Disabled Futures

Lorde and Engelberg both represent racialized disgender as a rethinking of the ideological role of the logic of futurity for bodies identified as wounded or vulnerable. The body that registers publically as racially disgendered, and thus potentially makes the broadly shared state of racialized disgender more perceptible to others, resists normative, future-oriented medical narratives in that racialized disgender exists in relation to the body as both a disruptive condition and simultaneously a condition that is not available for elimination, rehabilitation, or cure. As long as race and gender are constructed via idealized bodily norms and the reproduction of heteronormativity, racism, patriarchy, and other systems of power and privilege, there will be racialized disgender. Those structures can change, but the individual body itself can be neither the agent nor the site of that change. In the case of diagnoses of breast cancer, the medical prognosis often "operates to actively position the subject in relation to the precarious roulette of futurity" as a body "having diverged from normal operation" that needs to be put back on a proper future-oriented track (Ehlers 123). The path to futurity becomes one of individual recovery rather than a recognition of not only the systemic causes of cancer but also the continued disabling of bodies marked female and sick within current future-oriented, ableist, developmental, curative, progressive models of both gender equity and medical recovery.

As several critics of dominant rhetorics of breast cancer have noted, discourses surrounding breast cancer awareness campaigns function to individualize and naturalize breast cancer as well as to create a safe space for corporations to present themselves as "doing something for women, without being feminist" (Cindy Pearson, quoted in Ehrenreich 48). Multiple and intersecting gendered discourses surrounding breast cancer, its treatment, and its use in corporate culture work to individualize the experience of the disease and to obscure the racial, economic, and gender inequities that make certain bodies more vulnerable to the environmental pollutants that cause the cancer in the first place. This cure-oriented and palatable "pinkwashing" also leaves no room for those whose cancer has metastasized and who no longer fit the medical model of progression toward a normative or "healthy" future. Emily Waples notes of Engelberg's memoir, "Its end point of metastasis, rather than a return to health and 'normalcy,' highlights the disease's complicated, and terrifying, relationship to temporality" (158–159). Contra the individualizing white-dominated discourses of corporate breast cancer and positive narratives of recovery, both Lorde's and Engelberg's texts suggest that broader social structures of systemic inequality and narrative structures of normalizing futurity must change, not the individual ill body.

Normative racialized sex-gender systems often function conservatively as a site for the ideological reproduction of power. This has been true throughout U.S. history, certainly, in the case of ideals of true womanhood, white legal rights to the offspring of Black slaves, the American eugenics movement, the legal sterilization of women of color and people with disabilities, and anti-miscegenation laws as well as the restriction of legal access to marriage and parental rights (not to mention bathrooms) for African American, gay, lesbian, queer, and transgender people. Such discourses about who has access to legally legitimate and institutionally supported gender and sexual identities are often framed in relation to an idealized but never realized future. Lee Edelman argues that our current understanding of the political holds out a heteronormative fantasy of the future that figures the white, female, middle-class child as a symbol of our cultural vulnerability and possibility, in need of protection to ensure the stability of our future. This version of the political future reinforces conservative and antiqueer modalities of being as the only ways of being that enable positive and valuable futures.

Racialized disgender as a way of reading social identity can help us re-think the connection between marginalized social positions and logics of futurity such as Edelman's description of conservative heteronormative re-productive futurity. In Lorde's and Engelberg's narratives, attentiveness to racialized disgender helps the reader to reimagine a connection between wounded pasts and futures that might be disabled but are nonetheless worth living and therefore worth investing political energy in. This perspective is figured by both Lorde and Engelberg as one that situates us in relation to the future without it inherently presenting us with a promise, and thus can disrupt the logic of reproductive futurity that devalues and denies futurity to those who do not fit its hegemonic promise—those who are queer, disabled, Black, poor, or sick.

This nonpromissory future-oriented logic values what we might call looking on the dark side of things. When Lorde does not wear the suggested prosthetic, the representative from Reach for Recovery criticizes her for not "looking on the bright side of things" (57). Lorde experiences this as a disruption of her access to authentic positive thinking and self-validation by demanding a kind of affectation of positive thinking that serves others. "Looking on the bright side of things," writes Lorde, "is a euphemism used for obscuring certain realities of life, the open consideration of which might prove threatening or dangerous to the status quo" (76). Lorde's way of surviving with the knowledge of her wounded experience is to "integrat[e] this crisis into [her] life," to find ways *to integrate death into living, neither ignoring it nor giving in to it*" (8, 11, italics in original). As Sara Ahmed puts it, "looking on the bright side" can be a way "to avoid what might threaten the world as it is" (83). Looking on the dark side of things instead might be a way to hold on to aspects of one's experience that are legitimately painful and traumatic, to make both those experiences and an awareness of their causes a part of oneself and way of living. Such a way of looking might then open a space for an integrated way of experiencing one's dominant and oppressed positions and healthy and ill aspects of the self as opposed to a binary perspective that understands one path as healthy and future-oriented in opposition to another path that would involve illness, disability, or oppression and obstructs access to a worthwhile future.

Engelberg is similarly critical of positive narratives of healing or overcoming. She points out how these narratives set up expectations for women with cancer to perform in exceptional ways such that other people will not have to think about the dark side of things that these women's bodies represent. Engelberg specifically critiques the ideological work of the word "survivor" as a way of putting a positive affective spin on cancer. "What does [being a survivor] mean, exactly? Is it just a statement of fact?" Miriam asks in the caption to a panel showing a woman wearing a pink ribbon and pointing to a bed out of frame, saying, "I'm alive, She's not. Na na nana na!" In the following panel she asks, "Or is it a moral judgment?" Here the same woman with the pink ribbon says: "I'm alive because I'm a *SURVIVOR*. I've obviously done all the right things" ("Survivor"). To be a survivor is to present yourself in contrast and opposition to the sick and the dead, to participate in the narrative that if you have recovered or if you are healthy, if you have no "family history," if you are a woman who has both breasts and has not yet been raped, assaulted, or otherwise directly traumatized, that you are safe and do not need to think about your own personal or social vulnerabilities and lack of control.[8] And, of course, Engelberg's family members are survivors of another sort, being Jewish, and may not want to ideologically separate themselves from those who did not survive. Engelberg highlights how the discourses we impose on traumas, wounds, and experiences that cause negative affective and bodily responses attempt to recenter and reassure the not-yet-ill and (mostly) gender-normative body. Her Jewish identity as a descendant of survivors also makes clear that this reassurance is available for only those who begin from the position of not already considering part of their identity decentered and haunted by historical trauma.

Cancer does not mark a change, a better life, or a revelation for Miriam, despite the desires of those around her to turn it into something positive. Cancer is, Engelberg's memoir suggests, a permanent interruption, similar really to many of the most disabling aspects of our lives and identities. We will not overcome most of the many obstacles, inequities, dependencies, and oppressions we face in our lives. A sense of futurity that has room for only positive narratives of overcoming leaves many people futureless. My focus on the concept of racialized disgender here is an attempt to give more extensive and extended attention to what we think of and experience as the negative aspects of illness, impairment, and socially disabled identities, without assuming that these aspects decrease future possibility or trap us in victimized positions. My hope is that this focus can show us how the wounds of our identities have far from exhausted the possible knowledges that they have to offer us.

4

Speculative Disabled Futures

Octavia Butler's Xenogenesis *Trilogy*

It's a crip promise that we will always comprehend disability otherwise and that we will, collectively, somehow access other worlds and
futures. (McRuer 208)

The quotation above, in which Robert McRuer makes a future-oriented
crip promise, indicates a generic affinity between disability theory and
the genre of science fiction, which attempts to comprehend our current
world otherwise and provides narrative, if fantastic, "access to other worlds
and futures."[1] The quotation also suggests that disability studies offers a re-
thinking of what the social and political future and future-oriented politics
might look like. McRuer's promise to some extent relies on a political logic
of reproductive futurism, but one that undermines hegemonic and heteronormative values associated with a redemptive future. His promised future
announces itself as not straight but crip, and not about the reproduction and
protection of the child as fetishized product of a teleological drive but about
collective access and alternate understandings of bodies and ability. Octavia
Butler's science fiction *Xenogenesis* trilogy (*Dawn,* 1987; *Adulthood Rites,*
1988; and *Imago,* 1989) offers similar ways of comprehending otherwise via
access to other worlds and futures.[2] In this chapter, I read Butler's trilogy
through a critical lens of disability, combining queer, feminist, and critical
race approaches to the novels. In so doing, I suggest that Butler's trilogy
presents a disabled futurism that revalues injury, impurity, and lack, and
thereby resists "the compulsory narrative of reproductive futurism" (Edel-

man 21) while retaining a feminist narrative that values motherhood (specifically Black motherhood) as a historically determined, embodied, and racially disgendered social identity and political position.

Until quite recently, most critical work on Butler's trilogy argued that the novels provide alternate narratives of or critical narrative distance in relation to womanhood, Blackness, sexuality, social identity in general, and/or humanity. These approaches are generally poststructuralist and read the experiences of the main character, a Black American woman named Lilith Iyapo, in relation to the Oankali aliens as rewriting of narratives of colonialism, slavery, motherhood, and restrictive ideologies of pure or essentialist identity.[3] Though most of these critics note, as Donna Haraway puts it, that "catastrophe, survival, and metamorphosis" are "Butler's constant themes" (226), missing has been a study of these themes in relation to disability theory.[4] In the five years since I first published on Butler and disability,[5] this perspective has grown and produced a number of new and insightful readings of Butler's work. Such work uses a disability focus to explain, if not resolve, the paradoxes and contradictions that arise when queer readings of Butler's texts attempt to deal with race and when critical race and Black feminist readings attempt to deal with the trilogy's challenges to identifiable and consistent social identities. In an article published in the same year as an earlier version of this chapter, Therí Pickens makes the argument that "many of [Butler's] protagonists exist at the crossroads of race, gender, and disability" and that "despite critics' nod to 'mental strength' or illness, the scholarship on Butler neglects a fuller engagement with ability and embodied knowledge as significant within Butler's discussion of power—separate from yet interacting with racialized and gendered discourses" ("You're Supposed" 33–34). Pickens looks at not only ableism and racism as discourses that mutually reinforce one another but also places where "they contradict each other" thereby "expos[ing] their instability" ("You're Supposed" 34). Claire Curtis has also used disability theory to create a compelling reading of the *Xenogenesis* series as a "critical utopia" that does not give us a blueprint for a better future but rather is written out of an impulse toward a better future. Curtis's reading, like my own, understands disability theory as a way to theorize possibilities for more socially just futures and to awaken "the imagination that feeds the capacity to bring about radical change," while acknowledging the limitations of our current ideologies around betterment and perfection ("Utopian Possibilities" 32). Sami Schalk's reading of Butler's "The Morning, Evening, and Night" similarly uses an intersectional disability studies and critical race theory lens to argue that the disease that the main character has in the story "serves as a disability metaphor that demonstrates how ableism and antiblack racism operate in parallel and overlapping ways" ("Interpreting Disability" 140). This intersectional disability studies approach, Schalk argues, allows "us to explore the historical and material connections between disability and other social systems of privilege and oppression such as race, gender, sexuality, class, the nation, and more" and that "it is important that black disability studies scholarship consider how disability's intimate historical relationship to antiblack racism layers African American use of disability metaphors with multiple meanings" (140–141). As these critics demonstrate, a disability focus can help us revalue the histories of pain and interdependence that constitute the historical wounds and often communal pride of minority social groups and think through questions such as the ones I focus on below: How does one narrate racialized disgender without losing race and gender as sites of identity and identification? And what might a future look like in which racialized disgender undoes, to some extent, racial and gender identity as we know them?

Butler's *Xenogenesis* trilogy can be read as a speculative representation of accessibility and interdependence that revalues disease by presenting xenophobia and able-bodiedness as conditions of illness. As our main character in the first novel, Lilith, is made to experience inaccessibility in the alien Oankali society, she becomes more aware of the limitations of her able-bodied ideology. Ultimately she must learn to live within an interdependent public culture. Her race and gender figure as aspects of her identity that reinforce a reliance on ideals of able-bodiedness and independence as well as making her more adaptable. Her children's narratives in the second and third books rewrite, echo, and repeat Lilith's story, inheriting, if not precisely embodying, Lilith's racially disgendered social identities.

Butler does not present queer, critical race, and disability pride discourses and ideologies as neatly overlapping or always liberating. The price of interdependence and accessibility for the characters these novels follow is revealed to be a loss of historical identity, at least as we currently understand social identity to function. And the bodily and environmental changes needed to create a more interdependent and accessible future rely on practices of genetic engineering designed to eliminate humanity as a disabled species. The trilogy presents the racialized disgender that is revealed and continually ever more "dissed" as belonging to a type of "dismodern" future, though not an entirely celebratory one. The dismodern, according to Lennard Davis, is a politics or way of thinking in which "the ideal is not a hypostatization of the normal (that is the dominant) subject, but aims to create a new category based on the partial, incomplete subject whose realization is not autonomy and independence but dependency and interdependence" (30). Butler's trilogy examines what a dismodern future might look like and some of the paradoxes and violences one might find on the road to it and on the roads within it. I argue that ultimately she does present us with a possibility for an interdependent dismodern future, but this future is not future oriented in a utopian or dystopian teleological sense. It has to incorporate pain, loss, and impairment and also to appreciate the value of disability, both in terms of bodily difference and in terms of the histories of wounds and disablement that have contributed to the construction of many identity formations.

Why Critical Disability as Intersecting Narrative Perspective for *Xenogenesis*?

Xenogenesis unfolds as a story of, among other things, motherhood.[6] In *Dawn*, which is divided into sections titled "Womb," "Family," "The Nursery," and "The Training Floor," Lilith Iyapo awakes aboard an Oankali ship in a small, bare room with no doors, where she is interrogated by voices whose source she cannot see. The Earth has been nearly destroyed by human nuclear war. The Oankali, her alien captors, are working to repair the Earth as they keep those humans who survived in a naturally induced suspended animation sleep. As the novel unfolds, Lilith becomes part of an Oankali family, is made responsible for waking other humans and training them to live on Earth again, and eventually becomes pregnant with a human-Oankali baby conceived via her relationship with an ooloi (gender-neutral or third-gender Oankali) named Nikanj, and her now dead male human mate, Joseph.

The next two novels take place on Earth and follow the development of both human-Oankali hybrid communities as well as human-only resister communities. The hybrid communities live on biological part-ships that cover the surface of the Earth. They live in family models of five—a male and female human, male and female Oankali, and one ooloi, the third gender gene-mixing Oankali. The human-only communities are places of violence and sadness, largely because the Oankali have extended human life but made it impossible for humans to reproduce without mating with an Oankali. Their rationale is that it would be unethical to allow humans to reproduce due to a "genetic flaw"—an inherited combination of hierarchical tendencies and advanced intelligence that leads to violence and self-destruction. The Oankali, while physically drawn to humans in part because of this genetic anomaly, believe it is their moral duty to both repair any illness they find in individual bodies and to prevent a purely human line genetically programmed to destroy itself to continue to procreate.

Adulthood Rites is focalized through Akin, one of Lilith's male Oankali-human children (these children are first referred to as "hybrids," but for most of Books 2 and 3 as "constructs"). Akin is taken at an early age by resister humans and becomes sympathetic to their desire to continue the human race, despite genetic flaws. He lobbies and gets permission for a Mars colony of humans who will be given back their reproductive capabilities. The final novel, *Imago,* is the only one narrated in the first person. It is narrated by Jodahs, the first human-born ooloi construct. Jodahs has a fluid bodily form. It needs others, particularly human others, to have a coherent sense of self and often takes on physical characteristics in order to please the humans it desires to mate with. Jodahs finds a community of people who had not been altered by the Oankali—they had nonenhanced life spans and had been reproducing, but with the effects of the war, the small number of people in the town, and the presence of certain genetic diseases in the population, had bred children with more bodily abnormalities and higher rates of illness in their attempt to keep the human race alive. Some of these humans ultimately accept the human-Oankali ooloi as potential mates, beginning another cycle of theretofore unknown reproductive practices.

Once one begins to look at discourses of disability, health, reproduction, and medicalization in the trilogy, it becomes difficult *not* to perceive disability as affecting and infecting the feminist, postcolonial, and critical race narratives. Butler allegorizes rehabilitation and accessibility as models of social change, each of which resonates with different histories of African American social movements—rehabilitation most strongly with the Women's Club Movement and a politics of racial uplift and accessibility most strongly with the civil rights demands for equal access. Rehabilitation and accessibility also represent two of the most prevalent approaches to disability in the contemporary United States—the individual body–oriented medical approach and the socially oriented civil rights approach. The history of rehabilitation rhetoric in relation to disability is also heavily inflected by racial ideologies. As Paul R. D. Lawrie argues, the passing of the Vocational Rehabilitation Act in 1918, rather than helping to create more income equity between Black Americans and white Americans, actually increased labor and income segregation by mobilizing cultural assumptions about the inherent "colored diseases" carried by Black bodies to deny African American veterans access to vocational rehabilitation. Denial of these resources then led to stronger claims by many African American soldiers that they had the right to rehabilitation—that is, a social and political right to the resources for personal health, normative labor, and individual uplift (327–329). Jennifer C. James links rehabilitation in these contexts to literary representations as well, arguing that there is a "dearth of references to Black corporeal damage in African American war literature," which is a result of African American war writers' wish "for African men to be considered 'normal' rather than aberrant or damaged" (137, 139). This dearth, James argues, "can be considered a literary version of bodily rehabilitation, mimicking the purposes of rehabilitative technologies used to reconstruct bodies disabled and altered by war" (137). James further links this use of normativity in relationship to rehabilitation to Black women's attempts to "destigmatize their bodies by adopting the dominant culture's 'feminine' paradigms [and] striving to present themselves as physically and morally fit for domesticity" (140). Each of these appropriations of rehabilitation ideology is in an attempt to gain greater accessibility for Black people to the social and political rights of U.S. citizenship. Butler alludes to these complicated relationships to rehabilitation ideologies for disabled and Black people, while her narrative reveals how accessibility narratives often rely on aspects of the rehabilitation model—that is, to gain accessibility one often has to make an argument about the rehabilitative potential of one's body and/or identity group, rather than demand access for the bodymind and self that one is. It suggests that both models have the potential to reproduce ideals of bodily purity. And, resisting a narrative of either utopia or dystopia, it points to paradoxes that arise in imagining a shift from our world to a more accessible and interdependent one.[7]

Dawn begins with a set of oppressions based on physical lack of accessibility. The Oankali ships are made from organic material that responds to Oankali biochemical touch. This allows all Oankali aboard the ship to open and close doors; access food; and create beds, tables, separate rooms, and so forth. Lilith awakes aboard the ship in a room described in the following manner:

> The walls were light-colored—white or grey perhaps. The bed was what it had always been: a solid platform that gave slightly to the touch and that seemed to grow from the floor. There was, across the room, a doorway that probably led to a bathroom. She was usually given a bathroom. Twice she had not been, and in her windowless, doorless cubicle, she had been forced simply to choose a corner. (5)

While one might read this as a jail cell or slave quarters, Lilith's isolation and the description of the room as sterile, white/gray, and furnished with only a standardized bed, recalls a medical institutional site. The separate bathroom that she "usually" has access to indicates a space constructed through medicalized discourse, in which privacy is nominally acknowledged as important, but not consistently granted as a right to those marked as patients. Additionally, Lilith is not made to perform labor (though later she will be impregnated and perform reproductive labor without her verbal consent), nor is she being punished. She knows she has been operated on because of "the long scar across her abdomen," which turns out to be where the Oankali have removed a cancerous growth (6). Lilith finds herself in the position of a patient without full control of her own care, both grateful for her bodily health and angry at her lack of ownership over that body: "It enraged her . . . that there had been moments when she actually felt grateful to her mutilators for letting her sleep through whatever they had done to her—and for doing it well enough to spare her pain or disability later" (7). Here we can already notice the competing discourses of medical health and social accessibility. Lilith's situation can be read as an allegory of slavery, colonialism, and violence done to women's bodies. But each of these readings must also take into consideration that Butler puts Lilith in a position in which she must learn to live as an institutionalized, diagnosed subject, and with a dependent body that lacks the ability to affect her environment and achieve equal access to physical spaces and necessities.

Another way the trilogy prompts readers to consider intersections between discourses of disability and illness and those of race and gender is through the parallels that arise between Butler's Lilith and the historical figure Henrietta Lacks, whose story has been recently popularized by not only Rebecca Skloot's best-selling *The Immortal Life of Henrietta Lacks* (2010), a book of journalistic creative nonfiction based on the experience and treatment of Lacks and her family, but also the HBO movie of the same name (2017). Lacks's story would have likely been known to Butler, given her deep knowledge of both scientific and American cultural histories. Henrietta Lacks was an African American woman whose cancerous cells (which came to be known as the HeLa cells) proved to be an "immortal" line that became an essential tool in medical research vital to the discovery of a polio vaccine, and to in vitro fertilization, cloning, and gene mapping. Lacks's identity was not kept anonymous, but her family, though asked to provide their own bodily materials to science, was never compensated in any way for Lacks's contribution to medical science.[8] In Skloot's book, she notes that part of the excitement surrounding the HeLa cells was the possibility that they might hold the key to human life extension or to the making of "designer babies" (216–217, 214). She also notes the connections between the discovery of HeLa, debates over who owns a part of the body once it has been removed, and the bourgeoning ways of turning "bodies into businesses" through such processes as selling blood plasma or sperm (205, 203). The resonances between Lacks's story and Lilith's as Black women from whose bodies samples have been taken that become essential to major scientific discoveries, treatments, and reproductive possibilities suggest that these same questions about the value of illness and who has the right to benefit from it or determine its value are of central interpretive importance in Butler's trilogy.

The Oankali's interpretation of humanity as disabled also reinforces a medicalized reading of Lilith's experience. They believe they are helping the humans whose "own bodies handicapped them" (38). Lilith's job becomes to awaken and train the other humans kept by the Oankali. The Oankali hope the humans, after their rehabilitation, will voluntarily mate with them, but Lilith hopes that if the humans can learn about their captors, and learn to live on Earth again, they can escape. Lilith's rebellious plan reads as a parable for consciousness-raising and community building among the enslaved, the colonized, or the disabled who have been kept isolated from one another by oppressive power structures. Yet in the resister communities, the proclaimed disability is never addressed as a potentially shared characteristic or identity around which to build socially just practices, nor is the rigid medical discourse of the Oankali. While the humans do not want to have "alien" babies, they never discuss the Oankali's representation of humanity as illness but continue to treat their bodies as individual agential units over which control and ownership should be maintained at all costs. The disability politics that could help them survive and respond to the demands of the Oankali are not available as political or ideological resources. To some extent, Lilith's and the other humans' weakness is their treatment of their situation purely as one of race-based enslavement or colonization and their nonrecognition or inability to deal with the paradoxes of the medical and disability models involved in their subjection and captivity.[9]

While Butler does allow us to read the humans as oppressed by the medicalizing and isolating practices of the Oankali, the Oankali also present alternative discourses and lived models that enable a more universally accessible and interdependent world, based on a biological rather than a social model. The Oankali can communicate through sensation rather than speech. This allows them to connect to one another and come to communal consensus as a way of making decisions that affect them as a whole. They also, in their use of living materials for their ships and modes of transportation, have to maintain mutually beneficial relations between themselves and their environment. Their use of biochemical sensors to create doorways and make furniture allows multiple body types (of which the Oankali have many due to their history of gene trading) comfort and accessibility.

Additionally, the Oankali revalue disease and illness, ability and disability. While they understand humans as a species as carrying a genetic disease that they mark as disability, they perceive certain diseases, such as cancer, as bodily "talent" (22).[10] Their investment in human health is not about creating a perfect-looking body, or even a particular type of body, but one that can live well in its environment. The Oankali tell Lilith that she has "been given health" and that the "ooloi have seen to it that [she]'ll have a chance to live on . . . Earth—not just die on it" (33). For the Oankali, adaptability to environment and exchange of genes follows a biological imperative. It is not that accessibility is a civil, ethical, or individual right so much as that without the adaptability that cancer cells allow, the Oankali will not be able to sustain their existence. Thus, while cancer is revalued as useful, it does not necessarily follow that sick or disabled beings deserve full accessibility and the right to remain in a state that the majority conceptualizes as unhealthy or not forwarding the sustainability and health of the species as a whole.

What becomes clear is that both the social rebellion model of the humans and the medical health model of the Oankali rely to some extent on rehabilitative ideologies of ability and bodily perfection. To escape or to be allowed to go to Earth, the humans must be rehabilitated physically and mentally—a rehabilitation that, like U.S. historical models, relies on assumptions about not only the health but also the labor potential of raced, gendered, and dis/abled bodies. The Oankali assumption that humans could not be rehabilitated as humans but must be genetically altered to be functional in a way ethical and productive to society is not dissimilar from white doctors' contention after World War I that African American veterans did not deserve access to rehabilitative resources because they were "disproportionately afflicted with the ostensibly hidden wounds of 'colored diseases' such as venereal disease and tuberculosis" (Lawrie 328). Or, as James puts it, the historical "notion of the black body as congenitally disabled—inherently defective, afflicted by deformity and disease—was merely compounded by the attribution of another form of acquired disability: the black body as irreversibly impaired by the violence of slavery" (137). Both Lawrie's and James's arguments highlight how inherited disorders are always read and diagnosed through histories of power and often as well through the historical effects of violence on the diagnosed bodies. Any genetic disorders read as racially inherent are "fixed" by the Oankali via genetic manipulation and interspecies procreation—and any humans who do not cooperate or who demonstrate anger, mental instability, or violent tendencies (in response to captivity) are kept aboard the ship. These historical but decontextualized ideologies of health, purity, and inherited disease only increase in the next two books, *Adulthood Rites* and *Imago*, which take place on the more dangerous and unknown regenerating Earth. The human-Oankali communities on Earth are able to embrace physical and sexual fluidity, indeterminacy, and change. They have children who are mixed Oankali and human and who won't know their adult forms or genders until after metamorphosis. At the same time, they maintain fixed understandings of what a healthy body is and refuse to entertain the idea that disability can have value, believing that anyone who does not seek the medical attention of the ooloi is suffering from mental illness, again medicalizing and diagnosing the choice to live with a disability and to determine how one's body interacts with medical institutions.

Susan Wendell, in *The Rejected Body*, argues against this type of fixed ideology of ability, suggesting that while alleviating suffering is a project to take seriously, the drive to rid people of disabilities could amount to a great loss and relies on ways of thinking that marginalize and do violence to those with disabilities. Such an ideology conceptualizes people with disabilities as symbols of "imperfection, failure to control the body, and everyone's vulnerability to weakness, pain, and death" (60). It is not hard to understand how the Oankali, in their drive to alleviate suffering, could reproduce such a potentially oppressive ideology. Most Oankali consider the option of allowing the humans to reproduce without the Oankali (thereby not breeding out the genetic defect) ethically untenable. During a consensus session they think, "We've given them back the things they value—long life, freedom from disease, freedom to live as they wish. We can't help them create more life only to destroy it" (O. Butler 470). Here humanity itself is perceived by the Oankali's medical logic as itself disabled, in the sense that from a medical perspective a disability is a negative bodily state referring to impairment or illness. Without access to a disability rights perspective, the condition of being human is diagnosed as a disability and disease that the Oankali believe it is their ethical responsibility to cure. But diagnosing and "treating" this disease without consent is critiqued by Butler as ultimately a limiting and potentially violent response. Butler's novels push for more knowledge of the social construction of disability and the history of human patterns of behavior, not the erasure of any person who carries certain genes or reproduces potentially destructive patterns. Such erasures simply replicate the violence of hierarchy supported by intelligence and technology. Butler has stated in an interview that

> hierarchical behavior is definitely inborn and intelligence is something new that we've come up with and like I said, I happen to think that the combination is lethal. I think that it doesn't have to be lethal if we deal with it. But unfortunately, the ways in which we tried to deal with it in the past have not really acknowledged the problem. Too often when people start talking about inborn characteristics, they start talking about who shall we eliminate, who has the negative characteristics. And we get to decide what's negative and we get into the eugenics and the real nasty stuff where people use something that could be and is in fact part of behavior science as a reason to put somebody else down to get rid of your enemies, using science for hierarchical purposes. (Beal 17)

Like Wendell, Butler suggests that the assumption that we know what a genetic condition means and can make decisions for those who have it is not ethical and relies on a power-based hierarchical ideology of bodily control. The Oankali, while constructing what they believe to be an ethically minded approach to bodily health, still rely on a paradigm of control of the body in which some bodies are granted access if they conform to certain modifications or alterations, while others are not.

Not only are individual bodyminds oppressed in a power-based system of bodily control, but also social identities may be lost or devalued in a way that harms their members in their ability to inhabit that identity freely and openly. Wendell contemplates this:

> People who take it for granted that it would be a good thing to wipe out all biological causes of disability . . . are far more confident that they know how to perfect nature and humanity than I am. Even supposing that everyone involved in such an effort were motivated entirely by a desire to prevent and alleviate suffering, what else besides suffering might we lose in the process? (84)

The Oankali, even with what they may self-perceive as ethical intentions, are characters that suggest that there can be severe and unacknowledged loss as a result of medically oriented and nonconsensual models of bodily control—not only individual well-being but also potentially the well-being of humanity as some humans know and are attached to it. While Butler is not suggesting that the human tendency toward killing one another is by any means a trait to nurture, she also presents a distinction important to people with disabilities and other populations that have suffered eugenic "correction": Certainly most would want themselves and others to live long lives and be cured of pain and suffering, but the idea of curing the population by preventing those with disabilities from being born or persisting as they are carries with it its own kind of genocidal logic and produces its own pain and suffering.

Even the more human-oriented and human-activist Oankali and human-Oankali construct characters represented in the book understand disability and illness as evils that any rational and ethical person would seek to eliminate. "How stupid to be sick and know where there was healing and decide to stay sick," says Akin (O. Butler 318). Later Jodahs reflects, "There used to be Humans who adapted to not being able to see or hear or walk or move. They adapted. But I don't think any of them chose to be so limited" (609). Of course, Jodahs (and therefore implicitly Akin) is wrong, as any reader who is familiar, for example, with Deaf culture would immediately recognize.

Harlan Hahn and Todd Belt, in considering what they call the "health locus of control" (454), argue that personal identity is linked to communal identity and that the assumption that "all disabled people are presumed to want to eliminate their impairments and that nearly everyone would accept whatever doctors prescribe for them . . . may not be applicable to all populations" (462). A "quality life" should be defined by those whose lives are being judged, and social reasons why people with disabilities do not have access to a "quality life"—that is, exclusion and isolation from jobs, families, social networks—should be considered in addition to medical reasons such as pain and physical impairment. Butler's representation of the Oankali echoes Bruce H. Gross and Hahn's claim that "quality of life standards can be used to the disadvantage of people with disabilities" (133). Perhaps some humans will kill, die earlier than others, or get sick, and humans might possibly even die off as a species. But to not allow humans choice in their acceptance or refusal of medical treatment or to not recognize the psychological importance of existing as a group with a shared social identity is to take the medical model of control to violent and unethical lengths.

Butler's humans, in their willingness to accept disability in the form of illness, loss of reproductive capacity, and their choice to work through rather than alter their flawed human natures, nevertheless retain ideologies of racial health and wellness that rely on ideals of pure and normative bodies. There is, first of all, the general human reaction of xenophobia in relation to the Oankali, described largely as a discomfort with the Oankali's modes of attaining sensory information—the Oankali sensory tentacles; Akin's long gray tongue, which he uses to understand things and people through taste; and the various combinations of "human" and "alien" sense organs used by the Oankali-human construct children. The constructs, like the Oankali, learn to act as though they are using their sense organs in an able-bodied human way to avoid negative reactions from the humans. Two girl constructs are taken in *Adulthood Rites* by a human community that cannot have children. One of the girls, Shkaht, is described in relation to her multisensory body:

> She had a normal Human tongue, but each of her grey tentacles would serve her as well as Akin's long, gray Oankali tongue. Shkaht's throat tentacles gave her a more sensitive sense of smell and taste than Akin, and she could use her hands for tasting. Also, she had slender, dark tentacles on her head, mixed with her hair. She could see with these. She could not see with her eyes. She had learned, though, to seem to look at people with her eyes—to turn to face them and to move her slender head tentacles as she moved her head so that Humans were not disturbed by her hair seeming to crawl about. (373)

It is hard not to read this passage as explicitly incorporating disability discourses in relation to, at the very least, the human condition of blindness. Shkaht cannot see with her eyes, but this does not mean she cannot perceive the world by other means. But because humans associate "proper" bodily behavior and sense organ use with humanity as such, the constructs learn to mimic "human" sight in the same ways that many blind people do.

Shkaht's and her sister Amma's oppression within the human's own version of ableism does not stop here. Several of the townspeople want to surgically remove (without anesthesia) the girls' tentacles. This decision is rationalized by humans from a perspective of ableism: "They'll learn to use their human senses. . . . They'll see the world as we do and be more like us" (375). They cannot, according to Akin, "learn" to use their other senses. Their eyes simply are not made for seeing, while their tentacles are. As the humans organize for support to amputate the girls, the text demonstrates that this antidisability discourse is gendered and sexed as well. "It was criminal to allow little girls to be afflicted with such things," argues one of the townspeople. "Girl children who might someday be the mothers of a new Human race ought to look human—ought to see Human features when they looked in the mirror." Another asks, "How can little girls grow up to be Human women when their own sense organs betray them?" (391). Here the debate takes on connotations of not only sensory norms but also binary and essentialist sex norms as they intersect with racialized disgender. The humans use the same "quality of life" argument as the Oankali—that is, it would be "criminal" to allow one to be born or to live a life in which one would experience psychological and social pain and oppression. This presumed social marginalization comes from gaining access to a certain kind of racialized womanhood—to be fully human and acceptably female one must also perform able-bodiedness. This is not read as a set of interlocking social oppressions, but rather as an individual responsibility to make bodies conform so as to save them from those social oppressions, while doing nothing to change those power dynamics or systems of violence. While one might argue that the Oankali's approach is more benevolent than the humans' in this scenario, in that they are attempting to save lives, not just create docile and assimilated bodies, the text also reveals the parallel logics behind the human and Oankali approaches to bodies read as ill, impaired, or nonnormative. Neither approach takes seriously the possibility that more social change could lead to higher qualities of life; both look to "fix" bodies through medical intervention only.

Both the human and Oankali rationales echo historical arguments made in debates surrounding the ethics of performing surgery on intersex children. Anne Fausto-Sterling argues against infant genital surgery on the grounds that it is physically harmful and that it assumes natural biological binary gender, an assumption that is physically and psychologically harmful to many bodies, including but not limited to intersex ones. Fausto-Sterling points out that medical discourse on intersex children reproduces ideologies about ability and disability, health and illness: "Generally doctors inform parents that the infant has a 'birth defect of unfinished genitalia,' and that it may take a little time before they know whether the child is a boy or a girl. The doctors can and will, they assure the parents, identify the 'true' sex that lies underneath surface confusion" (50). Finding and bodily reflecting one's "true" sex, then, is a mark of physical ability and wellness.

Fausto-Sterling acknowledges that her argument is vulnerable to the "quality of life" attack. "Perhaps they think I am sacrificing the well-being of unfortunate children on the altar of gender politics," writes Fausto-Sterling. "How could I possibly consider using a poor intersexual [sic] child as a battering ram to assault the fortress of gender inequality?" (79). This rationale relies on a racialized and conservative logic of reproductive futurity—that is, that hope for a better future is to be found in a heteronormative model that produces, protects, and invests in able-bodied biological children in nuclear families—a logic that has historically served white adults by constructing queerness and racial nonwhiteness (and I would argue trans identities as well) as a threat primarily to the purity and safety of white women and girls. In many ways the Oankali also rely on the idea that the only way to produce a healthy future is via biological reproduction rather than social change, even if in their case this produces difference rather than reproduces sameness. Fausto-Sterling responds to the heteronormative logic that wants to eliminate intersex as an embodied experience or identity in a twofold manner. First she argues, like Belt, Gross, Hahn, and Wendell, that quality of life cannot be predicted ahead of time. On the basis of her research, she found that "Intersexual [sic] children who grow up with genitalia that seem to contradict their assigned gender identities are not doomed to lives of misery" (95). Second, she argues that medical attempts to surgically or genetically "cure" what is essentially a social problem can cause more injury than they alleviate. The "social imperative" of conforming to a two-sex system, Fausto-Sterling writes, "is so strong that doctors have come to accept it as a medical imperative, despite strong evidence that early genital surgery doesn't work: it causes extensive scarring, requires multiple surgeries, and often obliterates the possibility of orgasm" (80).

Butler's presentation of Amma and Shkaht echoes these concerns and complicates a reading of the trilogy as about racial oppression via heterosexual forced reproduction only, not by preventing us from perceiving the Oankali as colonizers or the humans as racist, miscegenation-fearing purists but rather by linking these oppressive ideologies to ableism and regimes of bodily normalcy. It helps us to understand that the ways social violence occurs do not always happen at the level of an abstracting, dehumanizing "othering," but can also appear in the guise of the humane and empathic, as an offer (however coercive) to allow bodies access into the realm of those who belong and are healthy. The humans cling to certain body types to reinforce a human identity. The Oankali also understand only a fixed, gendered combination of family units used to produce medically "better" bodies. Both of these readings rely on ideologies of racialized disgender, in that they highlight that how we gender bodies is always intersectional with ideologies of racial embodiment, has historically limited and done harm to bodies, and has no natural or ideal embodied form. Embodying racialized disgender from a position empowered by critical race theory/activism, gender and sexuality theory/activism, and disability theory/activism might lead to a dismantling of the violence done to bodies via normative understandings of race, gender, and able-bodiedness. While the humans have the possibility in their resistance to consciously identify with racialized disgender and use that to challenge their own limited understandings of "healthy" and "normal" bodies and to demand the right to determine their health care, reproductive choices, and bodily autonomy, they instead reinforce a violent system of racialized disgender that continues to demand that bodies conform to a "human" and binary understanding of raced and gendered norms.

Fundamentally, then, both the Oankali way of life that embraces diversity through genetics and biology and the human way of life that invests in maintaining a sense of cultural and racial identity by fighting their oppressors rather than being willing to change themselves rely on culturally heavily raced and gendered images of health and bodily purity. This is not to say that there is not something of great value both in searching for medical cures and in building communities on the basis of wanting to hold on to and reinforce a shared social identity. Yet both these drives, when unchecked, lead to practices that devalue and attempt to eliminate nonconforming bodies. Near the end of the trilogy, the group of humans who have had little contact with and have not been genetically altered by the Oankali still feel that "it was better to have no children . . . than to have un-Human children" (661). Jodahs responds by asking them, "Why should your people want to stay here and breed dead children or disabled children?" (637). Both approaches conflate a state of perceived disability with one of death. Here politics of assimilation or separatism as we might read them along racial lines become complicated by questions of disability. What in one reading looks like a political refusal to be forced into giving up reproductive freedom in ways that echo oppressions of U.S. slavery becomes in another reading its own form of genocidal drive to rid the world/universe of the bodily differ-ent.[11] What in one reading looks like a willingness to accept difference, oth-erness, fluidity, and change reveals in another a potentially genocidal drive to rid the world/universe of those with mental illness or cognitive or physical impairments.

Survival and Adaptability

Sherryl Vint uses Foucault's concept of biopolitics to describe how the mate-rial and the speculative have become "so entwined" in our current era "that neither can be understood in isolation" (161). There has been a shift, Vint argues, in our material ways of understanding the biological and physical world as they have become more heavily influenced by the science of engi-neering and thus the speculative possibilities for human and animal body-minds. Vint writes, "Biopolitics involves a new power over life, and a new relationship between sovereignty and life. While 'the right of sovereignty was the right to take life or let live,' the new right established with the rise of modern governance is 'the right to make live or let die' (Foucault, *Society* 241)" (162). Thus, in this era of the speculative material, one iteration of which Butler captures in her trilogy, the choice for those in power, in this case the Oankali, is never to "take life or let live," but always "to make live or let die." The trilogy asks what the ethics of this choice entail, how are those ethics different than a choice between killing and letting live, and how does this system of choice for power affect the individual bodies without it in this system? Is choosing life ever a choice for the subjected individual if it is al-ways dependent on one's society to let one live?

Near the end of the trilogy Lilith claims that she did have a choice re-garding her own life, even in her captivity. "I did [have a choice], oh, yes," she tells the fully human Jesusa, "I chose to live." Jesusa, a much younger woman who has just come into contact with the Oankali, disagrees: "That's no choice. That's just going on, letting yourself be carried along by whatever happens" (672). To a reader who knows the history of Lilith's fictional strug-gles and is aware of the historical struggles they represent, Jesusa's comment registers as ignorant and judgmental, particularly as she herself has done very little to get out of her own approaching forced participation in her human community's reproductive order.[12] Readers' knowledge of the social identities, including Black, female, and colonized, that Lilith represents com-plicates their understanding of "make live or let die," for yes, that is the choice as the Oankali understand it, and might well be the choice as medical institutions understand it in relation to ill or disabled bodies. To the indi-vidual for whom the choice is made, however, biopolitics also carries with it histories of oppression that make the choice to survive the conditions under which one is enslaved, marginalized, threatened, imprisoned, traumatized, or institutionalized very much an active one. Such individuals must learn how and why to choose life or not in a system that is very close at every moment to letting one die.

Reading the humans' situation in the trilogy through the lens of disability theory helps to clarify how and when living becomes a choice. Waking up and realizing one suddenly falls under the category of disabled and that one does not own one's body in the way one formerly imagined, as Lilith does, changes the terms of what it means to "just be carried along." She now needs to reconcile the lack of access and judgments of others that come with her positioning. Moreover, in the case of a severe disability or illness in oneself or someone one has medical proxy for, there may be a cultural expectation that the person would not want to "just go on" in that situation. In the context of prenatal screening for children with disabilities, for example—which provides a context for reading how Lilith at first perceives her pregnancy ("It won't be human," she says, "It will be a thing. A monster" [247])—parents are explicitly given a choice (likely framed as make live or let die) and expected to make one by physicians and medical institutions. This reading complicates Lilith's role as a woman of color who is forced to participate in the colonization of her people by reproducing with the colonizer. From the perspective of a rape victim and colonized person, thinking of the pregnancy as monstrous makes ethical sense as it is the result of what may be perceived as monstrous acts. From the perspective of a human who is part of an ableist culture, thinking of a baby who is bodily different from the parent as a monster contributes to violence against disabled bodies, those with nonnormative sex or gender, and in certain contexts those with darker skin.[13] By introducing the possibility of reading Lilith's choice to live and to have and care for her baby as being about the ethics of living with disability or caring for another who does not read as fully healthy or fully human, Butler opens up narrative possibilities for a colonized motherhood that is a choice made within highly restrictive, oppressive, and potentially self-negating circumstances.

This reading also complicates cultural understandings of racially disgendered motherhood more broadly. Rayna Rapp and Faye Ginsburg argue that American ideologies of gendered and privatized caretaking restrict possibilities for social inclusion and support for persons with disabilities. Rapp and Ginsburg present a "cultural dialect" between perfectibility and inclusion as opposing narratives generated by medical technology and disability activism. Identifying kinship as a primary site for assigning meaning to disability, they demonstrate how "choices" about children with disabilities are often presented as individual choices of mothers, without providing social context or support (544). Jennifer L. Barclay has looked more specifically at the historical context of slave mothers with children with disabilities to parse the complex historical "intersection[s] of race, gender, and disability in the antebellum South" (117). Barclay argues that a child with a disability could become an added risk for an enslaved mother and might be sent away or exploited for medical or spectacular purposes. In other cases, because children with disabilities were considered "useless," they might be left with their mothers; similarly, slave women with disabilities might be more likely to be allowed child-care roles. Barclay notes that "the very same devaluation of disabled bondspeople that highlights one of the most atrocious facets of racial slavery in the United States—equating people to property and judging their worth on their ability to labor for another—was the very same idea that often enabled enslaved mothers to remain with their disabled children" (139). She adds that mothering children with disabilities under slavery was an act of resistance and survival in which slave caretakers "rejected slave-holders' definitions of their children [and] adapted, resisted, and persevered to ensure that they mothered their 'useless' children to the best of their ability, despite living under an institution that inherently devalued them" (115). Lilith's reading of her child as "monstrous" then might carry all of these complex historical connotations. The conception may feel like violence, the body of the child may be perceived to be different and potentially rejected by other humans, but Lilith can still choose to make herself and the child live within two competing systems—human and Oankali—that devalue different aspects of them both.

In the trilogy as a whole, Butler stages the contradictory choices presented as part of our often paradoxical raced and gendered expectations for motherhood as a central narrative theme but does not reproduce what Jane Stemp describes as the science fiction and fantasy trope of holding out "the image of magical cure for wounds and disabilities" (n.p.). Nor does she repeat the common science fiction narrative of genetic revolution as a neo-eugenic dystopia of monstrous kinship. Traditional science fiction narratives often replicate the binary ethical framework at work in disability politics—that is, the harmful perspective of reproductive technology versus the liberating perspective of social movements to increase rights and access for those with disabilities. Butler provides a less dichotomous approach by taking seriously the possibility of looking at "monstrous kinship" through a queer lens as a form of non-normative kinship. We are made aware of the horrors Lilith experiences as her sense of bodily integrity is threatened and her options for survival are dictated by others who do not share her culture, history, or identity. We are also asked to recognize how a more communal, more interdependent model might take away the liberal American ideal of individual choice but also provide a model of family and community that is more accepting of bodily difference. Lilith's choice to embrace her newly defined racialized disgender as the "mother" of a new race might also be read as claiming the never fully chosen monstrosity of disgendered womanhood, as figured by Hortense Spillers.[14] Rather than trying to hold on to an idea of what it means to be a gendered human as defined by her culture on Earth, Lilith is willing to accept the reality of her new conditions, claim the agency she finds there, and resist on a larger scale what feels impossible to live with. The trilogy takes communal support and decision making seriously. It also shows how communal choice can injure and has injured individuals who lack agency within the community; how such decisions can take the form of racial oppression, lack of reproductive choice, and/or even rape; and how one might still claim a position of chosen survival and wounded identities within it. The novels suggest that it may be Lilith's wounded history as a Black woman that has given her the flexibility to survive and resist.

In order to both survive and resist, *Xenogenesis* suggests that we must both adapt to change and build an awareness in relation to change. Thus, the trilogy complicates our understanding of choice and of what it means to live well. It foregrounds adaptability, as opposed to assimilation or xenophobia, as a way of choosing life and as a necessity for living. Adaptability is presented as a personal, individual, and bodily oriented change, but one that is required of everyone in order to mediate the potentially violent effects of ideologies of health and wellness that reproduce restrictive understandings of ability/disability, human/other, and future/past. Akin and Jodahs, the protagonists of *Adulthood Rites* and *Imago*, respectively, represent and function as tools of exploration for the possibility of adaptation as life.

Akin is the first male construct born to a human mother. The Oankali perceive human males as exhibiting the most violent symptoms in relation to their genetic illness of hierarchical intelligence; therefore, a construct male born of a human mother might, they fear, have the abilities of the Oankali but the illness of the human. Akin is then an experiment in adaptability. The Oankali had previously been controlling the genders of the construct children. Nikanj, Akin's ooloi parent, tells Lilith that the ooloi "control children in ways we should not to make them mature as Oankali-born males and Human-born females. We control inclinations that should be left to individual children" (259). The Oankali have a queer understanding of gender to the extent that they conceptualize it as ideally fluid and individually choice-based, but in their fear of reproducing illness they have been enacting binary, transphobic, and racially coded models that restrict individual inclination. The Oankali also have a fluid and socially constructed model of race—both human and Oankali. The Oankali thrive on "gene-mixing" to create new racial forms and must do this to live—thus adaptability to new forms and identities is part of their understanding of themselves. Human understandings of race are also figured as historically constructed. Akin's male Oankali parent explains to him that "the differences [he] perceive[s] . . . between groups of Humans . . . are the result of isolation and inbreeding, mutation, and adaptation to different earth environments" (262). Of course, his reading leaves out adaptation to historical violences, oppressions, and geographical migrations. But as human readers, we can be assumed to add this to the natural sciences–oriented reading given by the Oankali. Given his inherited ideologies of race and gender, Akin should be one of the most open, adaptable, and accepting beings yet created. However, even he carries fears of otherness, not in relation to race, gender, or sexuality, per se, but rather in relation to bodies he perceives as ill or disabled. And these perceptions inevitably intersect with and impact readings of race, gender, and sexuality.

While Akin is curious to know more about the resister humans, he also is repelled by their lack of health and their decision not to go to the Oankali for treatment. "It was *wrong*," he thinks, "to allow such suffering, *utterly wrong* to throw away a life so unfinished" (326). It is not until Akin is abducted and forced to spend an extended period of time with humans (which causes him to lose the rich dynamics that his multispecies family would have provided, thereby injuring the connection between himself and his closest sibling) that he actually gains an understanding of the humans as "a truly separate people" (378). This captivity narrative recalls U.S. racial histories and highlights the ways captivity narratives both enable understandings of difference and disable normative modes of being in the world for the person taken captive. It is Akin's development of disabilities, as the Oankalis understand them, that gives him the ability to understand that there are truly different ways of perceiving and experiencing the world. After he returns from the resister village, he becomes an outsider, feeling that "his world was made up of tight units of people who treated him kindly or coldly as they chose, but who could not let him in, no matter how much they might want to" (429). This isolation is due in large part to the lack of development of Oankali ways of communicating and interacting: "He could remember a time when blending into others seemed not only possible but inevitable. . . . Now, though, because he had not been able to bond with [his closest sibling]," he "spent as little time as possible with it" (429). Akin has taken on human ways of being that read as impairment and would disable him within his own community but that also give him an experiential knowledge of otherness that cannot be learned even through Oankali sense organs. This helps him not only perceive human otherness as a real and legitimate way of experiencing the world but also adapt to and become more able in his current environment.

Akin also initially expresses fear and disgust in relation to other Oankali forms on the basis of their bodies and use or lack of use of sense organs. At a young age Akin is given a sensory image of an earlier "caterpillar"-like form of the Oankali that speaks "in images, in tactile, bioelectric, and bioluminescent signal, in pheromones, and in gestures" but whose "throat and mouth parts won't produce speech" and "is deaf" (262–263). To Akin, "this seemed terrible . . . Oankali forced to live in an ugly form that did not even allow them to hear or speak" (263). At this point Akin is unable to imagine experiences of those with different bodies and modes of perception. After his captivity, at which point he too feels not fully capable of communication, he is taken to the Oankali ship to meet one of the caterpillar creatures. Upon meeting the Akjai (unchanged, noninterspecies breeding) Oankali, Akin realizes that it is "as Oankali as Akin himself" (453). Akin does not learn about difference from this Oankali—he has already learned that from the humans—but about interdependence. Akin is afraid to merge with the Oankali because it would be an experience "greater than any blending Akin had perceived." He wonders how one can, in such a state of connection, "continue to think at all as [an] individual" (453). He wonders, "How did they not lose themselves?" (454). At first, this experience feels "like drowning" (454). Akin understands himself as a bounded individual body for whom the experience of merging is a threat to his sense of self. But he leaves the experience understanding that "no matter how closely he was joined to the . . . ooloi, he was aware of himself. . . . [S]omehow . . . he was still himself" (455). Akin takes away from his experience on the ship a willingness to give himself over to interdependence and the experiences and perspectives of others, as well as a new appreciation for the Akjai's body as "strong" and "versatile" rather than horrific (456).

Adulthood Rites ends with Akin successfully making the case for an Akjai (unchanged, noninterspecies breeding) human community on Mars. To be able to reach the point of changing his political perspective and making material social change, he has, like Lilith in *Dawn,* had to reconcile true acknowledgment of the experiential difference of others with a willingness to be affected by and even merged with others whose ways of being feel like a threat to his own or to his understandings of bodily health and integrity. Both of these ways of thinking come to him through a shift in his perceptions about ability and disability.

Jodahs, the ooloi protagonist of *Imago,* is also indoctrinated into the Oankali ideology of ability. It thinks of the human Mars colony as providing no future. It tells the humans, "If you want to see the future, take a look at some of the third- and fourth-generation constructs" who are "free of inherent flaws" (529, 530). By contrast, it thinks of the human plan to reproduce on Mars as a dead end: "They would suffer so. And in the end, it would all be for nothing" (530). Yet Jodahs's surprising metamorphosis, which reveals it to be becoming ooloi rather than male or female, puts its own body in a highly differently abled and potentially disabling position. Jodahs is perceived by the Oankali as a construct "gone wrong" (536). The worst outcome for Jodahs, according to the Oankali, would be if it were "flawed" in any way, if it did not have full control over itself:

A flawed natural genetic engineer—one who could distort or destroy with a touch. Nothing could save it from confinement on the ship. Perhaps it would even have to be physically altered to prevent it from functioning in any way as an ooloi. Perhaps it would be so dangerous that it would have to spend its existence in suspended animation, its body used by others for painless experimentation, its consciousness permanently shut off. (542)

The paradoxical logic, then, is that a differently abled body must be perfect and in control in every way so as to be safe and responsible to others. The only other choice is institutionalization and the Oankali equivalent of lobotomy. Yet Jodahs is not always completely in control. What keeps him from confinement to the ship is Nikanj's (in its role as same-sex parent) protection, guidance, and ability to think beyond what the Oankali would normally consider ethical or healthy. Nikanj changes its own perceptions of the world to make room for Jodahs. Jodahs understands this as learning to live with disability, if initially from a somewhat ableist perspective. "I was like a blind man," it says, "trampling what I could not see. . . . What I was missing was something I had never had—or at least, something I had never discovered" (569). Nikanj encourages Jodahs and its sibling, Aaor, who will also become ooloi: "Do what your bodies tell you is right. This is a new relationship. You'll be finding the way for others as well as for yourselves" (567). Nikanj's parental role leads it to deny what its own body tells it, to allow for the safety and well-being of its newly embodied offspring. It even goes so far at one point as to suggest Jodahs carry a machete for self-protection. This is a sign of adaptability and making live that is quite striking to the reader and disturbing to Nikanj's mates, for as the trilogy has stressed, the Oankali "had no history at all" of violence. "Violence . . . was against their flesh and bone, against every cell of them" (564).

Jodahs, it turns out, relies less on physical violence and more on physical desire. It can be in control of its body only when it has found mates. Thus, its safety and the safety of others is literally based on a sexually oriented inter-dependence. It spends most of the novel looking for human mates and fi-nally finding them in a colony of humans that have been reproducing among themselves and have been reproducing human illnesses and non-normative physical characteristics, including tumors and other skin growths. What Jodahs reads as a terrible and repulsive disability—not only the humans' disease of being human but also their "short" (i.e., pre-Oankali enhanced) lifespan—becomes essential in its ability to bond with them. First of all, it is Jodahs's body's queer (in the sense of being transgender from the reader's perspective and non-normative in its sexual behavior from both the reader's and characters' perspectives) and not entirely controlled reactions to its en-vironment that allow it to take on forms attractive to its chosen mates (fre-quently either male or female). And it is ultimately a mutual recognition based on nonnormative physical characteristics that allows Jodahs to be recognized and accepted by its new mates, Jesusa and Tomás, as itself—that is to say, as ooloi, construct, hybrid, and physically substantially and truly different from them. One of Tomás's early reactions upon seeing Jodahs in a less-controlled form (covered in scales after being away for too long from others who might stabilize it) makes Jodahs laugh. Tomás comments, "My god, man, you must frighten more people than we do!" (620). Similarly, Je-susa later identifies with Jodahs's Oankali sensory spots and tentacles via her own visible tumors, remarking, "Actually, I think mine are uglier" (648). Jesusa's and Tomás's experiences with their own disabled bodies allow them to accept and to some extent identify with Jodahs's ooloi gender identity, whereas other humans either insist the ooloi are male or find them some-what illegible creatures.

Jodahs as a person who must learn to deal with its body as something ultimately beyond current social categories, internal control, or individual agency is, like Akin, a rewriting of Lilith's story from a differently embodied position.[15] Jodahs is named after an Oankali who died helping the Mars emigration. His name memorializes a history that, like Lilith's, involves sac-rifice for a people one does not perceive as one's own. Additionally, "Jodahs," especially given Butler's use of biblical and mythological names throughout, recalls "Judas," thus suggesting a connection to betrayal in general, but also to Lilith more specifically, who constantly refers to herself as a "Judas goat" in *Dawn*. What are we to make of the fact that for the Lilith character to end up relatively happy, with a future of its/her own that to some extent it/she must be rewritten, stripped of her female, Black, and even human identity? One might read this as a call for a postidentity politics—a call to relinquish attachments to histories of victimization by moving beyond identity. I argue in the following section that Butler explicitly links possibility for ethical futures to histories of identity that are never fully escapable and that often rely on an identification with wounded pasts and modes of identification that might allow for nonideal but recognizably interdependent and more widely accessible futures.

Dissed Identities and Disabled Futures

The concept of the future has played a central role in contemporary critiques of liberal politics in both queer and disability studies. Many disability studies critics argue that liberalism as a social and political ideology is not sufficient for negotiating questions about the rights and citizenship status of those with disabilities.[16] Liberalism, as Hans S. Reinders points out in *The Future of the Disabled in a Liberal Society,* upholds "free choice and personal autonomy" as its central "procedural values" (35, 34). Reinders asks us to look elsewhere for the values we might rely on to make decisions in relation to those with disabilities and posits the experiences of parents of children with disabilities as models for ways to "sustain strategies of inclusion within a liberal model" (36). Good parenting here becomes a model for good citizenship. Seemingly this approach aligns with Butler's trilogy's use of a story of mothering to explore the ethics of reproduction. It also seemingly contradicts queer critiques of heteronormativity, such as Lee Edelman's analysis of popular ideologies of reproductive futurism that fetishize the child and present heteronormative family structures as core units for proper citizenship. Edelman's proposal is not to try to make a space for the homosexual within the order of reproductive futurism, but rather to embrace the potential of queer positionality, which he refers to as the space of "the inhuman" that will always be there no matter what bodies inhabit it (152). Thus, to some extent there are contradictions or at least differences between queer- and disability-oriented perspectives on family, citizenship, and identity-based politics.

Xenogenesis shows us how both of these seemingly contradictory approaches to political futures are necessary to think ethically about oppression in relation to bodily difference and minority identity. While focused on parenthood, and Black motherhood in particular, the trilogy complicates the parents as moral model paradigm by revealing the historically differential experiences of parenthood for different people, the power structures inherent in who gets to parent and how, and the ideologies of motherhood that reproduce certain forms of care but also limit mothers' autonomy in their ability to choose to care or not. Lilith as mother lies at what Edelman might term "the limits of intelligibility" and at the same time is a figure already conscripted into historical narratives of nonwhite womanhood and impure sexuality.

Regarding the latter, even in the far future, in outer space, and among a race of alien beings, she is read and reads herself as a version of the slave mother—the "Judas goat" woman of color whose sexuality is used in the service of forwarding white dominance, colonization, and the killing and exploitation of nonwhite bodies. The unavoidability of this narrative challenges models of reproductive futurism that figure the unprotected child as the model of and reason for a future. As a woman whose role as mother is coerced if not forced and who identifies with a genealogy of other such women, Lilith cannot fully perform reproductive futurity. Additionally, Butler's model of a speculative reproductive family unit presents desire and drive as part of coerced sexuality and motherhood *and* as part of the dynamic of care. After all, it is the irresistible chemical attractions between human and ooloi that enable Lilith's cooperation with the aliens, her pregnancy, and the later bonds developed between Jodahs and its mates. It is a desire that both reinforces a biological imperative for survival and figures a possible nonfuture for humanity itself.

In terms of Lilith's narrative representation as existing at the limits of intelligibility, the trilogy tells the story of a character without a story—a queer, Black heroine of science fiction and adventure narratives. This is not a narrative that has fully socially intelligible historical models.[17] In fact, Butler has to look to Lilith, the apocryphal first wife of Adam, to find a cultural figure analogous to Lilith Iyapo. Lilith in ancient Sumerian and Hebrew mythology was Adam's wife before Eve who refused his power over her and left him so she could bear a brood of demon children. She was thought to cause barrenness and to harm children. In some versions of the myth, she had to make a pact with God to see a number of her own children killed each day (Patai 296). The Lilith of mythology is a figure who is not entirely culturally legible, both in the sense that she is noncanonical and therefore unknown to many and in the sense that she is a nonidealized mother. As Michelle Osherow notes in her reading of Butler's use of the mythological Lilith, "We are culturally encouraged to maintain maternal idealizations to so great an extent that the mother we cannot idealize is unacknowledged" (77). In addition to the unintelligible complexity of the nonidealized mother, we also become aware, as Nadine Flagel suggests of Butler's *Kindred,* another novel that engages histories of woundedness and our complex relationships to them, that in our drive to access the experience of cultural traumas such as slavery, which is part of the history that formed Lilith's Black womanhood, we encounter a crisis of representation when we realize that we are relying on narrative and figurative accounts to gain access to the "real" of that formative wound.

Butler's use of the Lilith mythology recognizes both the necessary conscription to the narratives that precede us and the necessity for those conscripted to function at the limits of intelligibility. It reminds us that race and gender are themselves disabling and marginalizing and that women, and women of color in particular, often have to use others' texts for their social identities to exist at all. A sense of oneself as freer in relation to one's social identity (including but not limited to race, gender, and ability status) in the future relies on an understanding of one's social identity through the texts that construct that identity, and (particularly for those with minoritized identities) those texts are always authored by another. Butler's choice of Lilith as her model of the wounded history of nonpure (and therefore often read as nonwhite),[18] nonpassive, nonideal womanhood suggests not only a reappropriation of another's text but also a reliance on that text—oppressive aspects included—to make a space for the future. Butler's speculation is about survival into a future that does not rely on the logic of white reproductive futurity. The child is clearly not the fetishized symbol of the future for the mythical Lilith.[19] As James Bliss argues, "Black feminist theorizing anticipates or, rather, haunts the political imaginary articulated in [Edelman's] queer negativity." Bliss performs a racialized disgender–oriented reading of the relationship between discourses of Black feminist theory and queer antifuturity, arguing, "Neither Edelman nor his . . . critics seem willing or able to imagine a mode of reproduction that is not reproductive futurism; that is, Black reproduction. On this score, we can consider Hortense Spillers's seminal essay, 'Mama's Baby, Papa's Maybe: An American Grammar Book.' . . . On Spillers's reading, the father, the L/law, and the 'whole network of symbolic relations' that Edelman rejects in the name of the queer are foreclosed a priori for the Black" (85). Thus, we might read *Xenogenesis* as attending to Edelman's critique of the dominant model of the fantasy of futurity that is heteronormative, child-oriented, and exclusive of the very non-future-oriented jouissance that created and sustains it not as an embrace of queer negativity but as a speculative imagining of a futurity that includes the negative (in the sense of a priori foreclosed) modes of Black reproduction and its racialized disgendering of Black women and Black mothers. Butler mobilizes existing narratives of racial disgender—the interlocking and intersecting histories and experiences of Black, female, queer, disabled bodies—to offer speculative possibilities for reproduction that encompass multiple histories of wounded identity formation.

Ultimately Lilith's Black womanhood is represented in the novels not as a set of disabling wounded attachments but as an enabling set of understandings and strengths, an embodied racialized disgender, rooted in an inherited history of wounds.[20] Lilith's social "disabilities"—her womanhood, her

Blackness, her humanity—are identified with her resources for survival, passed down to Akin and, finally, Jodahs. "I could handle the intensity and complexity [of Oankali, human, and construct]," Jodahs tells us near the end of *Imago*. And it conceptualizes this complexity in terms of Lilith's natural hair: "The whole business was like Lilith's rounded black cloud of hair. Every strand seemed to go its own different way, bending, twisting, spiraling, angling. Yet together they formed a symmetrical, recognizable shape, and they were all attached to the same head" (742). Here, the complexities of human bodies and societies contradict the ideology of straightness, purity, and perfection reproduced by both the humans and Oankali in their various forms. Butler suggests that a future without pain is no future at all for many of us and that it is rather from our current and historical positions of racialized disgender that we may access survival and adaptability, not by somehow getting beyond or outside of these contexts and lived identities. The trilogy does not dismiss the possibilities for an ethics of accessibility or an ethics of medical bodily care in this context. But it does suggest that those ethics require that we not only accept but also expect and even, on some level, appreciate pain, disability, and painful memories as part of our temporal future, a future that looks neither to perfectibility of bodies nor to full redemption from our social and political pasts.

Coda

More That

Going Back for Our Bodies

Woolf

Midway through writing *Disabled Futures* I had a child whom I lost in the NICU after five hours. Woolf Erin Backer-Obourn was born at twenty-five weeks and five days at Strong Memorial Hospital in Rochester, New York. Woolf was delivered via an emergency and physically difficult cesarean but was healthy and viable if a bit weak and bruised up. I spent the first four hours after Woolf's birth high from painkillers and the idea that I was a parent, watching the snowfall, and looking forward to meeting my kid. I spent the next hour in the NICU as a team tried repeatedly to keep her vitals up after a routine blood transfusion punctured a frail artery in her leg. When that hour was over, despite my insistence they not stop trying (their initial, and I felt ableist, reasoning was that the internal bleeding might cause permanent disability even if she lived), they put her in my arms, and she died almost immediately.

Due to my age and solid, unionized state-employee coverage, my insurance had paid for a range of early genetic testing, which included finding out the sex chromosomes of the baby. Because of my background in disability studies I had been wary of genetic testing for fear it would inadvertently participate in a culture of preemptive decisions about the value of disabled life. Because of my background in queer theory and my own gender identifications (I am trans), I resist the idea of basing knowledge of a future human's gender identifications and ways of being in the world on their chromosomal makeup. Nevertheless, I did the tests. I chose to do them because

I thought it might help me prepare ways of accommodating this future person in the world. This feeling of needed preparation applied to the possibility of receiving any genetic information that might indicate the existence of a disability that I would want to learn more about or form communities in relation to. It also applied to the baby's interpellation into binary gender norms. Whether the child had biological and physical indicators that were intersex or that lined up along more traditionally defined male or female understandings of bodies, they would be read in certain ways by others, and those readings matter. I know that my reasons for identifying as transgender and nonbinary have as much to do with what I know about being raised as a white, middle-class American male or white, middle-class American female and the restrictions required in order to come into subjectivity as a boy or a girl with those intersecting identities in my particular social and cultural context, as they do with any inherent sense of a gendered self. These restrictions are socially dictated and ones whose influence and presence I could not avoid.

I also, and this is both hard and easy to admit, thought that I wanted a girl. What a strange thing to think after thirty-eight years of learning to resist the ideas of femaleness, girlhood, or gender itself as fixed or inherently meaningful concepts. But I couldn't imagine at the time how to address the male privilege my child would be given if read as a boy and then potentially a cisgender man. At the same time I told myself the baby was, of course, not yet gendered. Identified female at birth means nothing about the child's actual gender identifications, and these would remain as both open in my own mind and dictated by the child's race, socioeconomic status, ethnicity, nationality, disability status, and many other ways they would be inscripted into the world. I resolved to make as much space for sharing knowledge about and resisting co-optation into racialized disgendering as I could, knowing that I have internalized our cultural understandings of social identities in ways I cannot yet and may never access.

But then I lost her. Woolf never had a chance to self-identify or grow into and around and inside this world's strange and limited options for existing in a gendered way. She is frozen in time as a little baby girl because not giving her a gender truly did feel like denying her a personhood that had already been horrifically limited simply by the brevity of the time she got to be alive. This need to gender her in a binary way after death tells me more about the ways I have grown into gender and the ways it continues, as a structure, to dictate and determine who is fully human and who can be understood to be worthy of a future. The worthiness of living and having the right to a future is something I needed desperately to give Woolf, even as I know she (who could have been he or they or a pronoun I am yet to become familiar with) materially does not have one. At the time, it felt like the only recognizable lost future was one that envisioned her as culturally identifiably gendered.

Taking Bob Lujano to Church and Taking Students to Counseling

In November 2015, just before the first anniversary of Woolf's birth and death, Bob Lujano, one of the stars of *Murderball*—an MTV-produced film about a wheelchair rugby team that received attention for its portrayal of men with physical disabilities as tough, (hetero)sexual, and sometimes violent and thus subverted many stereotypes of disabled masculinity as passive, weak, or impotent—came to give a talk at my college. I was suspicious, I'll be honest. The idea of having a representative from this film that in many ways tries to prove the full humanity of its disabled players via hypernormative enactments of cis masculinity made me uncomfortable. It felt as if it worked against the arguments I was trying to make about the value of racialized disgender, in that it seemed to want to erase the complexities of everyone's masculinity in favor of showing that "anyone" (i.e., white, cis, straight, physically disabled men) can still be masculine in a way that allows them access to true manhood and therefore to full personhood.

Contrary to my preconceptions, I met a gentle and thoughtful man who, instead of our original plan to see the Erie Canal and go to lunch, wanted me to drive him to church, specifically to St. Mary's Roman Catholic Church in Holley, New York. I learned that Bob is both a practicing Catholic and a church tourist. Luckily, St. Mary's had an accessible entrance, the door was open, and the pews and sanctuary were empty. I wandered around looking at stained glass and crosses, while Bob prayed and took pictures. Afterward, as I was sitting in Bob's engaging talk about his work with the Lakeshore Organization, a nonprofit that promotes accessibility to a wide range of sports for people with disabilities, I reflected on my earlier assumptions and prejudices. I still think that cis men of any race and disability statuses enacting a certain kind of masculinity will continue to read to me as participating in a set of unnecessary and deeply ingrained cultural violences. But I also thought, How different really is my need to mourn Woolf as a girl child from performative enactments of masculinity in wheelchair rugby? How different is my need to establish a queer transmasculinity that is legible to others from *Murderball*'s use of hypermasculine players to establish humanity within gender norms? Isn't this all to some extent racialized disgender as I have been conceiving of it?

In wheelchair rugby, which is predominantly a male sport, women can play on men's teams and are "balanced" into those teams using the same point system of functional characteristic ratings used to create parity of athletic ability on each team. The rating system moves from 0.5 for least functional ability to 3.5 for most functional ability for each player, with a total of 8 points on the court at any one time. The International Wheelchair Rugby website explains, "Functional classification systems ensure that athletes with a combination of impaired or absent upper and lower limb movement have an opportunity to play the sport and that the strategies and skills of competing teams and athletes, rather than the amount of movement of the athletes, are the factors determining success in competition." The idea is that the rating system makes the game accessible to everyone, while acknowledging that players' bodies differ and affect the ways they participate in the game. Having a woman on a team allows that team an extra 0.5 points, functionally presenting women as 0.5 points less able-bodied than male players with the same functional classification. There is no rating for nonbinary or agender people, and I was unable find on the site what defined "male" and "female" as such in this schema. That half-point is not located on the female player herself. That is, it is not part of her functional characteristic rating but transfers to her team space, potentially allowing a more able-bodied male player to participate than would otherwise fit into the total point allowance. There was a time when my feminist-influenced politics would have recoiled from this system, which signifies women as more disabled than men. After working on this project, however, I think that maybe the transparency of gender and physical disability having assigned points on the wheelchair rugby court is as close to a schematic and honest a way as any to think about the levels of disability created by racism, ableism, athletic competition, and socialization of bodies along gendered lines. If, as I have argued, racialized gender is a kind of disability, then this point system reflects other ways women's bodies have been disabled and in so doing actually makes gender diversity in the game more desirable and likely to occur.

I want to juxtapose this reading of wheelchair rugby against the experience of encouraging a former student to seek mental health support and register with the Office for Students with Disabilities. Let me acknowledge first that while race plays a huge role in how professional and amateur athletics function in the United States, and while the sports industry is deeply embedded in who has access to what kinds of resources and futures as sorted particularly along racial and class lines, and while our dominant narratives of racialized disgender often figure Black Americans in particular as hyperableist in relation to sports that make primarily white people a great deal of money, there is no discussion on the wheelchair rugby site about how points might work along lines of racial identity. This might be understood as one way that the category of disability potentially includes "all" bodies—

making racial difference less meaningful in a shared community of disability. It might simply be a replication of ways racism and binary sexism/transexclusion work on a broader cultural level at our current historical moment—segregating de facto by race and de jure by gender. I would suggest that it is also a nonrecognition of the ways whiteness remains in play in the gendering of wheelchair rugby's players. The bodies that can reclaim a disabled gender via this sport need to have access to (1) money or insurance coverage for sports chairs; (2) time and mobility to play a sport that requires practice time and travel; and (3) the capacity, as Jasbir Puar might put it, that comes with not being part of an already debilitated population and thus increased likelihood of understanding playing a competitive sport as a reclaiming of access to a body and community.[1] That is not to say that all wheelchair rugby players are white but to say that racism is most certainly at work in the kinds of masculinity that are constructed through the culture of the sport, at least as represented by *Murderball*, and that racism is certainly at work in terms of who has access to adaptive sports.

At the time of Lujano's visit I was not thinking about how whiteness was at play in our conversations about *Murderball* or the benefits of adaptive sports programs. Maybe because Lujano is Latino. But more likely because he didn't talk about his racial identity. At all. And there is nothing in any of his online bios or in the reviews of his books about how growing up Latino in Kansas might have affected his relationship to gender or disability. Though he refers to his father as the "first Hispanic quarterback in an all-white high school" and how sports were the one thing he could bond with his father about, there is little exploration of how their shared racial and gender identities impacted their relation to bodies, and how that translated into Bob's investments in adaptive athletics (Lujano 3). I am sure Lujano has stories beyond the "rare blood disease" that figures at the center of popular narratives of Lujano's journey. I would argue that racialized disgender structured Lujano's entire visit to my campus but a dominant association between whiteness and successful programs by and for men with physical disabilities interrupted a conversation that might have illuminated those intersections more fully.

Several months later I was sitting with a Black student with whom I was meeting primarily to discuss his experience of racism on campus. He shared with me how much trouble he had getting to class and getting access to medication for his depression. This student explained to me that he was having trouble not only going to counseling but also registering with the Office for Students with Disabilities, though both of those resources might have helped him to return to class after feeling threatened and marginalized in his dorm. He told me that his family would not approve and that they had advised him as a Black male student not to participate in anything that might add to his experience of marginalization. As I tried to give him the disability rights pep talk—that disability is a cultural construct as well as a social identity that many people claim and take pride in, that accessibility is a right for every student, and that to feel ashamed of disability or illness can perpetuate one's victimization—I realized there was no good reason he should listen to me, this white, queer authority figure who had no solution for the ways that his Blackness and masculinity had been shaped by discourses of disability that were not addressed at all in the ways our campus offered accessibility services. The worst part, he told me, was that he could not get to lacrosse practice, the one place he felt part of a community and in positive relation to his body.

Marking Wounds

Not long after Lujano's visit, I was reworking a portion of what became Chapter 3 of this book on breast cancer and racialized disgender for the annual Modern Language Association conference. In an attempt to learn more about current narratives around breast cancer, I attended a grand rounds lecture at Strong Memorial Hospital in Rochester, New York, hosted by the chief of Surgical Oncology and director of Comprehensive Breast Care.[2] The presentation overlapped histories of women's rights and breast cancer treatments, implying that social identity movements focused on women as a political group and the attention and money given to breast cancer treatments are directly related. The talk ended with a section on the "Angelina Jolie effect"—a phrase used to describe the recent increase in women (or at least people read by the medical industry as women) with breast cancer asking to get double mastectomies even if their oncologist does not deem it necessary, presumably because that choice was popularized by the actress Angelina Jolie. The response from oncologists, or at least those present at this grand rounds, seemed to be that these requests are creating unnecessary surgical procedures. And yet, since there is always a chance of recurrence of breast cancer, it was hard to read the professional resistance as not a little bit about a culturally based assumption that women would rather lose part of or one breast than all of both. I cannot imagine this is not partially a projection of cisnormative disgendered ideals that perceive "real" breasts as constitutive of womanhood—an aspect of disgender that women and people of other genders might have a range of personal relations to and feelings about.

Just after I gave that MLA paper, a friend and colleague shared with me that she had had breast cancer and two mastectomies during the time that I was in my most distracted stage of mourning for Woolf. In return, I shared a working version of Chapter 3 with her, and she wrote her story into the margins. Things she had not yet voiced about her experiences with diagnosis and surgery and her personal responses were inserted as comments in the Word document I had sent her. It was one of the most beautiful responses I have ever had to anything I have written, and it helped me become aware of some of what was missing in my critiques of reconstructive surgery. This included in particular her statement about being visibly wounded after her mastectomy. She wrote:

> I was confident that I didn't want to stay unreconstructed. I had seen photos of unreconstructed mastectomy scars and they looked horrific to me . . . like a wound. I didn't want to see a giant wound every day. I'm sure that this is because of my desire to pass as normal in public settings. I remember saying to the plastic surgeon that I didn't want much, only to wear a swimsuit and feel "normal" and wear my clothes and feel "normal." I think some of it might be fear of being seen in a locker room, but the socially constructed woman that I am really wanted to put something in that place.

I thought about these comments a great deal while revising Chapter 3. They were a reminder to me that an important part of the concept of racialized disgender is recognizing that it is always already there. And that while there might be political value to acknowledging and sharing wounds in safe spaces, there is no getting outside our gendered reality no matter how much we might feel the gender options available to us do not fit personally, ethically, or politically. To carry a minority social identity, including womanhood, is already to be marked as vulnerable. To ask someone to increase that vulnerability by wearing it more publically and in unsafe spaces could translate to asking someone to process trauma with less safe space rather than more. Not to mention that as much as I and other masculine-of-center folks might disidentify with and/or feel dysphoric in relation to body parts like breasts, so too might feminine-of-center folks feel attached to them. One response to the body is no more or less dictated by racial, class, national, and cultural history and the racialized disgendering that happens from and in those spaces than the other.

What provoked this friend to originally share her experience was in part my tattoos. I covered both arms after Woolf's death as part of my own mourning process. It was a way of making space on my body for grief and of creating my own visible record of what were largely invisible wounds. While my friend did want reconstructive surgery, she did not want to pretend nothing had happened or to act like the reconstructed tissue was the same as the breasts she had had before surgery. Instead of the nipple tattoos that were recommended to her, she wanted something of her own choosing and came to me for advice about tattoo studios, artists, and design. I ended up recommending and then going with her to the same studio where I had had Woolf's name and birthday carved into my wrist a little over a year earlier. It was a local studio owned by a woman and employing three of my favorite female-identified artists. Both my friend and I, then, were invested in creating visible records of our woundedness by acts of choice and in a nonmedical community of people who are practiced in recording pain and aesthetically rebuilding bodies. To be forced to identify with a wound or a wounded self can truly be traumatic. Part of becoming more aware of patterns and individual experiences of racialized disgender has to be some agency over where and how we mark that woundedness as well as a broader cultural recognition of the knowledges that come from it. My friend chose to mark her wounds not with a scar or with a simulacrum of nipples she knew would feel nothing like her nipples, but with an image of the flowers that grew in the place she went for peace amid trauma. Thus she is marked not just by the history of her trauma but also by her agential relationship to it. She has also become great friends with that tattoo artist, who I imagine has become better at listening to the experiences of her clients through knowing my friend.

Racially Disgendered Reproduction: Testosterone and Estrogen in the Twenty-First Century

A little more than a year after Woolf's death, I reconnected with someone I had known in the past who also identifies as a nonbinary trans person and who had been on testosterone for about a year and was at the time considering top surgery. This person was to become my partner and the person with whom I would have another child, but more on that to come. My immediate emotional response to the changes in this person's face and voice, the idea of them losing their breasts, was sadness and loss. Though this reaction passed very quickly, it was surprising to me as a queer and trans person, as someone who thinks of themselves as an activist and ally for other queer and trans people, and as a person for whom testosterone and surgery are far from out of the question. Particularly because it did not line up with ways I think of and want to think of myself, I needed to register that it appeared and think about the possible reasons why. I thought it might have been about losing the time since I had last known them (we'd been out of touch for years), missing parts of their transition, the sense of loss that comes with knowing one could always be closer to the people one loves dearly and that life and choices keep us disconnected as we grow in other spaces. I also thought it might be about my own inability to transition in any physical way, because in trying to get pregnant again after losing Woolf I was back at the fertility clinic rotating every few months through another IVF round, stuffing myself with estrogen and progesterone, and still keeping silent at that time about my identification as transgender in medical settings for fear that they might no longer consider me worth supporting or that my insurance would stop covering my IVF. I also thought maybe it was because I have experienced so much hatred against women's bodies, and when they seemingly disappear I feel on some level it is the violence of the world wanting to erase women, even when I know it is a real and meaningful personal choice that I make every day through my out identification as a transmasculine person, which has resulted in no part of myself or gender history having disappeared. If anything, I and my gender and its history have more room to exist.

The thought that has stayed with me the longest, and one that still resonates around my frustrations with gender embodiment is that, as this person whom I love leaves a position of being socially (mis)read as a woman, I will feel left behind as Woolf was. This makes very little sense, equating myself to my dead child or death with transitioning. I most certainly do not mean to imply in any way that anyone dies when they transition. Let me try to explain. The emotional response is to this feeling that through our practices of cultural disgenderment, the girls all get left behind and structurally there is no world for them to fully inhabit. "Leaving the girl behind" was originally coined in a discussion with my partner in relation to a line from Dominique Christina's spoken-word poem, "Star Gazer," which is about reclaiming a relation to her body through consensual sex after a history of molestation. The line is "Glory be to the girl who goes back for her body." My partner said to me once, "Being on T made me feel like I could go back for my body." While Christina doesn't talk about "leaving the girl behind," in our conversation about her poem we began to use it as shorthand for what happens to girls through molestation, rape, the threat of rape, and the series of learned exclusions and body shaming that lead them to have to leave their relation to their bodies behind. Going back, as Christina's poem makes clear, can happen through a reclamation of the self through and not in spite of a history of racial disgenderment. Glory indeed be to the girl (or boy or nonbinary or trans or agender or gender-nonconforming person) who goes back. And when we go back, what knowledge do we take from the girl? And in what ways do we move toward a world that did not leave the girl behind? Since my partner and Christina have helped me to coin this phrase, I have come to live with it almost every day as shorthand for everything I write about in this Coda and every network and structure of feelings attached to what I write here. I know I do not want to be a part of leaving the girl behind. Even if she was created out of a sense of herself not being enough reason for love and happiness. Even if to be left behind is part of what creates girl- and womanhood. And even if girlhood itself as I experienced it was based on a white supremacist racialized disgendering that framed me as a white girl even as it erased the girlhoods of many women of color. All the more reason to make sure the girl does not get left behind. Identifying as trans is not leaving her behind. Changing my name is not leaving her behind. Even if/when I physically transition enough to look like I have left her behind, I can never leave her. The girl remains essential.

But what makes the girl? Is it, in fact, a history of disablement, violence, lack of access? Is it only a racialized, classed, and culturally dictated set of limitations on who can be what and who is assigned meaning how? And what is it that makes me read my experience of infertility and child loss through a gendered rather than a disability lens? After all, my medically female sexed/gendered body was impaired in that it would not produce a child without medical intervention and did not carry the child it did produce full term. And my personally and socially masculine gendered body is impaired in that it cannot create sperm to impregnate someone else. Moreover, what makes me read them through a gender rather than a racial lens? Because of my race, socioeconomic position, and nationality as a citizen of a first world country, and because of the cultural capital I carry via my profession and rank, which come directly from my educational opportunities and therefore from my race, socioeconomic class, and nationality, I have access to a medical industry that simultaneously erases me and makes ableist forms of reproduction accessible—in terms of both ridding me of the impairment of infertility and not being read socially as a disabled person. Was my use of the fertility clinic subversive as an often functionally single queer who uses it to their advantage? Or by participating in it was I accepting and reinforcing an ableist, hetero- and homonormative, white supremacist, and binary system? Am I participating in reproductive and rehabilitative models of futurity that violently racially disgender bodies as they reproduce their idealized versions of social reality? If I gave up trying to get pregnant and started taking T and had top surgery would I also be reinforcing medical models of transition and rehabilitative gender, even if I did not feel that way about my own identity? When am I trying to go back for the bodies of girls that I have felt pressured to leave behind—most prominently but far from exclusively Woolf's and mine? And when am I perpetuating a world that causes violence to all girls?

Perhaps this is why the chief of oncology did not want women to jump to double mastectomies. Maybe she wanted them to love their breasts more than it appeared such a decision would indicate. Maybe she wanted to protect breast cancer patients from a reconstructive surgery in which they would lie unconscious in a room with mostly male plastic surgeons who ask techs and nurses for their opinions on the aesthetics of the breasts they are making.[3] Maybe she read Audre Lorde describe her right breast as a lost, important "area of feeling and pleasure" (43). And maybe this is why this oncologist also became one of the primary local providers for FTM top surgeries. Yes, the same doctor who gave the lecture on feminism and breast cancer treatment does top surgery and was the doctor to whom my partner was originally referred. Maybe she needed to offer a feminist intervention into racially disgendered embodiment after an indoctrination to a field that did not appreciate the connections between feminist activism and women's health.

Over the course of writing this book, several queers, including me, have been in complicated relationships to one another and complicated relationships to our gender identities and have all been taking hormones in adulthood. Though the reasons are distinct and complex, including but not limited to fertility, gender identity, long-term health, and mental and emotional stability, we were all reliant on hospitals, medical professionals, insurance companies, and other people's ideas about what it means to live as a healthy gendered person in this world. The same is true for my friend who had breast cancer and now takes the estrogen blocker Tamoxifen.

To transition, to remain, to become closer in some affective way to what we are already are, to be physically able bodied, to be normal, to be queer, to contribute to reproductive futurity, to resist the fixity of a future dictated to us as racially disgendered people and as diagnosed bodies—decisions to inject and ingest sex hormones exogenously or medications designed to change the uptake of endogenously produced sex hormones relate to all of these things. As Paul Preciado has written in relation to his use of testosterone in our current biopolitical era, which he terms a "pharmacopornographic society," "The somato-political context of the body's technopolitical production seems dominated by a series of new technologies of the body (biotechnology, surgery, endocrinology, genetic engineering, etc.)" (77). In such an era, "the consumption of testosterone, like that of estrogen and progesterone . . . do[es] not depend on any ideal cultural constructions of gender that would come to influence the way we act and think." In such an era, "everything is a matter of doses, of melting and crystallization points, of the rotary power of the molecule, of regularity, of milligrams, of form and mode of administration, of habit, of praxis" (142). As Preciado's book makes clear, the forms of racialized disgender that have historically constructed political subjectivities are not undone so much as redone at the molecular level in an era of medicalization and hormone administration.

The years of writing this book have been years living gender as disability and as medical diagnosis in ways both limiting and possibility creating. I know lesbians taking T and trans men carrying children, and these sets of knowledge cut across and bring color to my knowledge of the limiting narratives of futurity that often link gender, health, body normativity, and fertility. Yet these have also been years of watching the effects of implicitly and, in the era of the Donald Trump presidency, often explicitly telling people that the only lives worth protecting the futures of are those of white, able-bodied, cis men or those who exist to support white, able-bodied, cis men. Sick and disabled people, lesbians, trans people, intersex people, people who do not parent, people who reproduce or care for people in a way that might not produce normative bodies, all are surviving against expectations of no future and in so doing are creating disabled futures that might hold enough space for us to truly live well. Ableism, racism, binary gender models, and heteronormativity harm us all—doctors, white people, cis people, men, those of us read as able-bodied and cognitively normative included. And thus we all might participate in creating more disabled space to match our racially disgendered selves, as we build futures counter to those that currently limit us so violently.

Allyship, Political Climate, and Possibility

Just before I signed the contract for this book, my second child was born. Also early, also at Strong Hospital, also in the NICU. My partner and I lived there with them for seventy-two days, and then we all went home together. Seventy-two days of medical monitoring and hoping for "normalcy." Seventy-two days of overhearing other parents be told about their child's disabilities. Seventy-two days of being told about the high risks of visual impairments, asthma, developmental disabilities. Seventy-two days of just really, really wanting this baby to live.

As I had hoped to do more faithfully with Woolf, we are not gendering this baby, and the ease with which they can exist as a perfect human without an assigned gender reinforces to me that my need to give Woolf a narrative of subjective legibility had everything to do with the fear of lost possibility and lost life, not of gender itself. The experience of not assigning our baby a gender has also illuminated so many ways that gender circulates as well as misunderstandings of the ways it circulates. One friend asked how our child would ever learn about male privilege and the oppression of women if we did not gender them. What I heard her saying was "If they don't internalize one of those binary identities, they can't know what gender privilege and oppression mean." I want to suggest through the readings I have offered here that they can and will, and not just because gender norming will happen to them despite our efforts to let them self-identify. Being thrown back into/having the great privilege of access to a NICU at a major medical research institute has left me even more ambivalent about my relationship to the medical industry than when I began this book. In the NICU, one baby was killed and one baby was made to live. Both were gendered, one against my will and the other with my gratitude for the ways it recognized her as human. In the NICU, my partner and I were misgendered on a daily basis and also treated like white, middle-class, professional people with whom the care of their baby could be openly and respectfully discussed. The fact of being there in many ways negated social segregations by race, religion, and geographic background—if a baby needed intensive care, it went to the NICU, despite socioeconomic status and other cultural and identity markers. But in many other ways, the racial disgendering of babies was so clearly legible—for example, we were told by more than one nurse that Black girl babies were the strongest and did the best and white boy babies struggled the most, thereby replicating cultural ideologies discussed in this book around strong Black womanhood and white male fragility. The racial identity of our baby was also discussed repeatedly by the staff, who did not have access to information about our donor. It occurred to me that an aspect of white privilege I had not before considered is that the whiteness of my baby, if the baby was presumed to be white, would not be so consistently remarked on. And if my partner and I appeared to be a cisgendered, straight couple, most likely that would have been the assumption.

It is far from the case that only my stay in the NICU was experienced through raced, gendered, and medicalized lenses. My identity as a queer person inflects my readings throughout this text, as does my current status as able bodied. And, most certainly, this book as a whole comes through an inevitably white lens. I have tried throughout the chapters to consider how nonwhite racial and non-Christian and non-Anglo ethnic identities might affect not only how someone reads gender and disability as mutually constitutive but also how my own whiteness limits the ways that I experience them as mutually constitutive. White privilege does not change the fact that Black, Indigenous, Latino/a/x, and Asian cis womanhood and cis manhood, trans womanhood and trans manhood, nonbinary, and agender identities have also been constituted and reinforced by disability in multiple senses, including restricted access to citizenship, public space, and power; hyper- and desexualization; medical intervention, institutionalization, violence perpetrated and supported by the state and medical institutions; and narratives of impairment and incapacity based in dehumanizing assumptions about nonwhite bodies and minds. It does change what I can perceive and interpret about the modes of that constitution and reinforcement. I come to the work of this book knowing that it is the intersections with racial whiteness—what I call my "sighted spots," where because of privilege I am not perceiving something, that are perhaps the most ubiquitous, the most limiting, and the most in need of articulation.

Rather than resting in a space of acknowledgment of our limitations based on social privilege, what I would like to use this book and its interrogations of racialized disgender to propose is that we build more radical models for allyship. If we all work to become more aware of our histories of racial disgenderment, we might build more roads into a shared understanding of the ways that power and oppression impact and disable all of us. My suggestion is emphatically not that we lose the specificities of those histories or the ways they are individually lived and embodied. In fact, I would hope that a raised awareness around racialized disgender would help those specificities and the knowledges they create become more subtle, complex, and broadly recognized. In addition to this improved knowledge base around lived identity and structures of oppression, what I think such an approach can offer is a more radical form of inclusion, one that does not ask anyone to assimilate to a norm but is rather available for change and adaptability to the new knowledges that are produced from multiple positionalities. In providing a structure for more radical inclusion, I also believe it can help us work toward improved and more effective allyship. For example, following this model, I want not only to become a better ally to people of color as a white person, though I do want that. I also want to become a better ally to other trans people, including trans people of color. I want to become a better ally to women, even as I disidentify with womanhood as someone constructed within it but for whom that does not fit. I want to become a better ally to people with disabilities and to perceive with politically useful clarity how I am both included and not included in that designation. And I want to be able to build these structures of allyship through a knowledge gained not only through my positions of marginalization but also through a knowledge of what I have lost through my constitution as a white and highly capacitated subject. I want to better understand the community I do not have, the bodily and emotional restrictions I have inherited, the trauma I have caused and covered in my own psyche. I want to better understand how my racially disgendered body has been constituted, capacitated, disabled, and wounded through racial and racist systems as well so that I can also be a better ally to other white people.

The 2016 election of Donald Trump to the presidency of the United States prompted many discussions about wounded whiteness and the feelings of rural and poor marginalization that led to Trump's victory. As more research has been done, this narrative has shifted from an argument that the marginalized, non-college-educated, and angry poor elected Trump because they believed he could help them gain economic and political power to an argument that white middle-class people who fear losing their privilege voted for Trump to help keep white supremacy intact. Diana C. Mutz, a political scientist at the University of Pennsylvania, has recently argued, "The 2016 election was a result of anxiety about dominant groups' future status rather than a result of being overlooked in the past." Specifically she argues that white Americans feel threatened by losing global economic power to China and by losing dominant racial status to other racial groups in the United States. "When confronted with evidence of racial progress," Mutz argues, "whites feel threatened and experience lower levels of self-worth relative to a control group. They also perceive greater antiwhite bias as a means of regaining those lost feelings of self-worth" (E4331). This resonates with my readings of representations of white male disability and rehabilitation in a post–civil rights area, detailed in Chapter 1. If we continue to perceive white cis manhood as disabled by the empowerment of women, queer people, and people of color, we find ourselves in a political situation that is, in fact, to use a common Trump figuration, "us versus them." Another way of approaching what appears to be a shift not away from but very much toward identity-based politics in the United States is to offer up the framework of understanding how we are all disabled by dominant power. What if, rather than countering the sexism and racism of the Trump administration with a Women's March, which while slowly becoming more intersectional still works out of what I understand as a limiting identity-based model, we built a politics around a "What We Can Learn from People Constructed as Women's Movement." I do not mean this tongue-in-cheek. What would a politics of knowledge embedded in identity experience versus a politics of identity as fixed subjecthood and associated with specific bodies look like? If, as I suggest in Chapter 1, there is a sense of wounded white manhood in circulation in dominant cultural narratives, rather than embracing marginalized disability as the identity that can allow white people to the multicultural table, we can use the insights of disability theory to think about not only the multiple ways that disability, gender, and race intersect to construct all of our social identities but also the ways that disabled identities can be sources of knowledge and insight in changing our social and political models to accommodate all of us. What if our politics were about self-knowledge, about mining our marginalized and dominant positions for an understanding of oppression and intersectionality, and about recognizing that there is a need for and a space for everyone's work to raise our awareness of the ways we are all impacted and disabled by power? This would necessarily lead to and require a huge restructuring of power, and it may feel like an unrealistic and idealistic way to end this text. Nevertheless, I feel the need to end not with yet another critique, something academics are at no loss for, but rather with a sense of real possibility.

Drawing on a recent article by Keguro Macharia, I want to end with a suggestion not of an overarching solution to oppression and the violences of the power structures in which we live, but of a way of approaching our work in relation to them that promotes a deep relationality with our distinct pasts, our wounds, our privileges, our limitations, and our, I believe, deeply shared desire to be in community with each other in some form or another. Macharia uses the concept of "the erotic" and "pleasantness" in Audre Lorde and Samuel Delany, respectively, to forward a third path that is not simply criticism (a "not this") nor a full solution ("not this, but that") but instead a way of living in complex relation to both deeply needed critique and livability of a present with hope for a sustainable future. He calls this "not this, more that"—an approach that can provide needed knowledge about the problems with the systems we currently inhabit as well as things we can do on the ground to improve our present and our relation to that knowledge, "a present quotidian that extends into a desired future, a 'more that' we claim and practice" (n.p.).

I, too, want to end with not only the "not this" that has emerged through readings of limiting racialized disgender but also a "more that" of how that knowledge can position us in relation to our disabled futures. Part of the work of building disabled futures is to build more space for everyone to live their socially constructed and very real and truly at times disabling identities without fear. It is to resist every discourse that says such spaces do not matter. I have tried to structure this Coda and the book as a whole as a series of attempts to expand my own awareness from various points of contraction, experienced and read, and to build structures of allyship from them. My hope is that the readings in this book offer a set of tools to use in a movement toward accessible futures, in which we feel valued and can exist in deliberate, critical, and desired relation to one another. This may be a radically different kind of future from any we are imagining in our current social and political landscape, and it may entail loss, but it will let us carry our wounded and resistant and resilient selves and it is one that many of us work to build in small but important ways every day.

Notes

INTRODUCTION

1. I combine sexism, cissexism, and heteronormativity because they are all needed to replicate normative binary gender assumptions and ideologies. While this book argues that ableism and racism are also needed for this practice, they are less clearly and directly linked. In the remainder of this Introduction, I use "(cis)sexism" to encompass the ways that sexism, transphobia/cissexism, and homophobia/heteronormativity mutually constitute a normative binary gender that privileges cisgender masculine-conforming men and oppresses all other gender identities.

2. For a discussion of and links to many of these illustrations, see Froehle, "The Evolution of an Accidental Meme."

3. I use the term "bodymind" here to reference the concept in disability studies that the mental, physical, emotional, and spiritual aspects of the self are one integrated unit and to avoid privileging certain kinds of disabilities and impairments over others. For a discussion of the origin of the term, see Price, "The Bodymind Problem."

4. My favorite variation on Froehle's illustration is one drawn by Angus McGuire, with figures who appear to be Black males, or rather people of color who are masculine presenting. Like Froehle's original, they are of differing heights—the tallest one has seven boxes, the medium-height figure has one, and the shortest figure is standing in a hole. The caption reads: "reality." This does strike me as our current reality in several ways: we cannot capture racial inequity using embodied metaphors—in general, female or femme-presenting persons are left out, though the concept of equity has a long history in feminist thought, and the histories of systemic violence and exclusion have constructed an environment in which not only does the person who could make the best use of the box not have one, but even if he gained access to one, because of the contextual inequity surrounding him, it would not help.

5. For a discussion of the term "racialized gender" and the ways gender is always a racializing construction, see Boris; Snorton. I also choose the prefix "dis" as a reference to José Esteban Muñoz's term "disidentification." Just as Muñoz's disidentification is neither an assimilation to dominant narratives nor a counter-identification, but a potentially subversive recircuiting of dominant narratives of identity, racialized disgender is neither an assimilation to dominant racial or gender identities nor a complete rejection of or removal from dominant narratives of race and gender, but rather a way of thinking about the complex and disabling ways that race and gender intersect with each other and with our other social identities. Muñoz also describes disidentification as a "survival strategy" in that one must exist within dominant narratives of identity whether or not those narratives line up with one's sense of themselves. Racialized disgender is also a survival strategy. We are all existing within dominant discourses of race and gender and become legible to others within them, whether or not we perceive ourselves in them or feel they are working for our safety and freedom. While disgender is a relationship and intersection that applies to all bodies, including trans, intersex, nonbinary, agender, and other non-cis identities, I do like the fact that it is only one letter in the English alphabetic sequence off from "cisgender," thus highlighting that it is often via assumptions around a sameness between one's assigned gender and one's experience of gender that a great deal of disablement may occur.

6. One might argue that when I am speaking of disability as the systemic harm done to some bodies along lines of social identity and political/geographic location, I am actually speaking of debility. As Jasbir Puar defines it, "debilitation" is distinct from "disablement" because "[debilitation] foregrounds the slow wearing down of populations instead of the event of becoming disabled" (*Right to Maim* xiv). While this distinction is important for Puar's argument, I opt to keep "disability" as a central term, in an effort to highlight not the distinction between the violence of debility as an act and the pride of disability identity but the violence in the creation of ALL social identity positions as well as the possibility for a pride in the knowledge gained from knowing that violence.

7. See Bilge; Puar, "I Would Rather Be a Cyborg"; and Nash, "Institutionalizing the Margins."

8. For a detailed discussion of the limitations and critiques of intersectionality, see Nash, "Re-thinking Intersectionality," "'Home Truths' on Intersectionality," "Practicing Love," "Feminist Originalism," and "Intersectionality and Its Discontents." Even as Nash critiques many uses and limitations of intersectionality, she also argues that there is value in intersectionality's "capacity to be mobilized to describe structure, subjectivity, identity, marginalization, multiple-marginalization, oppression and agency at once" (Falcón and Nash 4). For book-length discussions of the history of the concept and defenses for its continued importance, see Collins and Bilge; May; Hancock; and Carastathis.

9. As May and Ferri note, "By definitively asserting that women are *not* disabled by their sex, many feminists have simply replaced one subject-object dualism (male vs. female) with another: woman vs. disability" (120).

10. I am not framing intersectionality here as a fantasy of perfecting work around identity and justice but rather as a way of thinking and a series of questions that continue to produce better understandings of and ways of talking about collaborative and dynamic resistance to a power structure invested in divisiveness and single-axis thinking.

11. For a clear articulation of this critique from the early 1990s, see Wendy Brown, "Wounded Attachments." Brown's connection between a politics based in social identity and an attachment to suffering continues to be echoed by critics of identity politics and the concept of intersectionality. For example, Jennifer C. Nash's recent work on "love-politics" is framed as "eschew[ing] the wounded subject that lies at the heart of identity politics" ("Practicing Love" 18).

12. I take the term "epistemic privilege" from Paula Moya's "Chicana Feminism and Postmodern Theory," where she formulates what she terms "the latent epistemic privilege of the oppressed" (471). As Moya explains in a footnote: "Epistemic privilege refers to a special advantage with respect to acquiring knowledge about how fundamental aspects of our society (such as race, class, gender, and sexuality) operate to sustain matrices of power. The key to claiming epistemic privilege for people who have been oppressed in a particular way stems from an acknowledgement that they have experiences—experiences that people who are not oppressed usually lack—that can provide them with information we all need to understand how hierarchies of race, class, gender, and sexuality operate to uphold existing regimes of power in our society" (471).

13. As Alyson Patsavas argues, "When we recognize the leakiness of pain, we can begin to conceptualize bodies, desires, and experiences (painful, shared, and otherwise) within a system of connectivity" (214).

14. Crenshaw notes that her investment is both to "reveal how Black women are theoretically erased" and to draw out the "theoretical limitations" more broadly of feminist and antiracist critiques, such that "placing those who are currently marginalized in the center" expands "potential collective action" (139, 167).

15. See Kafer; Siebers; and Wendell. Throughout this text, I use the plural "they/them/their" to refer to any single person whose gender identity is unknown to recognize the range of possible gender identities people have and to avoid the implication that everyone uses "he" or "she" pronouns.

16. I am not alone in working on coalitional intersectional studies of race, gender, and dis/ability. Schalk notes, "Disability studies has a long history of borrowing from work in other fields and civil rights movements, but this borrowing tends to emphasize the difference or exceptionality of disability rather than its similarities or overlap—the places where disidentification across/between/among minoritarian subjects could occur" to form a "coalitional politics" of "minoritarian subjects disidentifying with other minoritarian subjects, representations, theories" ("Coming to Claim"). My sense is that the field is moving in this direction. At the 2016 Modern Language Association Conference in Austin, Texas, I saw a number of panels directed toward intersectionalities between race, gender, sexuality, and disability that took a distinctly nonwhite, queer, feminist perspective and in which scholars worked across and between identities for more coalitional disability studies. This work included Cameron Awkward-Rich's discussion of Jack Bee Garland as appropriating disability drag to open up alternate possibilities of lived gendered spaces, Simone Chess's paper on infertility as constructing crip sexual relations in Early Modern drama, Casie Cobos's work on Chicana (dis)claiming of mental disability, and Adam Newman's argument that racial Blackness functions as a narrative prosthesis to whiteness in American Renaissance literature.

CHAPTER 1

1. For this performance, Eddie Redmayne, the able-bodied actor playing Hawking, won not only the Oscar for best performance by an actor in a leading role but also a Golden Globe, a BAFTA, and a Screen Actors Guild Award. His sweep follows a long line of white male actors playing characters with illnesses and/or disabilities they themselves do not have and winning awards for it. Such actors include Dustin Hoffman in *Rain Man*, Tom Hanks in both *Forrest Gump* and *Philadelphia*, Al Pacino in *Scent of a Woman*, Russell Crowe in *A Beautiful Mind*, and Tom Cruise in *Born on the Fourth of July*.

2. For a more expanded theorization of racialized disgender, see this book's Introduction.

3. See Coston and Kimmel.

4. Tobin Siebers defines the model complex embodiment as a theory of disability that posits that it is both socially constructed and materially embodied. "The theory of complex embodiment views the economy between social representation and the body not as unidirectional as in the social model, or nonexistent as in the medical model, but as reciprocal" (25).

5. Brook notes that this multicultural aesthetic was largely in response to "the so-called 'lily white' controversy of 1999, which arose from media monitoring groups' aggressive attempt to reverse a perceived backslide in minority representation on network shows for the coming season. A convergence of pressure put on the networks by the monitoring groups, working together rather than separately for the first time, forced the networks not only to tilt their upcoming lineups toward greater diversity but also to commit to long-term upgrades" (333).

6. As Michaela D. E. Meyer and Danielle M. Stern note, "*Lost* has been touted as one of the most diverse shows on television; however, of the main characters featured on the first season only four are women: Kate, the ex-bank robber and felon; Shannon, the spoiled, rich princess; Claire, the pregnant lone Australian character; and Sun, the Korean housewife" (314).

7. The *Black Rock* is a reference to an actual historical ship discovered in 2004 in the Caribbean, the same year *Lost* began. It was actually named the *Trouvadore* and identified as a Spanish ship. Though in the series it is implied that the ship is mostly carrying European convicts, the reference to an actual ship carrying Africans meant to be sold into slavery as well as the name "Black Rock" and continued reference to it as a "slaving ship" creates a strong association between this ship and the history of chattel slavery in the United States as well as the experiences of the Middle Passage.

8. For further discussion of slavery and racialized disgender, see my discussion of Spillers in this book's Introduction.

9. While "Special K" is also slang for the drug Ketamine, I do not think that is how the use of "Special K" registers to an audience in this scene.

10. Sam Worthington, who plays Jake, was born to British parents and raised in Australia. *Avatar* is one of his first American films. It seems a notable choice that Cameron would use a relatively unknown Australian actor of British descent to play this American working-class everyman. Additionally, Worthington is not disabled. Given

the attention drawn to his disability in the film by the camera (his legs are often shot uncovered, looking substantially smaller than the rest of his body; he is also shown pulling his legs in and out of the avatar more frequently than he is shown being actively mobile in his wheelchair), it seems a more logical choice to use a paraplegic actor, particularly if one is going to use someone relatively unknown. What this casting choice suggests is that Worthington's universalizing white maleness is the most, if not the only, important factor in his casting. Particularly when juxtaposed against the rest of the cast, Worthington's national and ethnic identity is inconsequential compared to his racial whiteness. His disability status is also of little consequence because (1) his disability functions as a metaphor rather than a lived identity in the film and (2) technology can virtually give him a disability for the film (e.g., editing to make his legs appear atrophied) in the same way it takes his disability away in the film's plot.

11. David Brooks, a conservative neoliberal writer, may seem an odd citation for this particular argument, but I think his review only stresses that the racial politics of the film are fairly straightforward and that even someone who generally conceptualizes America as "postrace" is aware of the white savior mentality of the film. This suggests to me that the use of disability allows the film a kind of exemption from the critique of white supremacy it might otherwise receive because it represents white manhood as just as marginalized as the people of color that the white men colonize.

12. There have been numerous critiques of the use of "namaste" in Western culture due to the rise of the "yoga industrial complex" (Miller 2) as an offensive cultural appropriation of Hindu culture and religion. *Avatar*, in its reference to the Western appropriation of "namaste," also gestures toward the ways the yoga-industrial complex in the West often reinforces unhealthy body ideals as well as connections between able-bodiedness, whiteness, and idealized womanhood. One might say that yoga in the West is often used as a kind of rehabilitative prosthetic device for a spiritually damaged whiteness that participates in the simultaneous reinforcement of white privilege and the racial disgendering of bodies who attach to it as an ideal. For more on the relations between the yoga-industrial complex and cultural appropriation, see Bowers and Cheer. For discussions of the use of "namaste" as cultural appropriation, see Snow; Muddagouni.

13. "I see you" is also an ableist phrase to the extent that it metaphorically equates blindness with an inability to perceive others well.

14. For more on models of complex embodiment, see Siebers; for more on political/relational models of disability, see Kafer.

15. Walter Benn Michaels provides a good example of a critique of social identity politics that flattens differences between oppressions and opens a space for white masculinity as just as "wounded" or "disabled" as any other social identity. In *The Trouble with Diversity: How We Learned to Love Identity and Ignore Inequality*, Michaels dismisses social identity politics as a distraction from the real (read "important, true, white male inclusive") politics of class. To do this, Michaels needs to ignore the psychological power of racial, gender, sexual, or disability identity as well as the value of positional knowledges. The alternate perspectives and psychoanalytic, affective, and political archives, methodologies, and knowledges that the trouble of identity (in a positive Butlerian sense) opens up are devalued in this supposedly more realist, materialist revision of inequality.

CHAPTER 2

1. See Shinn.

2. See Couser; Mitchell and Snyder; Sontag; Vidali; and Schalk, "Interpreting Disability."

3. For a more expanded theorization of racialized disgender, see this book's Introduction.

4. Though there continues to be debate about using Chicanx in place of Chicano or Chicano/a, I choose to use it when not referring to a specific character in this text as a reflection of the work that I am trying to do with racialized disgender, part of which is to challenge a natural or even useful gender binary and to see all gendering as both intersectional and to some extent disidentificatory. Thus, making room for a gender-expansive or gender-inclusive way to talk about Chicanx identity in relation to disability is important, even as the authors and characters I discuss identify or are identified within a gender binary.

5. See Vidali.

6. For a discussion of the staging of Cerezita's character, see Davies.

7. For a definition of "epistemic privilege," see the Introduction, note 12.

8. See Ortíz; see also John Alba Cutler's discussion of surrogacy in readings of *The Rain God*.

9. For a fuller discussion of theories of femaleness as disability, see Chapter 3.

CHAPTER 3

1. In this essay Sedgwick claims, "with all a fat *woman*'s defiance," her identity "as a gay man" (256).

2. See Schultz.

3. For a more detailed explication of racialized disgender, see this book's Introduction.

4. For foundational discussions on the dominant ideologies of Black womanhood in the United States as they evolved from the system of chattel slavery in which Black women functioned as property, laborers, and the reproducers of property and labor, see Carby; Dill.

5. Trudier Harris argues that the historical stereotype of the strong Black woman makes its way into contemporary African American literature via positive representations of big, powerful Black women "who [are] more suprahuman than human" (11) but whose strength comes at a cost, "sometimes handicap[ping] the very tradition it seeks to perpetuate" (20).

6. Trans women who may have lived as men may not have as directly experienced this particular form of racialized disgendering for their entire lives.

7. Here I move between "women" and "bodies marked as female" in an attempt to attend to the fact that some trans men and nonbinary, genderqueer, agender, and other folks may have experienced such a form of racialized disgendering in relation to their bodies but also to note that racialized disgendering in this case happens specifically through the social construction of racialized forms of womanhood.

8. Ehrenreich goes so far as to call the cult of survivorhood a "mass delusion" that

"down-play[s] mortality and promot[es] obedience to medical protocols known to have limited efficacy" (50).

CHAPTER 4

1. While this affinity enables the readings that follow, I make no ultimate claims about intrinsic relations between science fiction as a genre and disability studies. Michael Bérubé's comment that he finds it "plausible that the genre of science fiction is as obsessed with disability as it is with space travel and alien contact" (568) should indicate that there is no single way of reading disability in science fiction.

2. I choose to focus on the *Xenogenesis* trilogy here not because Butler's other work does not address similar issues of disability, gender, sexuality, and race, but because the trilogy deals more directly with medical narratives of cure and resists both a utopian-dystopian dichotomy as much as if not more than her other novels and stories. It would be interesting and useful, however, to look at disability in Butler's other work, as it opens up our thinking about identity and political futures. For example, one might look at how Lauren Olamina's hyperempathy in *Parable of the Sower* can be seen as a revaluing of disease or disability. It is represented as painful and a hindrance to regular daily activity but also as potentially part of what makes Lauren a leader and someone who can relate to others and build communities, which the novel posits as more valuable than nuclear family units for securing humanity's future. Claire P. Curtis at least implicitly acknowledges the possibilities for thinking about a nonideal future-oriented politics in *Parable of the Sower* in her reading of the novel as an exploration of dystopia that replicates what is useful about a utopian vision that accepts flaws but realizes things can be better ("Rehabilitating Utopia" 153–156). Other works of Butler's that would prove interesting to read along these lines include novels in the *Patternist* series (specifically looking at how telepathy, mutations, and lack of disease are treated as abilities or disabilities), the short story "Bloodchild" (in particular how it deals with gender, reproductive bodies, and interdependence), and the novella "The Evening and the Morning and the Night" (especially the complex and ambivalent ways that medical cures for diseases and genetically inherited illness are treated in the text).

3. For example, Amanda Boulter reads the trilogy as a rewriting of Black womanhood via "homeopathic reworking that imbibes the violent structures of the past to create something new" (181). Éva Federmayer reads it as an allegory and critique of U.S. slavery that also acknowledges the Black female body as a "bridge" between master and slave, human and Oankali (98). Naomi Jacobs argues that the Oankali-human hybrids represent a hope for a posthuman future that no longer "clings to" the sense of individual agency and identity that troubles Lilith (93). Elizabeth Billinger reads the trilogy as a narrative estrangement from humanity that provides a perspective from which to perceive and critique it. Frances Bonner reads it as an anti-utopian slavery allegory that explores the troubling "intermingling of slavery and desire" (53). Patricia Melzer reads the books as introducing a multiplicity of simultaneous discourses that "juxtapose affirmation of difference with experiences of colonization and slavery" (36). Both Melzer and Traci Castleberry read the ooloi as representations of alternate sexualities. Several critics, including Stacy Alaimo, Christina Grewe-Volpp, and Boulter, read the trilogy as a deconstruction of the nature-culture binary that has historically underwritten oppres-

sions of women and people of color. Finally, and perhaps most famously, Donna Haraway argues that *Dawn* "draw[s] on the resources of Black and women's histories and liberatory movements" to "interrogat[e] the boundaries of what counts as human" and to create a cyborg heroine in Lilith (226).

4. One critic, in fact, performs a clearly antidisability reading when she suggests that the *Xenogenesis* trilogy reveals "the weakness of the human form" as "a universal dissatisfaction and one which any consideration of the human race would seek to transcend" (Billinger 98).

5. See Obourn.

6. In fact, the trilogy is currently published under the title *Lilith's Brood*. Motherhood has been noted as a central trope by many critics of Butler's work, leading them to read Lilith either as an allegorical figure of Black women's historical sexual oppressions or as a role model for and originator of a freer, postidentity future. For examples of the former reading, see Federmayer; Bonner; and Melzer. For examples of the latter, see Boulter; Jacobs; and Parisi.

7. Curtis has noted that a "crucial utopian reading" is appropriate for the series, which "embraces the messy ambiguity of critical utopia" ("Utopian Possibilities" 22). I find this reading compelling, though my point here is that the messiness creates a narrative in which we cannot read any particular community or approach as ideal nor as substantially different in its desires and practices to those many of us have and value now; thus the narrative is neither utopian nor dystopian in their commonly used senses.

8. Pricilla Wald has also noted this connection and suggests that "Octavia Butler has much to contribute to an understanding of the ethical dilemmas raised by the case of Henrietta Lacks and the HeLa cells. With her interest in science and race, Butler was almost certainly familiar with the famous donor. But whether or not she had Henrietta Lacks explicitly in mind when she created the protagonist of a series of science fiction novels written in the 1980s, the series, which would become known as the xenogenesis trilogy, addresses the ethical questions surrounding the famous case" (1908).

9. This same nonrecognition of disability models leads to limitations in some critical readings of the trilogy as well. For example, Bonner, who reads Lilith as a figure of the enslaved woman, can't understand why Butler and Lilith would accept the "rape" of the humans by the Oankali. She writes, "It seems to me quite reasonable to apply [the term 'rape'] to the early instances of inter-species sexual activity. . . . Yet the language used would not be all that inappropriate at the getting-to-know-you party" (57). Part of Bonner's frustration comes, I think, from reading race and enslavement without the intersecting discourses of disability and queer politics at work in Lilith's relation to both the Oankali and the other humans.

10. Again, however, this echoes the treatment of Henrietta Lacks's cancerous cells as a medical miracle while denying medical care, knowledge, or monetary reimbursement to her or her family.

11. Such logic is reproduced in critical readings such as Boulter's "Polymorphous Futures." Boulter's focus on the trilogy as a homeopathic reworking of violence against Black women's bodies causes Boulter to overlook other kinds of violence against bodies in the novels and ultimately entails a reliance on an ideology of ability and health to heal the wounds of African American history.

12. While one could read Jesusa as representing the limitations of institutional religion, I think it makes more sense to read Jesusa and Lilith as a rewriting of Christian and pre-Christian mythology. In some versions of the Lilith myth, Jesus's coming will end Lilith's (the slave-woman) relationship with God, which she has tricked him into. Here Jesusa learns from Lilith's experiences, revaluing connections between women in a patriarchal mythology that has denied their importance. More on the mythology of Lilith below.

13. I am thinking of scenes primarily from African American literature, such as the one in Nella Larsen's *Passing* in which Gertrude shares her fear of having a "dark" baby and assumes this to be a cultural truth when she states to Irene and Claire, "Nobody wants a dark child" (60).

14. For a fuller reading of Spillers, see this book's Introduction.

15. It is also worth noting Butler's use of the term "imago" as the title to book three of the trilogy. Critics frequently point to its scientific meaning—that is, an insect after its last metamorphosis. Certainly Butler had this definition in mind. But there is little attention paid to the psychoanalytic meaning of the term. (Grewe-Volpp notes the Webster's definition as "idealized mental image" but does not trace this to its source in psychoanalysis). Jodahs, I would argue, is a performative model of the Lacanian mirror stage. It constantly and repeatedly takes on its imago from its erotic relations and its environment. In this way "imago" means both final stage and constantly emerging sense of self that is taken on as an image from one's environment and the others in it.

16. In addition to Reinders, discussed below, Rapp and Ginsburg and Burtt explicitly address liberalism's ineffectiveness for addressing questions of social equality and disability.

17. When I taught *Dawn* in 2009, more than half the class argued that the book did not provide enough evidence to prove that Lilith was Black. Boulter has also noted that readers of *Dawn* have interpreted Lilith as white. Boulter attributes this misreading to the hegemony of white male perspectives in science fiction reading and writing communities. I suggest that the threat to human culture and memory and the recontextualization of humanity in relation to the Oankali also disrupts many of the sign systems that allow Black womanhood to register. Either way, this reinforces my reading of Lilith as a representation at the limits of intelligibility.

18. Osherow suggests that "in the science fiction genre, the revisioned Lilith reflects the myths and experiences of alien minorities, namely, Jewish and African American women" (68).

19. In an interview, Butler says the following in relation to reproduction and the future: "In one neighborhood the girls living on both sides had decided that they wanted to prove they were women, so they got pregnant, and one of them more than once. I looked at them both, and I saw *no future*" (Mehaffy and Keating 70, italics mine). Here she makes clear the important gender and racial dynamics at play in the kind of reproductive futurism Edelman critiques.

20. As Federmayer notes, "[Lilith's] textual figuration . . . is kin to those other 'sturdy black bridges,' including Harriet Jacobs's grandmother in *Incidents in the Life of a Slave Girl*, Claudia's mother in Toni Morrison's *The Bluest Eye*, or, for that matter, Octavia Butler's strong grandmother, Sister Butler, who, under most adverse conditions, managed to sustain life as well as hope in their community" (105).

CODA

1. Puar argues that, for some populations, debility is normative, not exceptional—"a banal feature of quotidian existence that is already definitive of the precarity of that existence" (*Right to Maim* 16)—and that the "recapacitation of a debilitated body . . . is based on the assumption it was supposed to be better" (*Right to Maim* 10–11), an assumption not available to those for whom debility is the norm.

2. Grand rounds are a practice in teaching hospitals during which senior physicians present on cases or general concepts for medical students and junior colleagues. They can take the form of a lecture, which was the structure of the one I attended at Strong.

3. This scenario occurred in a story I heard from a surgical resident.

Works Cited

Ahmed, Sara. *The Promise of Happiness*. Durham, NC: Duke University Press, 2010.

Alaimo, Stacy. "Displacing Darwin and Descartes: The Bodily Transgressions of Fielding Burke, Octavia Butler, and Linda Hogan." *Poetry Criticism* 35 (2002): n.p.

Alexander, Elizabeth. "'Coming out Blackened and Whole': Fragmentation and Reintegration in Audre Lorde's *Zami* and *The Cancer Journals*." *American Literary History* 6.4 (1994): 695–715.

Anzaldúa, Gloria. *Borderlands/La Frontera: The New Mestiza*. San Francisco: Aunt Lute Books, 1987.

Barclay, Jennifer. "Mothering the 'Useless': Black Motherhood, Disability, and Slavery." *Women, Gender, and Families of Color* 2.2 (2014): 115–140.

Beal, Frances M. "Black Women and the Science Fiction Genre: Interview with Octavia Butler." *Black Scholar* 17.2 (1986): 14–18.

Beauboeuf-Lafontant, Tamara. *Behind the Mask of the Strong Black Woman: Voice and the Embodiment of a Costly Performance*. Philadelphia: Temple University Press, 2009.

Bederman, Gail. *Manliness and Civilization: A Cultural History of Gender and Race in the United States, 1880–1917*. Chicago: University of Chicago Press, 1995.

Bell, Christopher, ed. *Blackness and Disability: Critical Examinations and Cultural Interventions*. East Lansing: Michigan State University Press, 2011.

Bernier, Celeste-Marie. "'A Fabricated Africanist Persona': Race, Representation and Narrative Experimentation in *Lost*." In *Reading Lost: Perspectives on a Hit Television Show*, ed. Roberta Pearson, 241–259. New York: Palgrave, 2009.

Bersani, Leo. "Is the Rectum a Grave?" *October* 43 (Winter 1987): 197–222.

Bérubé, Michael. "Disability and Narrative." *PMLA* 120.2 (2005): 568–576.

Bilge, Sirma. "Intersectionality Undone: Saving Intersectionality from Feminist Intersectionality Studies." *Du Bois Review* 10.2 (2013): 405–424.

Billinger, Elizabeth. "After Earth: How Far Away Does the Far Future Have to Be? Estrangement and Cognition in Clarke and Butler." In *Earth Is but a Star: Excursions through Science Fiction to the Far Future,* ed. Damien Broderick, 96–106. Crawley: University of Western Australia Press, 2001.

Bliss, James. "Hope against Hope: Queer Negativity, Black Feminist Theorizing, and Reproduction without Futurity." *Mosaic: A Journal for the Interdisciplinary Study of Literature* 48.1 (2015): 83–98.

Bonner, Frances. "Difference and Desire, Slavery and Seduction: Octavia Butler's *Xenogenesis.*" *Foundation* 48 (1990): 50–62.

Bordo, Susan. *Unbearable Weight: Feminism, Western Culture, and the Body.* Berkeley: University of California Press, 1993.

Boris, Eileen. "From Gender to Racialized Gender: Laboring Bodies that Matter." *International Labor and Working-Class History* 63 (2003): 9–13.

Boulter, Amanda. "Polymorphous Futures: Octavia E. Butler's *Xenogenesis* Trilogy." In *American Bodies: Cultural Histories of the Physique,* ed. Tim Armstrong, 170–185. New York: New York University Press, 1996.

Bowers, Hana, and Joseph M. Cheer. "Yoga Tourism: Commodification and Western Embracement of Eastern Spiritual Practice." *Tourism Management Perspectives* 24 (2017): 208–216.

Brook, Vincent. "Convergent Ethnicity and the Neo-Platoon Show: Recombining Difference in the Post-network Era." *New Television Media* 10.4 (2009): 331–353.

Brooks, David. "The Messiah Complex." *New York Times,* January 7, 2010. http://www.nytimes.com/2010/01/08/opinion/08brooks.html?_r=0.

Brown, Laura S. "Not outside the Range: One Feminist Perspective on Psychic Trauma." In *Trauma: Explorations in Memory,* ed. Cathy Caruth, 100–112. Baltimore: Johns Hopkins University Press, 1995.

Brown, Wendy. "Wounded Attachments." *Political Theory* 21.3 (1993): 390–410.

Burtt, Shelley. "Is Inclusion a Civic Virtue? Cosmopolitanism, Disability, and the Liberal State." *Social Theory and Practice* 33.4 (2007): 557–578.

Butler, Judith. *Undoing Gender.* New York: Routledge, 2004.

Butler, Octavia E. *Lilith's Brood.* New York: Grand Central Publishing, 1989.

Carastathis, Anna. *Intersectionality: Origins, Contestations, Horizons.* Lincoln: University of Nebraska Press, 2016.

Carby, Hazel V. *Reconstructing Womanhood: The Emergence of the Afro-American Woman Novelist.* New York: Oxford University Press, 1987.

Carroll, Hamilton. *Affirmative Reaction: New Formations of White Masculinity.* Durham, NC: Duke University Press, 2011.

Caruth, Cathy. *Listening to Trauma: Conversations with Leaders in the Theory and Treatment of Catastrophic Experience.* Baltimore: Johns Hopkins University Press, 2014.

Castleberry, Traci N. "Twisting the Other: Using a 'Third' Sex to Represent Homosexuality in Science Fiction." *New York Review of Science Fiction* 21.5 (2009): 13–17.

Christina, Dominique. "Star Gazer." https://www.youtube.com/watch?v=PmLyumKQr4M.

Clare, Eli. *Exile and Pride: Disability, Queerness, and Liberation.* New York: South End Press, 2009.

Collins, Patricia Hill. *Black Feminist Thought: Knowledge, Consciousness, and the Politics of Empowerment.* 2nd ed. New York: Routledge, 2000.

Collins, Patricia Hill, and Sirma Bilge. *Intersectionality.* Malden, MA: Polity, 2016.

Combahee River Collective. "A Black Feminist Statement." In *Words of Fire: An Anthology of African-American Feminist Thought,* 232–240. New York: New Press, 1995. First published 1977.

Coston, Bethany M., and Michael Kimmel. "Seeing Privilege Where It Isn't: Marginalized Masculinities and the Intersectionality of Privilege." *Journal of Social Issues* 68.1 (2012): 97–111.

Couser, G. Thomas. "Disability as Metaphor: What's Wrong with *Lying.*" *Prose Studies* 27.1–2 (April–August 2005): 141–154.

Crenshaw, Kimberlé Williams. "Demarginalizing the Intersection of Race and Sex: A Black Feminist Critique of Anti-Discrimination Doctrine, Feminist Theory, and Anti-racist Politics." *University of Chicago Legal Forum* 140 (1989): 139–167.

Curtis, Claire P. "Rehabilitating Utopia: Feminist Science Fiction and Finding the Ideal." *Contemporary Justice Review* 8.2 (June 2005): 147–162.

———. "Utopian Possibilities: Disability, Norms, and Eugenics in Octavia Butler's *Xenogenesis.*" *Journal of Literary and Cultural Disability Studies* 9.1 (2015): 19–33.

Cutler, John Alba. "Prosthesis, Surrogation, and Relation in Arturo Islas's *The Rain God.*" *Aztlán: A Journal of Chicano Studies* 33.1 (2008): 7–32.

Davies, Telory W. "Race, Gender, and Disability: Cherríe Moraga's Bodiless Head." *Journal of Dramatic Theory and Criticism* 21.1 (Fall 2006): 29–44.

Davis, Angela Y. *Women, Race, and Class.* New York: Random House, 1981.

Davis, Lennard. *Bending Over Backwards: Disability, Dismodernism and Other Difficult Positions.* New York: New York University Press, 2002.

DeShazer, Mary K., and Anita Helle. "Theorizing Breast Cancer: Narrative, Politics, Memory." *Tulsa Studies in Women's Literature* 32.2/33.1 (Fall 2013/Spring 2014): 7–23.

Diedrich, Lisa. *Treatments: Language, Politics, and the Culture of Illness.* Minneapolis: University of Minnesota Press, 2007.

Dill, Bonnie Thornton. "The Dialectics of Black Womanhood." *Signs* 4.3 (Spring 1979): 543–555.

Dolmage, Jay Timothy. *Disabled upon Arrival: Eugenics, Immigration, and the Construction of Race and Disability.* Columbus: Ohio State University Press, 2018.

Downs, Jim. *Sick from Freedom: African-American Illness and Suffering during the Civil War and Reconstruction.* New York: Oxford University Press, 2012.

Dyer, Richard. *White.* New York: Routledge, 1997.

Edelman, Lee. *No Future: Queer Theory and the Death Drive.* Durham, NC: Duke University Press, 2004.

Ehlers, Nadine. "The Dialects of Vulnerability: Breast Cancer and the Body in Prognosis." *Configurations* 22.1 (Winter 2014): 113–135.

Ehrenreich, Barbara. "Welcome to Cancerland: A Mammogram Leads to a Cult of Pink Kitsch." *Harper's Magazine,* November 2001, 43–53.

Engelberg, Miriam. *Cancer Made Me a Shallower Person: A Memoir in Comics.* New York: Harper, 2006.

Erevelles, Nirmala. *Disability and Difference in Global Contexts: Enabling a Transformative Body Politic.* New York: Palgrave, 2001.

Falcón, Sylvanna M., and Jennifer C. Nash, "Shifting Analytics and Linking Theories: A

Conversation about the 'Meaning-Making' of Intersectionality and Transnational Feminism." *Women's Studies International Forum* 50 (2015): 1–10.

Fausto-Sterling, Anne. *Sexing the Body: Gender Politics and the Construction of Sexuality.* New York: Basic Books, 2000.

Federmayer, Éva. "Octavia Butler's Maternal Cyborgs: The Black Female World of the Xenogenesis Trilogy." In *Anatomy of Science Fiction,* ed. Donald E. Morse, 95–108. Newcastle, UK: Cambridge Scholars Press, 2006.

Flagel, Nadine. "'It's Almost Like Being There': Speculative Fiction, Slave Narrative, and the Crisis of Representation in Octavia Butler's *Kindred.*" *Canadian Review of American Studies/Revue canadienne d'études américaines* 42.2 (2012): 216–245.

Foucault, Michel. *The Birth of Biopolitics: Lectures at the College de France, 1978–1979.* Trans. Graham Burchell. New York: Picador, 2009.

Froehle, Craig. "The Evolution of an Accidental Meme: How One Little Graphic Became Shared and Adapted by Millions." *Medium,* April 14, 2016. medium.com/@CRA1G/the-evolution-of-an-accidental-meme-ddc4e139e0e4.

Garland-Thomson, Rosemarie. *Extraordinary Bodies: Figuring Physical Disability in American Literature and Culture.* New York: Columbia University Press, 1997.

Gerschick, Thomas J. "Toward a Theory of Disability and Gender." *Signs: Feminisms at a Millennium* 25.4 (Summer 2000): 1263–1268.

Grewe-Volpp, Christa. "Octavia Butler and the Nature/Culture Divide: An Ecofeminist Approach to the *Xenogenesis*-Trilogy." In *Restoring the Connection to the Natural World: Essays on the African American Imagination,* ed. Sylvia Meyer, 149–173. Münster, Germany: Lit Verlag Forecaast, 2003.

Gross, Bruce H., and Harlan Hahn. "Developing Issues in the Classification of Mental and Physical Disabilities." *Journal of Disability Policy Studies* 15.3 (2004): 130–134.

Hahn, Harlan D., and Todd L. Belt. "Disability Identity and Attitudes toward Cure in a Sample of Disabled Activists." *Journal of Health and Social Behavior* 45.4 (2004): 453–464.

Hancock, Ange-Marie. *Intersectionality: An Intellectual History.* New York: Oxford University Press, 2016.

Haraway, Donna J. *Simians, Cyborgs, and Women: The Reinvention of Nature.* New York: Routledge, 1991.

Harris, Cheryl. "Whiteness as Property." *Harvard Law Review* 106.8 (1993): 1707–1791.

Harris, Trudier. *Saints, Sinners, Saviors: Strong Black Women in African American Literature.* New York: Palgrave, 2001.

Harrison, James, James Chin, and Thomas Ficarrotto. "Warning: Masculinity May Be Dangerous to Your Health." In *Men's Lives,* ed. Michael S. Kimmel and Michael A. Messner, 271–285. 2nd ed. New York: Macmillan, 1992.

Herndl, Diane Price. *Invalid Women: Figuring Feminine Illness in American Literature and Culture 1840–1940.* Chapel Hill: University of North Carolina Press, 1993.

———. "Our Breasts, Our Selves: Identity, Community, and Ethics in Cancer Autobiographies." *Signs: Women's Journal of Women in Culture and Society* 32.1 (2006): 221–245.

———. "Reconstructing the Posthuman Feminist Body Twenty Years after Audre Lorde's *Cancer Journals.*" In *Enabling the Humanities: A Sourcebook for Disability Studies in Language and Literature,* ed. Rosemarie Garland-Thomson, Brenda Brueggeman, and Sharon Snyder, 144–155. New York: MLA, 2002.

hooks, bell. *The Will to Change: Men, Masculinity, and Love.* New York: Washington Square Press, 2004.

International Wheelchair Rugby Foundation. "Classification." Accessed July 1, 2016. http://www.iwrf.com/?page=classification.

Islas, Arturo. *The Rain God.* New York: Harper Collins, 1984.

Jacobs, Naomi. "Posthuman Bodies and Agency in Octavia Butler's *Xenogenesis.*" In *Dark Horizons: Science Fiction and the Dystopian Imagination,* ed. Raffaella Baccolini and Tom Moylan, 91–111. New York: Routledge, 2003.

James, Jennifer C. "Gwendolyn Brooks, World War II, and the Politics of Rehabilitation." In *Feminist Disability Studies,* ed. Kim Q. Hall, 136–158. Bloomington: Indiana University Press, 2011.

Jarman, Michelle. "Dismembering the Lynch Mob: Intersecting Narratives of Disability, Race, and Sexual Menace." In *Sex and Disability,* ed. Robert McRuer and Anna Mollow, 114–139. Durham, NC: Duke University Press, 2012.

Kafer, Alison. *Feminist, Queer, Crip.* Bloomington: Indiana University Press, 2013.

Kim, Eunjung. *Curative Violence: Rehabilitating Disability, Gender, and Sexuality in Modern Korea.* Durham, NC: Duke University Press, 2017.

Kimmel, Michael S. *Guyland: The Perilous World Where Boys Become Men.* New York: HarperCollins, 2008.

König, Christiane. "Not Becoming-Posthuman in the Ultimate Postfilmic Posthuman Male Fantasy: Queer-Feminist Observations on James Cameron's *Avatar* (2009)." *Gender Forum* 32 (2011): 1–16.

Larsen, Nella. *Passing.* Ed. Carla Kaplan. New York: Norton, 2007.

Lawrie, Paul R. D. "'Salvaging the Negro': Race, Rehabilitation, and the Body Politic in World War I America, 1917–1924." *Disability Histories,* ed. Susan Burch and Michael Rembis, 321–344. Chicago: University of Illinois Press, 2014.

Lorde, Audre. *The Cancer Journals.* San Francisco: Aunt Lute Books, 1980.

———. *Zami: A New Spelling of My Name.* Freedom, CA: Crossing, 1982.

Love, Heather. *Feeling Backward: Loss and the Politics of Queer History.* Cambridge, MA: Harvard University Press, 2007.

Lujano, Bob. *No Arms, No Legs, No Problem.* Write with Grace Publishers, 2014. www .NoArmsNoLegsNoProblem.com.

Macharia, Keguro. "Not This. More That!" *New Inquiry,* July 23, 2018. https://thenewinquiry.com/blog/not-this-more-that/.

Magill, David. "The *Lost* Boys and Masculinity Found." In *Looking for Lost: Critical Essays on the Enigmatic Series,* ed. Randy Laist, 137–153. Jefferson, NC: McFarland, 2011.

Martínez Falquina, Silva. "'The Pandora Effect': James Cameron's Avatar and a Trauma Studies Perspective." *Atlantis (0210–6124)* 36.2 (December 2014): 115–131.

Martinot, Steve. *The Machinery of Whiteness: Studies in the Structure of Racialization.* Philadelphia: Temple University Press, 2010.

May, Vivian M. *Pursuing Intersectionality, Unsettling Dominant Imaginaries.* New York: Routledge, 2015.

May, Vivian M., and Beth A. Ferri. "Fixated on Ability." *Prose Studies* 27.1–2 (2005): 120–140.

McRuer, Robert. *Crip Theory: Cultural Signs of Queerness and Disability.* New York: New York University Press, 2006.

McRuer, Robert, and Abby L. Wilkerson. "Cripping the (Queer) Nation." *GLQ* 9.1–2 (2003): 1–23.

Mehaffy, Merilyn, and AnaLouise Keating. "'Radio Imagination': Octavia Butler on the Poetics of Narrative Embodiment." *MELUS* 26.1 (Spring 2001): 45–76.

Melzer, Patricia. *Alien Constructions: Science Fiction and Feminist Thought.* Austin: University of Texas Press, 2006.

Meyer, Michaela D. E., and Danielle Stern. "The Modern(?) Korean Woman in Prime-Time: Analyzing the Representation of Sun on the Television Series *Lost*." *Women's Studies* 36 (2007): 313–331.

Michaels, Walter Benn. *The Trouble With Diversity: How We Learned To Love Identity and Ignore Inequality.* New York: Metropolitan Books, 2006.

Michaelson, Jay. "The Meaning of Avatar: Everything Is God (A Response to Ross Douthat and Other Naysayers of 'Pantheism')." *Huffington Post,* December 22, 2009. www.huffingtonpost.com/jay-michaelson/the-meaning-of-avatar-eve_b_400912.html.

Miller, Amara Lindsay. "Eating the Other Yogi: Katheryn Budig, the Yoga Industrial Complex, and the Appropriation of Body Positivity." *Race and Yoga* 1.1 (2016): 1–22. escholarship.org/uc/item/2t4362b9.

Millner, Michael. "Post Post-Identity." *American Quarterly* 57.2 (2005): 541–554.

Minich, Julie Avril. *Accessible Citizenships: Disability, Nation, and the Cultural Politics of Greater Mexico.* Philadelphia: Temple University Press, 2014.

Mitchell, David T., and Sharon L. Snyder. *Narrative Prosthesis: Disability and the Dependencies of Discourse.* Ann Arbor: University of Michigan Press, 2000.

Mollow, Anna. "Is Sex Disability? Queer Theory and the Disability Drive." In *Sex and Disability,* ed. Robert McRuer and Anna Mollow, 285–312. Durham, NC: Duke University Press, 2012.

Moraga, Cherríe. *Heroes and Saints. Heroes and Saints and Other Plays.* Albuquerque, NM: West End Press, 1994.

———. "Queer Aztlán: The Re-formation of Chicano Tribe." In *Queer Cultures,* ed. Deborah Carlin and Jennifer DeGrazia, 224–238. Upper Saddle River, NJ: Pearson, 2004.

Moraga, Cherríe, and Gloria Anzaldúa, eds., *This Bridge Called My Back: Writings by Radical Women of Color.* Watertown, MA: Persephone Press, 1981.

Mousoutzanis, Aris. "'Enslaved by Time and Space': Determinism, Traumatic Temporality, and Global Interconnectedness." In *Looking for Lost: Critical Essays on the Enigmatic Series,* ed. Randy Laist, 43–57. Jefferson, NC: McFarland, 2011.

Moya, Paula M. L. "Chicana Feminism and Postmodern Theory." *Signs* 26.2 (2001): 441–483.

Muddagouni, Kamna. "Why White People Need to Stop Saying 'Namaste.'" *Sydney Morning Herald,* April 1, 2016. www.smh.com.au/lifestyle/why-white-people-need-to-stop-saying-namaste-20160401-gnw2xx.html.

Muñoz, José Esteban. *Disidentifications: Queers of Color and the Performance of Politics.* Minneapolis: University of Minnesota Press, 1999.

Mutz, Diana C. "Status Threat, Not Economic Hardship, Explains the 2016 Presidential Vote." *Proceedings of the National Academy of Sciences of the United States of America,* April 23, 2018, E4330–4339. https://doi.org/10.1073/pnas.1718155115.

Nash, Jennifer C. "Feminist Originalism: Intersectionality and the Politics of Reading." *Feminist Theory* 17.1 (2016): 3–20.

———. "'Home Truths' on Intersectionality." *Yale Journal of Law and Feminism* 23.2 (2011): 445–470.

———. "Institutionalizing the Margins." *Social Text 118* 32.1 (2014): 45–65.

———. "Intersectionality and Its Discontents." *American Quarterly* 69.1 (2017): 117–129.

———. "Practicing Love: Black Feminism, Love-Politics, and Post-Intersectionality." *Meridians* 11.2 (2011): 1–24.

———. "Re-thinking Intersectionality." *Feminist Review* 89 (2008): 1–15.

Obourn, Milo [Megan]. "Octavia Butler's Disabled Futures." *Contemporary Literature* 54.1 (Spring 2013): 109–138.

Ortíz, Ricardo. "Arturo Islas and the 'Phantom Rectum.'" *Contemporary Literature* 48.3 (2007): 398–422.

Osherow, Michelle. "The Dawn of a New Lilith: Revisionary Mythmaking in Women's Science Fiction." *NWSA* 12.1 (2000): 68–83.

O'Toole, Joan Corbett. "The Sexist Inheritance of the Disability Movement." In *Gendering Disability,* ed. Bonnie G. Smith and Beth Hutchison, 294–300. New Brunswick, NJ: Rutgers University Press.

Parisi, Lusiana. "Essence and Virtuality: The Incorporeal Desire of Lilith." *Anglistica* 4.1 (2000): 191–212.

Parker, Patricia. "Metaphor and Catachresis." In *The Ends of Rhetoric: History, Theory, Practice,* ed. John Bender and David E. Wellbery, 60–73. Stanford, CA: Stanford University Press, 1990.

Patai, Raphael. "Lilith." *Journal of American Folklore* 77.306 (1964): 295–314.

Patsavas, Alyson. "Recovering a Cripistemology of Pain: Leaky Bodies, Connective Tissue, and Feeling Discourse." *Journal of Literary and Cultural Disability Studies* 8.2 (2014): 203–218.

Pickens, Therí A. *New Body Politics: Narrating Arab American and Black Identity in the Contemporary United States.* New York: Routledge, 2014.

———. "You're Supposed to Be a Tall, Handsome, Fully Grown White Man": Theorizing Race, Gender, and Disability in Octavia Butler's *Fledgling.*" *Journal of Literary and Cultural Disability Studies* 8.1 (2014): 33–48.

Poniewozik, James. "Preparing for Life after *Lost.*" *Time,* May 24, 2010. http://www.time.com/time/magazine/article/0,9171,1989123,00.html.

Preciado, Paul (Beatriz), and Bruce Benderson. *Testo Junkie: Sex, Drugs, and Biopolitics in the Pharmacopornographic Era.* New York: The Feminist Press at CUNY, 2013.

Price, Margaret. "The Bodymind Problem and the Possibilities of Pain." *Hypatia* 30.1 (2015): 268–284.

Puar, Jasbir K. "'I Would Rather Be a Cyborg than a Goddess': Intersectionality, Assemblage, and Affective Politics." European Institute for Progressive Cultural Policies website. January 2011. https://transversal.at/transversal/0811/puar/en?hl=puar.

———. *The Right to Maim: Debility, Capacity, Disability.* Durham, NC: Duke University Press, 2017.

Rapp, Rayna, and Faye Ginsburg. "Enabling Disability: Rewriting Kinship, Reimagining Citizenship." *Public Culture* 13.3 (2001): 533–556.

Reinders, Hans S. *The Future of the Disabled in a Liberal Society: An Ethical Analysis.* Notre Dame, IN: University of Notre Dame Press, 2000.

Root, Maria P. P. "Reconstructing the Impact of Trauma on Personality." In *Personality and Psychopathology: Feminist Reappraisals*, ed. Laura S. Brown and Mary Ballou, 229–265. New York: Guilford Press.

Schalk, Sami. *Bodyminds Reimagined*. Durham, NC: Duke University Press, 2018.

———. "Coming to Claim Crip: Disidentification with/in Disability Studies." *Disability Studies Quarterly* 33.2 (2013): n.p.

———. "Interpreting Disability Metaphor and Race in Octavia Butler's "The Morning and the Evening and the Night." *African American Review* 50.2 (Summer 2017): 139–151.

———. "Metaphorically Speaking." *Disability Studies Quarterly* 33.4 (2013): n.p.

Schultz, Eliza. "The Grim Reality behind the Pink Ribbon." *Talk Poverty,* November 2, 2015. https://talkpoverty.org/2015/11/02/grim-reality-pink-ribbon/.

Schwab, Gabriele. *Haunting Legacies: Violent Histories and the Transgenerational Trauma*. New York: Columbia University Press, 2010.

Sedgwick, Eve. "White Glasses." In *Tendencies,* 252–266. Durham, NC: Duke University Press, 1993.

Shinn, Christopher. "Disability Is Not Just a Metaphor." *The Atlantic,* July 23, 2014. https://www.theatlantic.com/entertainment/archive/2014/07/why-disabled-characters-are-never-played-by-disabled-actors/374822/.

Sideris, Lisa Hatton. "I See You: Interspecies Empathy and 'Avatar.'" *Journal for the Study of Religion, Nature and Culture* 4.4 (2010): 457–477.

Siebers, Tobin. *Disability Theory*. Ann Arbor: University of Michigan Press, 2009.

Skloot, Rebecca. *The Immortal Life of Henrietta Lacks*. New York: Crown, 2010.

Smith, Barbara, ed. *Home Girls: A Black Feminist Anthology*. New York: Kitchen Table: Women of Color Press, 1983.

Snorton, C. Riley. *Black on Both Sides: A Racial History of Trans Identity*. Minneapolis: University of Minnesota Press, 2017.

Snow, Jason. "Why I Stopped Saying Namaste." *Steemit.* Accessed May 30, 2019. steemit.com/yoga/@jasonsnow/why-i-stopped-saying-namaste.

Sontag, Susan. *Illness and Metaphor and AIDS and Its Metaphors*. New York: Picador, 1990.

Spillers, Hortense. "Mama's Baby, Papa's Maybe: An American Grammar Book." *Diacritics* 17.2 (1987): 64–81.

Stemp, Jane. "Devices and Desires: Science Fiction, Fantasy and Disability in Literature for Young People." *Disability Studies Quarterly* 24.1 (2004): n.p.

Thandeka. *Learning to Be White: Money, Race, and God in America*. New York: Bloomsbury, 1999.

Tillman, Terry. "'I See You': How Avatar's Writers May Have Based the Idea on the Beautiful Customs of an Actual African Tribe." *Finerminds.* https://www.finerminds.com/consciousness-awareness/samburu-greeting-terry-tillman/.

Tyler, Dennis, Jr. "Jim Crow's Disabilities: Racial Injury, Immobility, and the 'Terrible Handicap' in the Literature of James Weldon Johnson." *African American Review* 50.2 (2017): 185–201.

Vidali, Amy. "Seeing What We Know: Disability and Theories of Metaphor." *Journal of Literary and Cultural Disability Studies* 4.1 (2010): 33–54.

Vint, Sherryl. "Introduction: Science Fiction and Biopolitics." *Science Fiction Film and Television* 4.2 (2011): 161–172.

Wald, Priscilla. "The Art of Medicine: Cognitive Estrangement, Science Fiction, and Medical Ethics." *Lancet* 371.9628 (2008): 1908–1909.

Wanzo, Rebecca. "Apocalyptic Empathy: A Parable of Postmodern Sentimentality." *Obsidian III* 6.2 (2005): 72–86.

Waples, Emily. "Avatars, Illness, and Authority: Embodied Experience in Breast Cancer Autopathographics." *Configurations* 22.2 (Spring 2014): 153–181.

Wendell, Susan. *The Rejected Body: Feminist Philosophical Reflections on Disability.* New York: Routledge, 1996.

Young, Iris Marion. *On Female Body Experience: "Throwing like a Girl" and Other Essays.* New York: Oxford University Press, 2004.

Index

Milo W. Obourn, Associate Professor of English and Women and Gender Studies and Chair of the Department of Women and Gender Studies at The College at Brockport, State University of New York, is the author of *Reconstituting Americans: Liberal Multiculturalism and Identity Difference in Post-1960s Literature.*

www.ingramcontent.com/pod-product-compliance
Lightning Source LLC
Chambersburg PA
CBHW051433270326
41935CB00018B/1814